Urbanisation: Changing Environments

Second Edition

Corrin Flint

Head of Geography, King Edward VI High School for Girls, Birmingham

David Flint

Senior Lecturer, Newman College of Higher Education, Birmingham

LANDMARK GEOGRAPHY

D0453072

Contents

1 Urbanisation

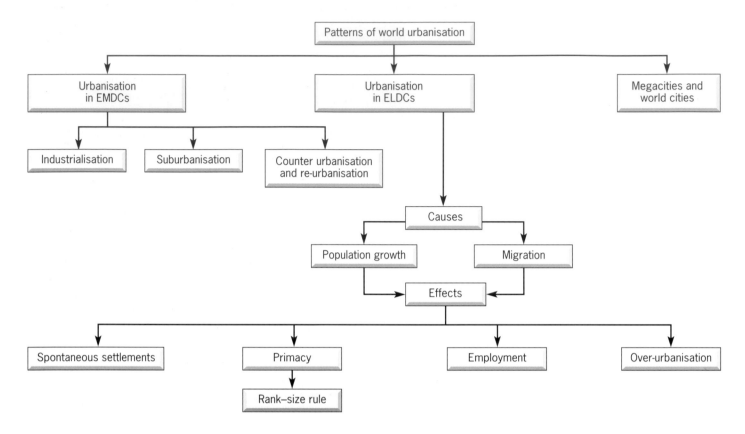

1.1 Introduction

Most people in Europe, the USA, Asia and Latin America live in towns and cities. Otherwise, people live in rural areas but work in cities and depend on them for services, such as shops. The process of becoming an urban society, that is **urbanisation**, is a key feature of life for most of the world's population. Urbanisation is the process of change from a rural society in which people live scattered across the landscape, to an urban society where people are concentrated into thickly populated nodes.

An urban area is therefore a concentration of people, buildings, infrastructure and economic activities. Rural areas, in contrast, have a much more dispersed pattern of settlement. We can interpret urbanisation in three main ways, according to its causes and effects:

• If we look at urbanisation from the viewpoint of population geography, it is a process by which an increasing percentage of the population lives and works in places that are defined as urban. **Migration** from rural to urban areas is one demographic cause of urbanisation (see section 2.8). Internal population growth within cities is another.

• Seen from the viewpoint of socio-economic geography, urbanisation is often caused by changes that accompany industrialisation. Cities perform important commercial functions, and serve as locations for new forms of production, distribution and exchange. They also involve social structures that are different from those of rural societies.

• Seen from the viewpoint of human behaviour, urbanisation results in changes of human behaviour and attitudes towards society. Such changes may include increasing self-interest and a breakdown of family structure (see Chapter 5).

1.2 Historical trends in urbanisation

It is important to realise that cities are not a recent phenomenon and are not historically concentrated in today's economically more developed countries (EMDCs), like Britain. For example, Asia has an urban tradition going back at least 5000 years. The early kingdoms of south-east Asia were based on the city as the apex of civilisation. From about 2500 BC, royalty extended its power from cities such as Mohenjo-Daro on the River Indus, in today's Pakistan (Fig. 1.1). Surrounding rural areas then sent gifts and tithes, e.g. food, jewellery and people, to these political centres. Major religious centres developed across Asia well into the first century AD, including the Buddhist sites of Angkor in Cambodia (Fig. 1.2) and Sukhothai in Thailand. At its height, Angkor was much bigger than ancient Rome.

These early cities in Asia, Africa and Latin America were located inland, often at the centre of fertile plains – such as the Valley of Mexico where Teotihuacan, the centre of classic Maya civilisation, dominated the region from AD 250 to AD 750 (Fig. 1.3). The importance of such early cities was often political and religious rather than economic. In fact, cities represented the height of religious life for civilisations. Political systems centred on them and were closely linked to religion. Sometimes ancient cities, such as Angkor and Mohenjo-Daro, were centres of complex irrigation works which stimulated food production in the surrounding area. They also had specialist artisan trades, such as jewellery production and metal work (see Chapter 2).

Figure 1.1 Ruins of Mohenjo-Daro, *c.* 3000 BC: the city had streets 10 m wide lined with houses, shops and restaurants; underneath ran drains and sewers

Figure 1.2 The ancient Buddhist city of Angkor, Cambodia, built *c.* AD 1000

Figure 1.3 Temples at Teotihuacan, Mexico: between *c.* AD 100–750 the city state had between 125 000 and 250 000 inhabitants, covered 13 km^2 and included more than 23 temple complexes

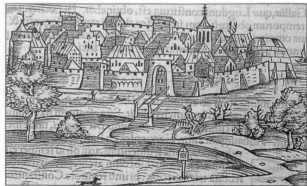

View of the walled city of Florence, Italy, 1493 (*top*)

Medieval walled city with moat and drawbridge, 1553 (*top right*)

Map of London, 1572 (*right*)

Figure 1.4 Medieval representations of early European cities

?

1a On a tracing of Figure 1.5, mark and name the castle; the town walls; gates through the town walls; estuary; bridge; main road; the church of St Mary in the town centre.
b What features make it clear that Conway was a planned town?

Early Europe

The growth of cities in Europe came several thousand years after their first expansion in parts of Africa and Asia. Early European cities grew particularly fast with the development of trade during the Middle Ages. Towns grew within walls which provided protection from invaders and could be extended to allow for further growth. The layout of such towns was unplanned, with buildings linked and separated by a network of narrow winding streets. Behind many of the town houses were long narrow plots of land which were intensively cultivated (Fig. 1.4).

However not all medieval towns in Europe grew from an established economic base. Some, like Conway in Wales (Fig. 1.5), were built in a single operation according to a development plan. It was King Edward I of England who established the new town of Conway in the late thirteenth century to consolidate his conquest of Wales.

Recent worldwide urbanisation

Despite the long history of city growth in many parts of the world, the recent pattern of urbanisation is very different. Urbanisation in the twentieth century created a new scale of city, namely one with over a million inhabitants (Fig. 1.6). In 1950 there were 70 cities with populations of over a million. By 1995, 18 per cent of the world's population lived in the 276 cities which had over one million people (Fig. 1.7).

Percentage of total population

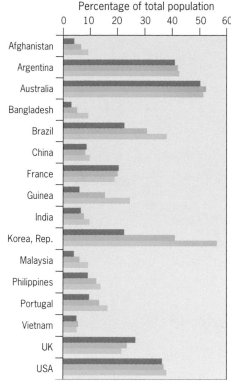

Figure 1.6 Distribution of the million cities by region, 1965–95 (*Source:* Hirsch, 1995)

Countries with cities over a million inhabitants	1965
	1980
	1998

Percentage of population living in cities

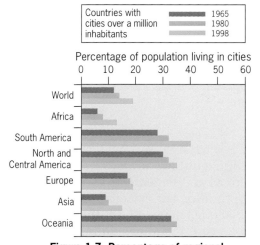

Figure 1.7 Percentage of regional populations living in million cities, 1965–99 (*Source:* Philip's Geographical Digest, 1998–99)

Figure 1.5 Conway, Wales

Additionally, in the first half of the twentieth century the world's major cities were concentrated in Europe and North America. By 2000, eight out of the largest sixteen cities were in Asia and several of the world's **megacities** (with over 10 million people) were also located there and in economically less developed countries (ELCDs)(Fig. 1.8). The interpretation of figures relating to urbanisation raises two important questions:

• how do we define urban settlements?

• how reliable are figures relating to urban settlements and urbanisation?

1.3 Defining urban settlements

Geographers look at settlements and tend to divide them into rural or urban. Underlying this division is an assumption that it is relatively easy to distinguish between rural and urban settlements. However, this is more complicated than you might think. For example, in 1990, Carter's attempt to distinguish rural from urban settlements describes villages as places in which 'most people work in agriculture', whilst in towns 'most people work in industry or other non-agricultural occupations'. But villages have many non-agricultural occupations, such as shopkeepers, publican and priest. In addition, people living in villages of the developed world commute to work in towns. So differences between town and village, urban and rural become complex.

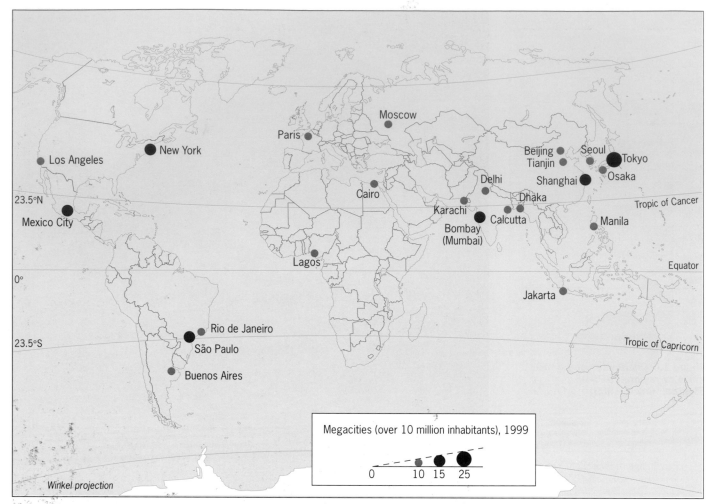

Figure 1.8 Cities with over 10 million inhabitants (1999)
(*Source:* Adapted from Philips Geographical Digest, 1998–99)

2a Describe the pattern of megacities for the year 1999 shown in Figure 1.8.

b Suggest reasons why, despite the growth of megacities in ELDCs, the global economy in 2005 will still be managed from cities in EMDCs, such as London, New York and Frankfurt.

So what is urban?

Given the problems of definition outlined so far, it is hardly surprising that different countries employ different methods of distinguishing 'urban' from 'rural'. In fact, the criteria for separating urban from rural settlements vary greatly in length and complexity from country to country. For example, in Israel 'urban' means all settlements with over 2000 inhabitants, except those where at least one-third of the heads of households earn their living from agriculture. In Norway, by contrast, 'urban' means any settlement of 200 or more inhabitants. Generally, there are four main ways of defining urban areas.

Definition 1: population size

This is the commonest and simplest definition. However on a world-wide basis, the problem is whether countries reach agreement on the minimum population size at which a settlement stops being a village and becomes a town. The contrasts in such a size range from 200 people in Norway to 50 000 in Japan. This shows that international comparisons of 'urban' statistics can be potentially very misleading.

Sometimes, as in Sweden, in addition to the minimum population size, a 'town' has to have a limited distance between houses. This is a measure of its compactness or density. In Sweden, built-up areas have 200 inhabitants and not more than 200 metres between houses.

Definition 2: employment

Some countries use the presence of agricultural employment as a measure for separating villages from towns. So, for example, in the Netherlands an urban

?

3a Look at Figures 1.9 and 1.10 and identify which is a town, which is a village.
b Justify the basis for your decision.
4a Look at a 1:50 000 Ordnance Survey map of your area. Divide the settlements into:
• towns; and
• villages. Keep a note of the criteria you use to make this division.
b Compare your criteria with those of other students. How far do you agree? In what aspects do you disagree?

Figure 1.9 Settlement, Norfolk, UK

Figure 1.10 Settlement, Worcestershire, UK

5a For each of the four main approaches to defining urban areas outline:
• the main advantages;
• the problems and disadvantages.
b Work out a definition for urban settlements which uses a combination of all four approaches. Now apply this to the settlements in your area. How well does it work?

area has to have at least 2000 people with less than 20 per cent of the economically active male population engaged in agriculture.

Definition 3: facilities and functions

In countries such as the Czech Republic, settlements which contain basic amenities are called towns. Here, urban areas are defined as 'having 5000 inhabitants, piped water and a sewerage system for the major part of the town, at least five physicians and a pharmacy, a nine year secondary school, an hotel with at least 20 beds'.

Definition 4: government legislation

Some governments, such as in Iraq, designate certain administrative areas as being 'urban'. However, there is the additional problem in some countries of unreliable census information. To make things even more complicated, there is no guarantee that the administrative units used in a census coincide with the actual built-up area. The unit may include much more land than the town. This situation is called **overbounded**. If the town is much bigger than the administrative unit, as was the case of Manchester (in the 1890s), an **underbounded** situation exists. These problems usually result from the rapid growth of cities and the need for administrative units to be redefined to keep pace with this expansion.

Clearly, statistics showing the urban percentage of a country's population need to be treated with great care because of variations in definition, the unreliability of some census data and problems of under or overbounding.

1.4 The world pattern of urbanisation

The process of urbanisation was very important in the EMDCs of western Europe during the nineteenth century, and in North America during the early twentieth century. Urbanisation is a phenomenon today of most ELDCs and of the post-socialist countries of eastern Europe (see section 1.8). The key questions we therefore need to ask about this process are:

6a Divide the countries in Table 1.1 into at least four major groups. Give these groups titles and justify your results.
b Now compare your grouping with that of other students. How far do you agree on titles, group members or reasons for the grouping?
c Try to agree on a general grouping which you can all justify.

Table 1.1 Total population and urban percentage for selected countries
(Source: Philip's Geographical Digest, 1999)

	Total population (millions)	Percentage urban
Argentina	34.6	89
Australia	18.0	85
Belgium	10.2	97
Bolivia	7.4	65
Brazil	157.8	81
Burma (Myanmar)	44.8	28
Czech Republic	10.4	66
Ecuador	11.5	62
France	58.1	73
Hungary	10.2	67
India	942.9	29
Mozambique	17.4	41
Poland	38.6	63
Russia	147.5	75
Sudan	28.1	23
UK	58.6	89
USA	263.2	78

- What features characterised the urbanisation process in the capitalist countries of western Europe and North America?

- What phenomena are associated with urbanisation?

- Is the current urbanisation process in Africa and Asia the same as it was in nineteenth-century western Europe and North America?

1.5 Urbanisation in EMDCs

Generally, more developed countries have over 70 per cent of their population living in urban areas (see Table 1.1). In the UK, the percentage of urban dwellers rose from 33.8 per cent in 1801 to 78 per cent in 1901. Today, it is 89 per cent.

Industrialisation

The urbanisation process in many EMDCs was closely associated with industrialisation in the nineteenth and twentieth centuries (see section 2.6). Because of the Industrial Revolution, society gradually changed from being dependent on agriculture to depending on industry. These industries were mainly located in towns. In the UK, massive industrial growth was based on the development of markets at home and abroad (such as the USA), together with the ability to harness new technological developments, such as steam and electric power. This industrial growth in turn attracted large numbers of people to live near the factories that produced the new specialised commodities (Fig. 1.11). A process of cumulative growth (Fig. 1.12) began in which industry not only attracted workers to the growing towns but also services such as roads, railways and sewage systems. These then gave advantages which attracted more factories and so stimulated further invention and innovation.

It was the largest UK towns, such as London and Manchester, which grew fastest in the nineteenth century. In 1801 there was only one city with over 100 000 people, namely London, accounting for 32 per cent of the total population. By 1901, there were 33 cities over 100 000 accounting for 56 per cent of the population.

Suburbanisation

A second feature of urbanisation in capitalist countries during the nineteenth and twentieth centuries was the rapid development of suburbs. City centres became noisy, dirty, congested and dangerous places packed with factories and

?

7 Study maps from the nineteenth century of a city in your region. (These are available in Record Offices and the reference section of main libraries.)
a When did the main spatial growth of the town take place?
b How far did population growth parallel this spatial growth? (Local libraries will have census figures.)
c Which industries were responsible for the growth?
d Where were most nineteenth-century factories located?

Figure 1.11 Colliers' cottages, Tyneside, c. 1850

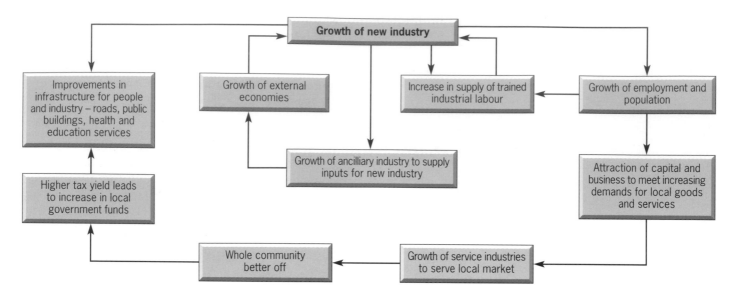

Figure 1.12 Cumulative growth of cities

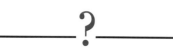

8 Study Tables 1.2 and 1.3.
a Briefly describe the main trends shown in the different types of urban area in the UK and in the USA.
b Explain the implications of the trends you have identified in relation to planning within settlements for the future provision of:
• hospitals;
• clinics and general practitioners;
• public transport;
• patterns of shopping;
• leisure facilities;
• business parks.

often plagued by disease (Fig. 1.13). As a result, those people who could afford it moved to live at the edge of town. This **suburbanisation** process became possible because of the development of mass transit systems, such as trams and railways. Thus towns spread outwards in leaps and bounds, leading to a constant attempt by local government to extend town boundaries to take in the new settlements and the rate revenue they produced.

Counter-urbanisation
The third, more recent, process of urban development in capitalist countries is called **counter-urbanisation**. This involves people abandoning cities in favour of areas which are essentially rural in character. Nonetheless, although people may relocate, they tend to continue with habits and lifestyles used in their previous urban environments. There is, though, a pattern of inner city decline and growth of population in small towns and villages in the countryside (Tables 1.2 and 1.3). Two factors encourage this process:

• easier movement as a result of rising car ownership and the construction of motorways;

• developments in information technology and telecommunications which allow people to communicate easily over long distances.

Table 1.2 England and Wales: population percentage changes, 1961–91

	1961–71	1971–81	1981–91
Conurbations			
Greater London	–6.8	–10.1	–8.1
Merseyside	–8.5	–11.0	–7.5
S-E Lancashire	–1.4	–6.2	–6.3
Tyneside	–5.9	–9.2	–6.1
West Midlands	–0.3	–5.4	–4.1
West Yorkshire	+1.4	–3.0	–5.2
Towns outside conurbations			
Over 100 000	+2.6	–1.16	–0.9
50 000–100 000	+9.4	2.2	5.1
Under 50 000	+13.0	5.5	7.8

Table 1.3 United States of America: population percentage changes, 1980–90

	Central city	Suburbs and beyond
Chicago	–12.5	+13.6
Cleveland	–26.2	+1.2
Detroit	–21.0	+8.6
Houston	+25.2	+79.0
San Diego	+26.1	+51.1
USA average	–5.1	+17.1

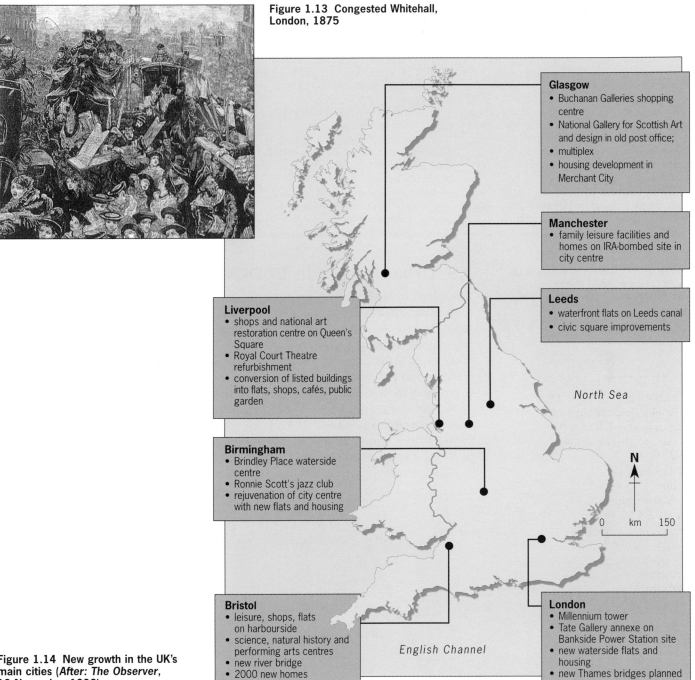

Figure 1.13 Congested Whitehall, London, 1875

Glasgow
• Buchanan Galleries shopping centre
• National Gallery for Scottish Art and design in old post office;
• multiplex
• housing development in Merchant City

Manchester
• family leisure facilities and homes on IRA-bombed site in city centre

Leeds
• waterfront flats on Leeds canal
• civic square improvements

Liverpool
• shops and national art restoration centre on Queen's Square
• Royal Court Theatre refurbishment
• conversion of listed buildings into flats, shops, cafés, public garden

Birmingham
• Brindley Place waterside centre
• Ronnie Scott's jazz club
• rejuvenation of city centre with new flats and housing

Bristol
• leisure, shops, flats on harbourside
• science, natural history and performing arts centres
• new river bridge
• 2000 new homes

London
• Millennium tower
• Tate Gallery annexe on Bankside Power Station site
• new waterside flats and housing
• new Thames bridges planned

North Sea

English Channel

N

0   km   150

Figure 1.14 New growth in the UK's main cities (*After: The Observer*, 10 November 1996)

The result is population dispersal over large areas, creating what seem to be dispersed cities. This further complicates any attempt to separate 'urban areas' from 'rural areas' (see section 1.3). In effect, the two are now interlinked in a complex regional system towards which more and more capitalist countries are moving.

Re-urbanisation

Fourthly, and most recently, cities in EMDCs have shown their ability to survive and start growing again in a process called re-urbanisation (Fig. 1.14). In this case, cities give themselves a face-lift by redeveloping their centres or decayed inner city zones. As a result, people are attracted back into areas where the population was declining (Fig. 1.15).

SOMETHING is stirring in Britain's cities. For two decades, millions of people have fled from their crime, pollution and squalor. But slowly, subtly, they are once again becoming desirable places in which to live.

From Glasgow to Birmingham, Liverpool to Bristol, Newcastle to London, the stampede to the countryside has slowed to a trickle. In some big cities, Manchester and London among them, the trend is starting to be reversed: people are moving back to the urban hub.

The residents re-colonising the cities are led by the affluent middle-class. They are mostly under 40, singles or childless couples, and working in the professions. These are the people buying the expensive lofts and warehouses, on waterside developments – London's Docklands, Manchester's quayside, Liverpool's Albert Dock – and in classily converted listed buildings.

But local authorities and developers say older people are interested, too. Divested of their children and eager to live close to cities' cultural and gastronomical delights, they are – albeit in small numbers – selling the family house and moving into town, perhaps buying a small rural retreat for weekends. One crucial factor is green politics. Labour and the Conservatives publicly accept that we must protect our countryside from destructive development. Last week both parties affirmed their view that at least half of the 4.4 million homes the Government believes this country needs by 2016 should be built in urban areas.

There are also fears that the colonisation of cities by a wealthy minority will be socially divisive. Most of the new homes are security 'fortresses' in warehouses or 'executive estates' hidden behind tall gates and intercom systems.

Figure 1.15 Civic pride grows in UK cities (*Source:* David Harrison, *The Observer*, 10 November 1996)

1.6 Urbanisation in ELDCs

Urbanisation in the European countries was a relatively gradual process, but in most economically less developed countries (ELDCs) the change is much more rapid. In fact, Figure 1.17 shows that, on a world scale, the proportion of population living in urban areas (as defined by the United Nations) is growing more rapidly than ever before. A closer examination of the data reveals that it is the urban population of the ELDCs in Asia, Africa and Latin America which is growing most swiftly (Figs 1.16–1.18, see Figs 1.6, 1.7). Between 1800 and 1850, the world's urban population grew on average by 22.5 per cent per decade. Between 1980 and 1990, it grew by 41.2 per cent. The speed and scale of this urban growth in ELDCs is a new phenomenon for the world and is the result of a series of interrelated factors.

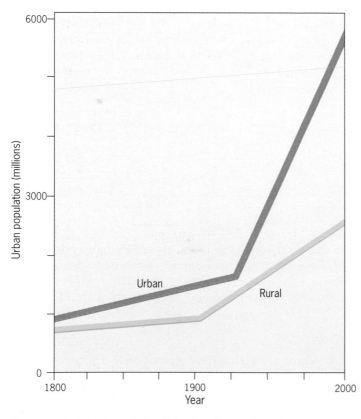

Figure 1.16 World population living in urban and rural areas

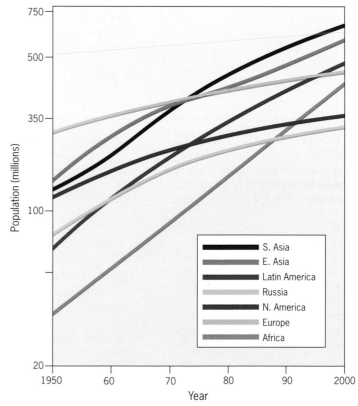

Figure 1.17 Urban growth by continent

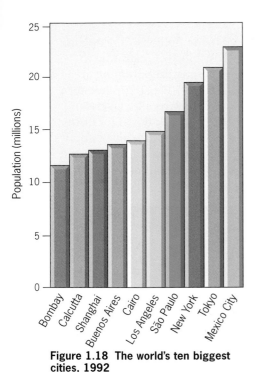

Figure 1.18 The world's ten biggest cities, 1992

Rapid population growth
Increased global population growth results from rapidly lowered death rates, combined with slowly declining birth rates. This then contributes to the urbanisation process both as the cities themselves grow (through lowered death rates), and as the pressure of population in relation to the resources in rural areas increases. This forces people to migrate into cities (Fig. 1.18). For example, Kenya's population grew from 5.4 million in 1950 to 15.3 in 1959 and 18.8 in 1983. By 1995, Kenya's population had reached 28.3 million and was 37 million by the year 2000. In line with this national growth, the population of the capital Nairobi doubled between 1980 and 1990 (Fig. 1.19).

Modernisation of agriculture
Much rural change in ELDCs has seen a shift towards higher capital input and relatively high technology. As a result, fewer agricultural workers are needed and therefore many people looking for work migrate to cities. Similarly, many ELDCs, such as Zimbabwe, Kenya, South Africa and Chile, have switched to producing more cash crops, e.g. coffee, tea, flowers and vegetables. These countries aim to generate export revenues to meet their burden of debt to Western banks. In order to compete in world markets, these export crops have to be produced on a large scale and as cheaply as possible. So, once again, fewer labourers are required. This highlights an important difference between modern urbanisation in ELDCs and its nineteenth-century equivalent in EMDCs. In EMDCs, the agricultural revolution took place alongside an industrial revolution and the two processes were closely related. By contrast, current agricultural change in ELDCs pushes people to the cities, but there is only limited industrial development to support them.

Industrial competition
EMDCs, such as the UK and USA, are urgently seeking new markets in the poorer ELDCs. The ELDCs import manufactured goods, ranging from pots and pans to cars, tractors and chemicals, but with this, their own traditional industries are destroyed. These traditional industries, such as leather-making, textiles and metal-working, are unable to compete with the low-cost, mass production of their Western equivalents. So the traditional craft economy disintegrates, displacing people in both cities and the countryside, who are forced to search for better opportunities.

9 Study Figures 1.16 and 1.17.
a Describe the pattern of world urban development in 1992, making particular reference to the differences between world areas and between cities.
b Now use Figure 1.17 to predict the likely pattern of urban development by the year 2020, paying particular attention to:
• variations in growth rates between world areas;
• likely future trends;
• the implications of these trends for countries in the regions shown.

Figure 1.19 Migrants (environmental refugees) crowd one of Nairobi's wealthy districts

Improved communications

Media, and especially the spread of television, have made millions of people in ELDCs aware of urban living standards and of the possibility of migrating to share them. People all over ELDCs now watch television, even in remote areas where community centres provide them for whole villages (Fig. 1.20). Western soap operas feature widely on such televisions, glamorising city life. Overall, television, radio and magazines widen people's horizons, break down localism, generate discontent with local conditions and build new (often unrealistic) hopes for a better lifestyle in cities. In addition, news from people who have migrated to cities spreads information and ideas which reinforce the chain of migration.

Figure 1.20 Communal television-watching, Rajasthan, India

1.7 The effects of rapid urbanisation in ELDCs

One result of recent rapid urbanisation is that cities lack the economic growth to support large and increasing populations. This **over-urbanisation** is clearly visible in cities such as Calcutta (see Chapter 10) and Mumbai in India, where development of manufacturing and service industries has not been fast enough to keep pace with population growth. In Mumbai, with 12.5 million people, only 3.4 million are employed in industry.

Primacy is a second important feature of urbanisation in ELDCs. Primacy is the degree to which a country's largest city dominates all other cities. So, for example, Dakar in Senegal contains 18 per cent of the country's population, 80 per cent of its industry and 75 per cent of its commercial workers. Urbanisation then contributes to primacy as more and more people and activities move into the first city. However, historical factors also play a part in primacy. This is because cities such as Dakar, Singapore or Lagos were developed during colonial times as centres for trade, industry and political power. Such centres tended to be ports, because the emphasis in the colonial era was on exporting raw materials, e.g. cocoa, tin or rubber, and importing manufactured goods. Thus coastal sites became the best location for many colonial cities, which were also centres for political control. Dakar, therefore, in the nineteenth century was the political and economic centre for much of what used to be French West Africa. When such countries regained their independence, the primacy of cities like Dakar was so firmly established that they continued to grow and to dominate the surrounding area.

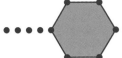

Rank–size rule

The study of the numerical relationship between the size and importance of towns and cities began in EMDCs. The rank–size rule was first introduced in 1913. By 1941, Zipf claimed that the size of settlements is inversely proportional to their rank. Thus, the population of the second city of a country will be about half that of the largest city. Similarly, the population of the third largest city will, in theory, be about one third the size of the largest city, and so on down the urban hierarchy. The rank–size rule suggests that in any settlement system there will be very few large places and very many small places – few cities and many villages. This supports the central place theory (see section 3.2).

Variations from the rank–size rule

While we can see that the rank–size rule seems to work quite well in European countries, it is much less appropriate for many ELDCs. For example, Dakar has 1.3 million people but Thies, the next largest town, has only 132 000 people. Thus although Dakar is a primate city, it is at least *three* times larger than we might expect from the rank–size rule. This same pattern can be found in many other ELDCs. In Figure 1.21, city size has been plotted against rank order for four countries on a semi-logarithmic scale. A straight line sloping from left to right at 45° indicates that the cities of a country fit the hypothetical rank–size rule. A very steep slope to the graph, as in the case of Mexico, indicates a **primate**

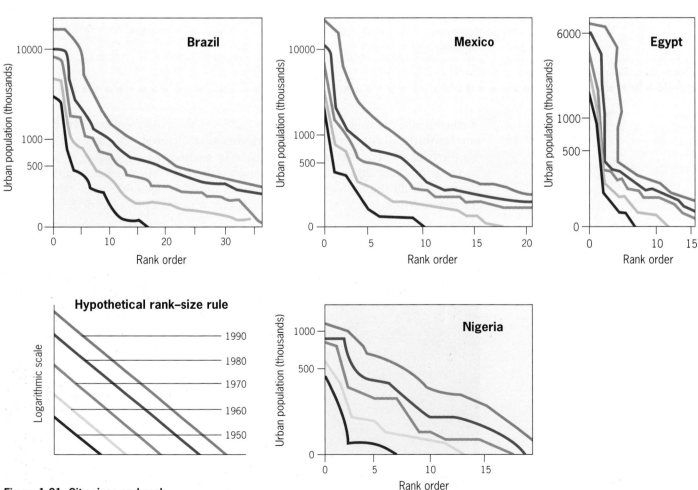

Figure 1.21 City sizes and rank

pattern with one dominant city. The primate city is a rapidly growing metropolis attracting large numbers of in-migrants. This is representative of the early to middle stages of the development process. Brazil and Egypt have two major cities in the urban hierarchy and this is called a **binary (bi-primate) pattern**, which refers to the later stages of development as regional and local centres emerge.

Table 1.4 Growth of cities in Pakistan, Argentina and Colombia, 1950–95 (thousand people)

	1950	1960	1980	1998
Pakistan				
Karachi	1086	1884	3499	9863
Lahore	826	1262	2165	5085
Hyderabad	232	419	628	1107
Multan	182	344	642	1257
Rawalpindi	147	277	615	1290
Peshawar	148	214	268	1676
Argentina				
Buenos Aires	4231	7000	9900	10990
Rosario	560	672	955	1096
Córdoba	426	589	982	1199
Mendoza	256	427	597	780
La Plata	325	414	562	690
Santa Fé	217	260	287	427
Colombia				
Bogotá	607	1241	2855	5026
Medellín	341	579	1160	1621
Cali	269	486	990	1719
Barranquila	287	414	692	1064
Cartengena	124	185	355	746
Manizales	123	167	232	333

?

10 Use the data in Table 1.4 to construct semi-log graphs showing the rank–size pattern of cities in Pakistan, Argentina and Colombia. Comment briefly on:
a The main changes in the nature of the urban system in each country.
b The key differences between the urban systems.

A third result of rapid urbanisation in ELDCs is the growth of **squatter settlements**, also known as **spontaneous settlements**. The huge influx of people from the countryside means that city authorities are unable to provide services for everyone, especially housing for the poor. As a result, migrants are forced to build themselves basic shelters on the least desirable sites, often on the urban fringe. These sites usually lack any water supply, electricity or a

Figure 1.22 Shanty housing built into the sea, Salvador, Brazil

11 What similarities are there in the main features of urban growth in EMDCs and those in ELDCs? What are the main differences?

12a On two world maps use Fig 1.23 to plot the distribution of megacities in 1970 and 2000
b What were the main changes in the number and distribution of megacities between 1970 and 2000?
c Explain the changes you describe in **b**

13 'Megacities create more problems than they solve'. How far do you agree with this statement? Refer to specific examples in your answer.

sewerage system (Fig. 1.22, see also Fig. 1.19). Spontaneous settlements house 46 per cent of the total population of Mexico City (see Figs 2.24–2.25), 33 per cent of Calcutta's population and 25 per cent of Jakarta's population.

In parts of Africa, Asia and Latin America, we can see that a fourth result of rapid urbanisation is a combination of **unemployment**, **underemployment** and the growth of employment in the **informal sector**. It is difficult for large numbers of migrants arriving in cities in ELDCs to find jobs. Despite some growth in manufacturing industry, many factories are highly automated and so employ relatively few people. As a result, people may seek work in the service sector, especially administration. National and local government are major employers, giving people jobs ranging from administering public works to collecting taxes. But even this sector cannot provide jobs for all city dwellers, and with more workers than there are formal jobs, people are forced to work in the informal sector. Here, they have no job security, receive no permanent wage or recognition by the state (for tax purposes) and are self-employed. Much of the nature of informal work, in both less and more developed countries, is that it is seasonal, or temporary. For example, street vendors in large cities, such as Bombay in India, depend on tourists to boost their income. Obviously, their wages will be higher during the 'tourist season'. Similarly, people may work as fruit or vegetable sellers, barbers, or even prostitutes in order to survive in the city (see section 7.3). Because of the seasonality and insecurity of the informal sector, many people are actually underemployed and only able to work for part of the year.

1.8 Megacities and world cities

The very rapid growth of cities in ELDCs has also led to the creation of megacities. These are cities whose population is over 10 million. In 1950 New York and London were the world's only megacities, but by 2000 there were 27 in this category. Of these, 22 were in the poorer ELDCs (Fig. 1.23). These megacities have expanded from million-city status to their present size as a result, in some cases, of becoming capital cities (Dhaka and Istanbul).

Figure 1.23 Cities and urban areas with over 10 million people 1970–2000 (*Source:* Philips Geographical)

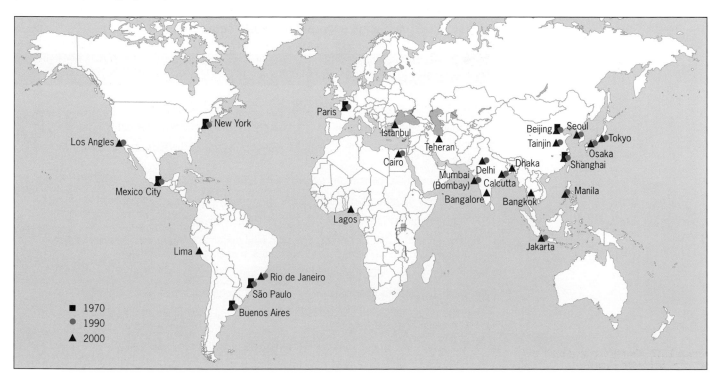

■ 1970
● 1990
▲ 2000

Figure 1.24 Photo of Bangkok, showing air pollution

Other megacities have expanded as a result of rapid industrialisation (Seoul, São Paulo), or have become centres for inward investment from richer EMDCs (Bangkok).

The growth of megacities has created benefits such as a large market for industrial goods, together with a resource of skilled labour for new companies looking to locate in the area. Services such as education and health are usually better in megacities than in surrounding areas, as are electricity supplies, postal services and the availability of piped water. Employment opportunities in megacities in both the formal and informal sectors are generally better than in small cities, and self-help housing schemes do allow people to find basic accommodation.

However, the growth of megacities has not been uniformly good. Employment opportunities in megacities draw in thousands of people from other, smaller cities, which leads to overcrowding in megacities and a labour shortage in some smaller towns. Rapid industrialisation has created massive air, land and water pollution in places such as São Paulo, Bangkok (Fig. 1.24) and Calcutta.

Megacities are home to some of the richest people in their countries, but they are also home to some of the poorest. These inequalities in terms of wealth and access to services are becoming more pronounced in megacities such as New York, Mumbai and Manila, and may lead to political and social unrest. Public administration in many megacities is difficult because of the sheer size of the urban area and the multiplicity of different municipalities. This leads to delays, inefficiency and dissatisfaction. Environmental problems in megacities in many ELDCs have become so great that their Brown Agenda (see pages 173–80) has become very important. Problems of water supply, sewage disposal, air and water pollution together with poverty make these environmental problems particularly difficult to solve.

World Cities

World cities are centres of global capitalism, that is the places where command and control is exercised over the global economy. World cities are important because of their economic power. They are usually the base for transnational companies operating in the area and also have a wide range of financial offices and business services. London, New York, Tokyo, Berlin, Mexico City and Rio de Janeiro are good examples of world cities.

Summary

- Urbanisation is an important aspect of life in all parts of the world.
- Urbanisation has demographic, socio-economic and behavioural aspects.
- Cities have existed for thousands of years and some of the earliest cities were in today's ELDCs.
- Recent urbanisation is more rapid than its earlier forms and has created million cities.
- Definitions of 'urban' and 'rural' areas vary greatly from country to country.
- Statistics on world urbanisation have to be treated with caution.
- Average world statistics on urbanisation hide important differences between slower urbanisation in EMDCs and very rapid rates in ELDCs.
- Urbanisation in EMDCs was often accompanied by industrialisation.
- Recently, counter-urbanisation has become a feature of urban areas in EMDCs.
- Rapid urbanisation in ELDCs has resulted in over-urbanisation, primacy and the growth of spontaneous settlements.
- Megacities and world cities are becoming more and more important.

2 A historical perspective of the growth of cities

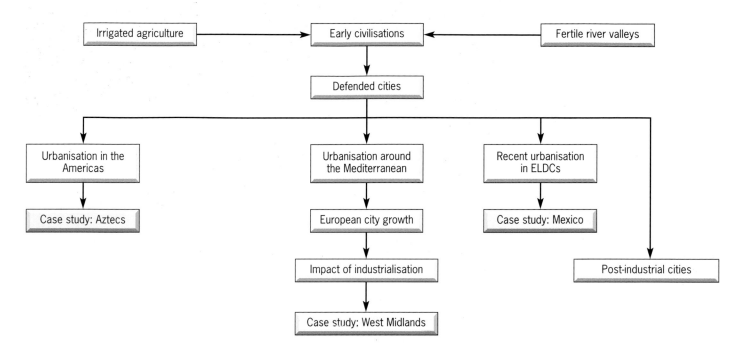

```
Irrigated agriculture ──────────► Early civilisations ◄────────── Fertile river valleys
                                          │
                                          ▼
                                   Defended cities
                                          │
        ┌─────────────────────────────────┼──────────────────────────────────────┐
        ▼                                  ▼                          ▼            │
Urbanisation in the              Urbanisation around        Recent urbanisation    │
    Americas                     the Mediterranean              in ELDCs           │
        │                                  │                          │            │
        ▼                                  ▼                          ▼            ▼
Case study: Aztecs               European city growth       Case study: Mexico   Post-industrial cities
                                          │
                                          ▼
                                 Impact of industrialisation
                                          │
                                          ▼
                                 Case study: West Midlands
```

2.1 Introduction

In this chapter we examine historical processes in the development of cities. We will consider both pre- and post-industrial urbanisation while contrasting areas in the developed and developing worlds. The aim is to aid understanding of urban structures and residential segregation.

2.2 Ancient river-valley cities, 3500–1000 BC

The world's earliest cities began to develop around 5000 years ago in four separate areas of intense agricultural activity. Here, along the banks of large rivers, a number of dispersed farming villages evolved into towns and grew into cities (Fig. 2.1). Then, 2000 years ago cities also began to grow in Middle America and south-west Nigeria.

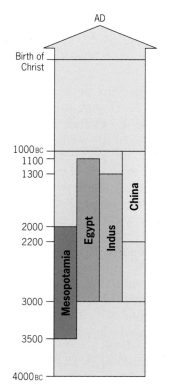

Figure 2.1 The early river-valley civilisations, 4000–1000 BC

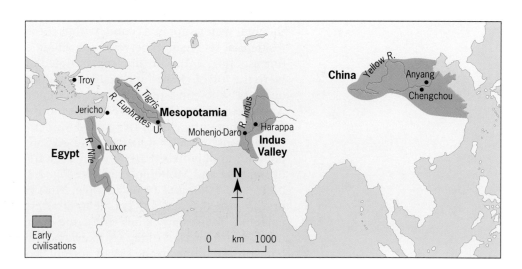

Figure 2.2 Remains of Jericho: an early farming settlement in the Jordan Valley, Israel, which grew into a prosperous city, *c.*7000 BC

Class pyramid

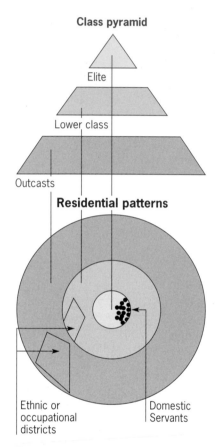

Figure 2.3 Characteristics of the pre-industrial city (*After*: Sjoberg, 1960, and Radford, 1979)

A secure agricultural base was vital to the creation of these early city cultures. It provided a surplus of food which allowed people to work in areas other than farming. Hence, specialisation of labour took place as craftsmen and traders did not need to depend on the soil for their livelihood. The form of these early cities reflected their origins, in that most were walled. One of the earliest known cities, Jericho *c.*7350 BC (see Fig. 2.1), grew from a farming village to a town of four hectares surrounded by a substantial stone wall with a ditch and guarded by towers (Fig. 2.2).

These defences illustrate that agricultural prosperity and wealth demanded permanent, static defences. In addition, they reveal the ability of early farmers to organise themselves collectively. As community sizes increased, so it became necessary to increase agricultural production. In the Near East, the main method for increasing crop yields was through irrigation, by digging canals and contructing dams.

Structure of early cities

The city walls also showed an important division between the protected and unprotected parts of the settlement, and illustrate the developing urban hierarchy. First, because the protection of the walls had to be funded, they marked the control of the ruling élite. This élite supervised the collection and distribution of surplus food as part of the power they exercised over the rest of the people. The élite maintained their political and religious hold by controlling the vital water supply. Second, within these early city walls there was marked residential segregation between the ruling élite, the lower classes and the outcasts (Fig. 2.3). The élite concentrated around the city centre. Further out were the lower classes of merchants and artisans and further out still were the outcasts, who consisted of slaves and minority ethnic and religious groups. Archaeological evidence reveals that most of these early cities were not large. For example, the city of Ur (part of Sumer – the earliest of all known civilisations), in Mesopotamia, covered about 50 ha and probably had a population of between 10 000 and 34 000 (Fig. 2.4). Similarly, the Indus cities of Harappa and Mohenjo-Daro (see Fig. 2.1) covered about 200 ha and housed between 10 000 and 15 000 people. Most early cities also led a rather precarious existence, susceptible to disasters such as flood, earthquake, war or epidemic. Many early cities fell to one or other of these disasters. For example, in the north-west of today's Turkey, excavations reveal nine cities buried one beneath the other on the site of ancient Troy (Fig. 2.5).

Figure 2.4 The ziggurat of Ur, southern Mesopotamia, c.2100 BC: standing three stories high, trees may once have grown on the terraces, while the summit was crowned by a temple.

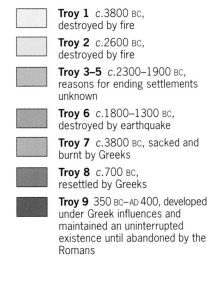

Troy 1 *c.*3800 BC, destroyed by fire

Troy 2 *c.*2600 BC, destroyed by fire

Troy 3–5 *c.*2300–1900 BC, reasons for ending settlements unknown

Troy 6 *c.*1800–1300 BC, destroyed by earthquake

Troy 7 *c.*3800 BC, sacked and burnt by Greeks

Troy 8 *c.*700 BC, resettled by Greeks

Troy 9 350 BC–AD 400, developed under Greek influences and maintained an uninterrupted existence until abandoned by the Romans

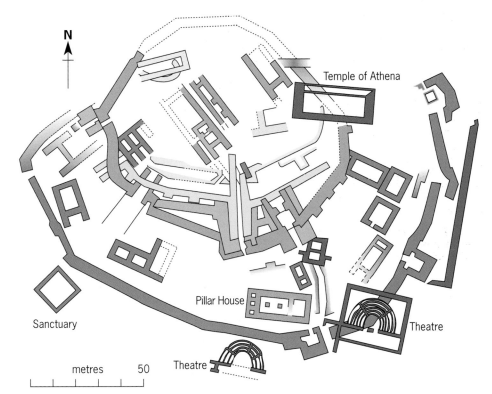

Temple of Athena

Pillar House

Sanctuary

Theatre

Theatre

metres   50

Figure 2.5 Troy: its many falls and rebuildings

2.3 Graeco-Roman cities, 600 BC–AD 600

The ancient cities, up to 1000 BC, were handicapped by technological, political and transport restrictions. The impact of war and conflict also limited the cities' survival. As a result, most declined. The next important phase of urban growth took place between 600 BC and AD 400 in the Mediterranean region.

Between 3000 BC and 1000 BC, the ideas of city life passed from Mesopotamia and Egypt to Crete and then Greece. It was developments in production, trade and colonisation which assisted the growth of Greek cities

Erechtheum

Gateway

Roman theatre

Parthenon

Walls and fortifications

Greek theatre

Formal walkway

Figure 2.6 The Acropolis, Athens, Greece

Figure 2.7 Remains of the Forum, Rome, Italy: markets were held in the large square which formed the centre of social life in Rome

?

1a Make a list of the main reasons for the foundation and growth of the earliest cities.
b Now reorganise your list so that it is written in order of most important factors. Mark against each factor: P (for political), E (for economic) or M (for military) to identify the main influence on each city.
2 Suggest reasons why Greek and Roman cities began to decline.

within a framework of city-states. Athens was the largest city with a population of 180 000 by the fifth century BC, while most other cities were much smaller.

Greek cities developed impressive citadels, i.e. defensive places, of which the Acropolis in Athens is the best known (Fig. 2.6). Temples and market squares, surrounded by a maze of narrow streets, were other important features of Greek cities. Where areas had been devastated by war or natural disaster, the cleared site allowed comprehensive planning for rebuilding. This usually involved a rectangular pattern of city layout, such as the rebuilt city of Miletus.

However, it was the Romans who built not only a great empire but also the largest city of the classical world. Rome began as a village of shepherds about 760 BC. Later, a temple was built on Capitol Hill and a market place developed outside the walled town on reclaimed marshland. The Romans developed very successful building techniques using concrete, brick and marble (Fig. 2.7). Roman engineers also built roads, bridges, aqueducts and docks all over Western Europe.

By the second century AD, Rome had a population of about a million people. However, as the city grew so did the problems of supplying it with food and water, as well as the difficulties of traffic jams. From about AD 200, though, the Roman Empire began to decline. Like earlier city-states and urban civilisations (see section 2.2), internal divisions weakened the empire's structure. Collapse of the Western Empire by the fifth century was inevitable.

Although both the Greek and Roman worlds had large cities, it is not true to say that urbanisation was an important trend. This is because only a minority of the total population actually lived in cities. The majority remained based in rural areas and working in agriculture.

2.4 Pre-colonial Americas

The civilisations which appeared in the Americas were cut off from all contact with other human life by the Pacific and Atlantic Oceans. Urban developments were therefore unique and not influenced by city growth in the rest of the world. And yet here we can see the same urban processes taking place, even in one of the later civilisations.

Urban development in the Aztec Empire, AD 1325–1500

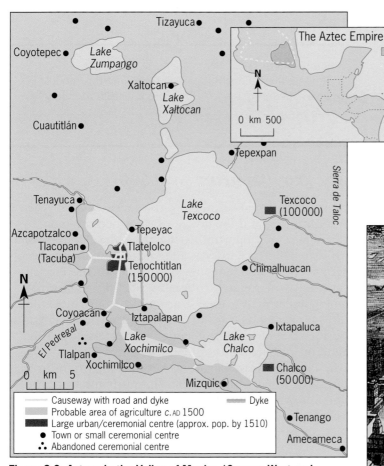

Figure 2.8 **Aztecs in the Valley of Mexico (*Source*: West and Angelli, 1966)**

Valley of Mexico

- Approx. 40–60 km long
- At the centre of the Aztec realm
- The most densely populated part of Middle America by 1500, with 1–2 million people in settlements concentrated on the narrow plain around the five lakes.
- Settlements were supported by an intensive system of agriculture, based on the cultivation of maize, beans and squashes, providing a balanced diet.
- Large cities are one of the key features of the valley.

Figure 2.9 **Reconstruction of Tenochtitlán, Mexico**

The Aztec Empire developed during the late fourteenth and early fifteenth centuries in central Mexico. The empire's focal point was the high, fertile Valley of Mexico (Fig. 2.8) where intensive irrigated farming was possible around the lakes. When the Aztec tribe arrived in the valley from the north, all available land around the lakes was already occupied by other farmers. The Aztecs therefore settled on a small island near the western shore of Lake Texcoco. Here, in 1325, they established a village and ceremonial centre called Tenochtitlán. Within a century, this grew into a magnificent city and capital. The central square of present-day Mexico City lies over the ruins of Tenochtitlán.

Tenochtitlán developed as the core of the Aztec Empire, dominated by its huge ceremonial square, temples and pyramids in the city centre (Fig. 2.9). It was also a focus of power, which was legitimised by religion. The ruler was seen as being close to a god, or even a god himself, and so people worshipped him. His palace was at the heart of the city, where lived the rich, powerful and also the priests. Servants and slaves saw to their needs. Peasants were forced to give part of their crops and produce as tribute to the city's élite. This was often stored in Tenochtitlán's temples. Further away lived the lesser nobility, merchants and craftsmen, whilst the remaining slaves lived at the city's edge. The island city was linked to the mainland by causeways. Each causeway was both a road and a dyke which helped to prevent flooding by Lake Texcoco.

From 1428 onwards, the Aztecs pushed out the boundaries of their empire through a series of alliances and military conquests. They transformed themselves into a well-organised state, and within 75 years the Aztecs controlled most of the area from the Rio Grande in the north to Guatemala in the south.

The Aztecs held fierce military control over conquered peoples and extracted rich payments from them, e.g. grain, gold, textiles, or cacao. These were carried back to Tenochtitlán and placed in the ruler's store-houses, or divided between the nobility. Although the Aztecs established a few military garrisons at strategic points, they made no attempt to impose their language, religion or culture on the defeated people.

3 Study Figure 2.3.
a How far does Tenochtitlán seem to follow this model?
b In what ways is Tenochtitlán different from the model?

Figure 2.10 Champs-Elysées with the Arc de Triomphe in the far distance, Paris, France

2.5 European city growth after AD 1600

The popularity of classical styles persisted throughout the seventeenth, eighteenth and nineteenth centuries, and the layout of cities became more geometric, with avenues and piazzas. Opportunities for the redevelopment of medieval cities, such as in seventeenth-century Rome, or for new urban areas, as in Bloomsbury or Belgravia in London, encouraged this trend. The French capital, Paris, in particular, shows the squares, fountains, obelisks and formal gardens which had become popular by this time. During its reconstruction in the Second Empire, after 1848, Paris was transformed from a medieval city into an Imperial showpiece on the scale of London, Vienna or St Petersburg. This involved building vistas and open spaces, including the Champs-Elysées (Fig. 2.10), L'Etoile and the Place des Invalides. However, it is important to remember that these cities show urban growth rather than urbanisation. The proportion of people living in towns and cities had not, in fact, changed greatly over the preceding thousand years. It was industrialisation which brought about real changes in cities' size and structure.

2.6 The Industrial Revolution and urbanisation

The Industrial Revolution began in Britain about 1750 and continued to influence society there until 1900. Industry arrived later in the rest of Europe, the USA and Japan, but throughout all regions it led to an accelerated growth of urban settlements. This was for two main reasons. First, new industrial techniques using steam power and coal, together with mechanisation and mass production, encouraged industrial agglomeration. It was more economic for factories to locate close to both their source of power and each other. This in turn led to the growth of factory towns. Second, industrialisation began a chain reaction which led to the expansion of tertiary occupations, especially in transport, communications, commerce, finance and scientific training. As even more jobs were created, so towns and cities expanded rapidly.

Figure 2.11 Back-to-back factory workers' housing, Leeds, UK

Urban slums

In Britain, for example, in 1801 only 17 per cent of the 10 million population lived in towns of over 20000. By 1891, 54 per cent of a population of 33 million lived in similar sized towns. Therefore, not only did total population increase, but there was also a shift in population distribution towards the coalfields and away from the rural, agricultural areas. The result of the growth of new urban settlements and developments in existing towns was large-scale changes in the appearance of nineteenth-century British cities. Gasworks, factories, smoke stacks, terraced houses and railways all became increasingly common.

For a time, it seemed as if civic design had been forgotten in the haste to build new houses and factories. Thousands of kilometres of back-to-back houses were constructed as cheap housing for factory workers (Fig. 2.11). There was tremendous overcrowding, coupled with a totally inadequate system of public health and sanitation. Not surprisingly, diseases were rampant with a death rate in the 1840s of 36 per 1000 people and a life expectancy of 30 years.

Conditions in both British cities and factories only improved after long periods of militant reform. The first Public Health Act was passed in 1848 and the first Dwellings Act, of 1875, laid down minimum standards for house building. Other urban construction involved typical Victorian monuments, such as the town hall, clock tower and railway station.

Figure 2.12 Almshouses built by the Cadbury family, Birmingham, UK

4a Study Figure 2.13 then describe and explain the layout of Bournville in terms of:
• location and size of open spaces
• landscaping • location of schools, shops and church hall • transport links • garden provision.
b What criticisms might modern urban planners make of this type of layout?

Figure 2.13 Layout of Bournville, 1915, Birmingham, UK (*Source*: The Bournville Village Trust)

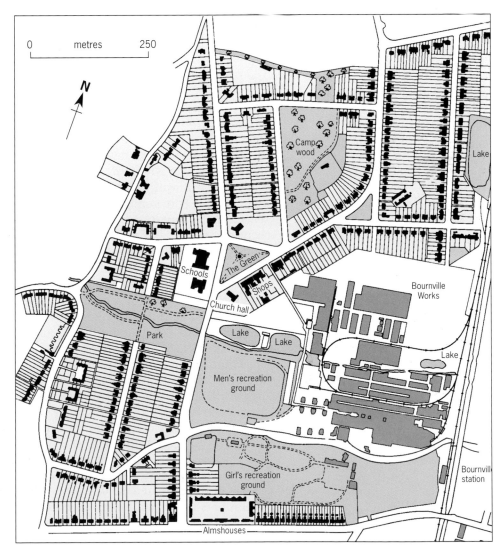

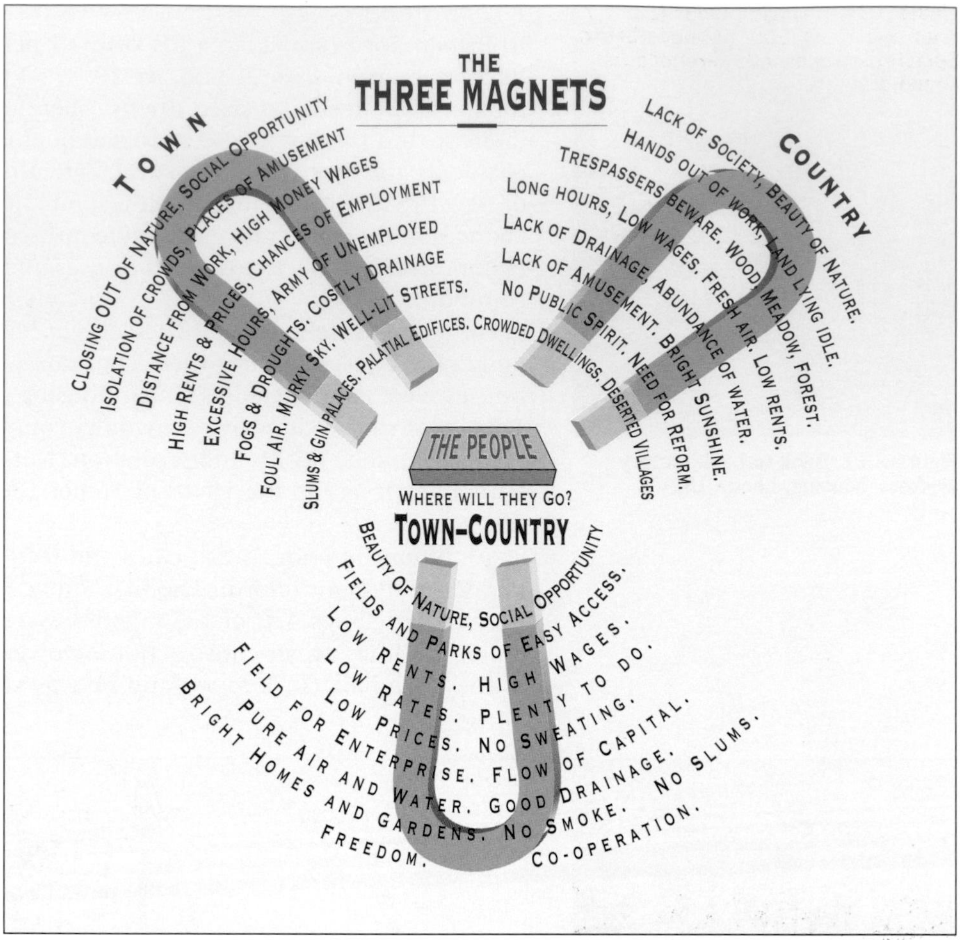

Figure 2.14 Howard's ideas for a garden city

Suburban planning

Some industrialists, however, did attempt to build better urban areas. Robert Owen, as early as 1800, developed New Lanark in Scotland. In 1851, Titus Salt built Saltaire near Bradford, and in 1879 the Cadbury brothers planned Bournville in Birmingham (Figs 2.12–2.13). Similarly, in 1880 the Lever brothers built Port Sunlight near Liverpool. The aim of all these schemes was to create a better environment for employees in which to live and work. The motives of the industrialists varied, though, from a real intention to improve social conditions to the aim of merely maximising profits.

A major step forward in urban reform came in 1898 with the publication of Ebenezer Howard's *Garden Cities of Tomorrow*. Howard argued that new cities should be built in the countryside on agricultural land. He believed high land values in existing cities and high rents encouraged overcrowding and high-density building. On the other hand, rural areas, despite having clean air and open space, lacked transport, employment and housing. So he aimed to combine the advantages of both environments in a 'garden city' (Fig. 2.14). Thus began the garden city movement which was responsible for the construction of Letchworth from 1906 onwards and Welwyn Garden City from 1919 onwards. This pioneer movement was belatedly recognised by the 1946 New Towns Act which led to the creation of the UK's new towns (see Chapter 8).

2.7 Post-industrial cities

Geographers have spent much time examining the urban structure of cities which can be described as **'post-industrial'**. The term is used to include cities such as Los Angeles, where manufacturing industry has long ceased to be the

Figure 2.15 Changing Cities (*Source*: Knox and Pinch (2000) 4th edn Urban Social Geography, p69, Prentice Hall, London)

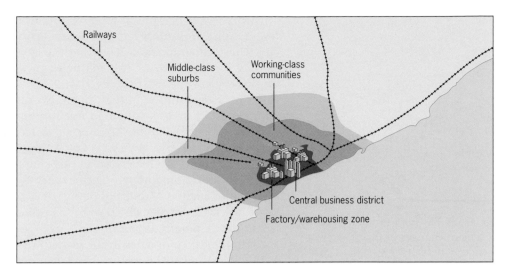

a) **Classic industrial city 1850s**

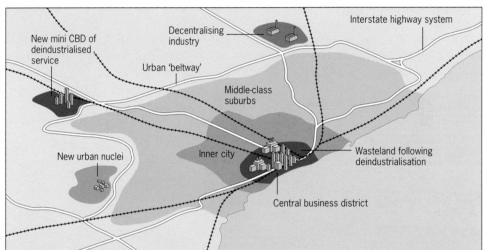

b) **The industrial city in the period 1945–75**

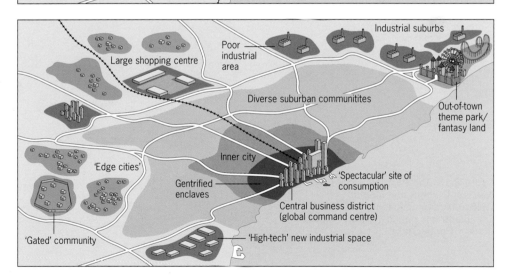

c) **The post-industrial city**

main factor in economic, social and cultural change. In the late twentieth and early twenty-first centuries, geographers have recognised that large cities are changing, adapting and becoming very different from their earlier counterparts (Fig. 2.15). In the post-industrial city, tertiary, quaternary and quinary activities take over as the bases of urban economic growth. In the case of Los Angeles, for example, recent growth is based on animation, the motion picture industry and hi-tech defence-related industries.

This recent geographical research argues that cities like Los Angeles are fragmenting and this is creating a new economic and social geography of the city. These geographers believe that the city as a single, coherent structure is ceasing to exist. Instead, it is splitting as a series of independent cities emerge on the edge of the existing city (Fig. 2.16). These are therefore called Edge Cities or Stealth Cities, in that they grow rapidly but cover several administrative areas so often do not crop up on statistics.

These modern ideas of the internal structure of cities have been criticised. In particular, critics ask: how far is Los Angeles typical of other metropolitan areas in the world? As we have seen in this chapter, cities have very different histories, so it would be wrong to expect Los Angeles to provide a model for other cities such as Mumbai, London or São Paulo. However, this work on the post-industrial city does help us to focus our attention on recent trends in urban development, especially:

- the importance of cities in the growth of an inter-connected world economy;
- the growth of social, cultural and economic inequalities in cities;
- the rise of 'paranoid' architecture, based on protection, surveillance and exclusion; and
- the growth of simulation in urban areas, especially the image of alternatives to the 'terrible reality' of cities. These simulations are often theme parks or themed shopping malls.

?

5a Study Fig. 2.15 then identify the main changes in urban structure between 1850 and 1945.
b Now describe the main changes in urban structure between 1945 and 2000.
c Outline the main factors behind the changes you describe in **b**.

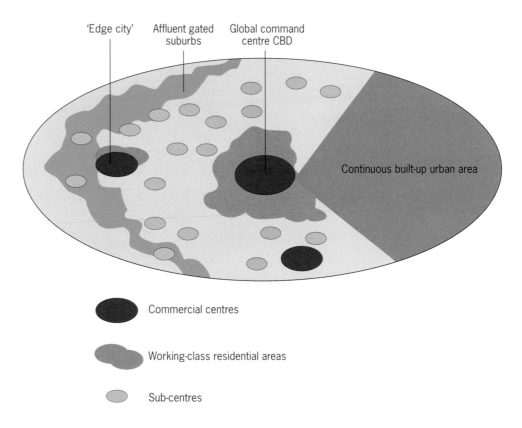

Figure 2.16 The Post-industrial City (*Source*: Graham and Marvin 1996:Telecommunications and the City: Electronic spaces, Urban Places. London, Routledge)

The urban doughnut
The internal structure of cities throughout the world is changing rapidly. Another term which has become part of the urban geographer's vocabulary is the **urban doughnut**. This refers to the structure of cities in the twenty-first century, whose **central business district** (CBD) has emptied of people and economic activities and has become the empty centre of an urban doughnut. People and economic activity have moved out to suburban or even edge city areas where improved telecommunication and transport developments allow them to retain links with the city centre, without having to live there.

2.8 Urbanisation in ELDCs

The speed and scale of the current urbanisation in ELDCs is much greater than it was in nineteenth-century EMDCs (see Chapter 1). In 1995, 36 per cent of people in all ELDCs lived in cities compared to 73 per cent in EMDCs. But these figures for ELDCs conceal great differences. For example, in Latin America 70 per cent of the population lived in cities, whilst in Africa the figure was only 32 per cent (1995). There are two main components in the growth of cities in ELDCs. In 1995 there was a 63 per cent population increase in urban areas due to **natural growth** (increase). **Migration** was the cause of the other 37 per cent population increase.

Natural increase
Cities in ELDCs have a predominance of younger people, especially in the 19–30 age range. This, together with advances in medical technology, e.g. immunisation, results in a decreasing death rate and a high birth rate. Consequently, cities in ELDCs will continue to grow rapidly because of this natural increase – even if migration from rural areas decreased or stopped.

?

6 Study Figs. 2.17 and 2.18. Compare the population pyramid for Mexico City with that for Puebla, a poor rural area. In particular, mention the age groups 0–14, 19–30 and over 55, as well as the differences in male/female ratio.

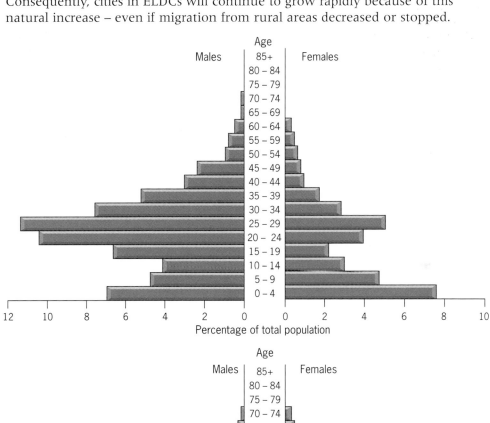

Figure 2.17 Population pyramid: Mexico City, 1991
(*Source*: Blakemore and Smith, 1992)

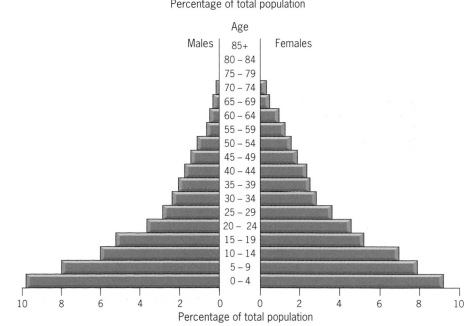

Figure 2.18 Population pyramid: Puebla, 1991
(*Source*: Blakemore and Smith, 1992)

Figure 2.19 The main causes of urban growth in ELDCs

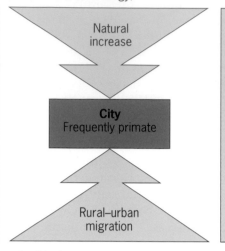

Increasing population accounts for approx. 60% of the rise in urban population, caused by high birth rate but a decrease in death rate (medical technology).

Natural increase

Push Factors
- Lack of job opportunities in countryside
- Lack of investment by government in rural areas
- Monotony and harshness of rural life
- Increased commercialism and mechanisation of agriculture causes lower demands for agricultural labour
- Problems of crop failure, etc. results in rural famine
- Insufficient land reforms and over-population causes lack of suitable land in rural areas

City
Frequently primate

Pull Factors
- Better health care in cities
- Greater educational opportunities
- Better provided services e.g. piped water/electricity in cities
- Perception of excitement, pace and bright lights of city life
- More public and private investment in cities gives greater job opportunities
- Higher wages/greater job availability in cities
- Cumulative influence of success of relatives in cities

Rural–urban migration

Rapid migration accounts for approx. 40% of the rise in urban population.

Rural-to-urban migration

Migration is the permanent (one year or more) movement of people from one place to another. This involves a complete change of address. Rural-to-urban migration is a major feature of many ELDCs and at one time was believed to be the principal cause of urbanisation. However, research in the 1980s established the dominance of natural increase in city growth (see above). In addition, this research identified some of the main factors operating in the process of rural-to-urban migration (Fig. 2.19).

Migration out of rural areas, Mexico

Puebla is a poor, rural region just to the east of Mexico City (Fig. 2.20). Here, labour is divided along traditional lines, with women caring for animals and children, and men growing potatoes, maize and beans (Fig. 2.21). There is no alternative employment. As a result, migration to Mexico City is the only answer for many people to find a livelihood. Half the population of Puebla does not reach the end of primary school, so the literacy rate is only 50 per cent. Two-thirds of the people lack proper housing; 80 per cent have no clean water and 33 per cent have no access to medical care.

In the 1960s and 1970s medical services did improve in the area, which meant that the death rate fell from 36 deaths per 1000 people to 12 per 1000. However, with little contraception, the rural population is growing at a rate of 24 live births per 1000 people a year, higher than India or Brazil. The results of this growth mean first, that there is less food for each person to eat. Second, people are therefore forced to farm more marginal land, which often increases soil erosion in areas of steep slopes. Third, it means that

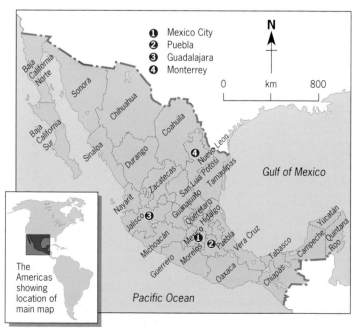

Figure 2.20 Mexico

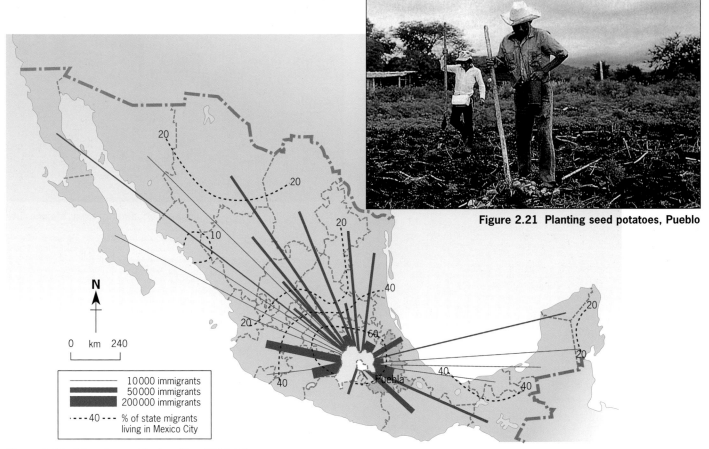

Figure 2.21 Planting seed potatoes, Pueblo

Figure 2.22 Migration to Mexico City, 1980–90

there is insufficient land available for people wanting to farm (despite land reform in the 1970s and 1980s). Crop failures in the early 1990s added impetus to people surging into the city (Fig. 2.22).

Figure 2.23 Easy access to healthcare: the family planning association for Mexico, MEXFAM, arranges for doctors to work in the poor districts of Mexico City. They provide healthcare and advice on family planning.

Pulled to Mexico City

By contrast, over 80 per cent of people in Mexico City have better access to health care (Fig. 2.23). There are also more schools and educational opportunities, including colleges and universities. Over 60 per cent of people in Mexico City have access to piped water and 75 per cent have access to electricity. Mexico City is investing heavily to attract more industry, especially in its inner areas.

The clear imbalance in both economic activities and services between Puebla and Mexico City creates the 'push' and 'pull' factors causing migration. People living in rural areas see and hear on national television and radio 'perceived opportunities', which they believe exist in cities. This increases their desire to move to urban areas. The results of the move are mixed.

?

7a Describe the pattern of migration to Mexico City shown in Figure 2.22.
b Suggest reasons for the pattern you have described.

8a How far do the causes of migration from Puebla to Mexico City follow the pattern outlined in Figure 2.19?
b What are the main differences?

Figure 2.25 Shanty town, Mexico City

Spontaneous settlements:
- Poor electricity supply
- Lacking sewage system
- Poor clean water supply
- Overcrowded
- Housing often built of scrap materials
- Housing often built illegally
- Few schools or clinics

0   km   8

⬚ Federal district   ═══ Main roads

▨ Spontaneous settlements

Figure 2.24 Mexico City: spontaneous settlements

Migrants to Mexico City learn to develop new skills, such as making sandals from used car tyres or selling water to tourists. In fact, because there is a relatively small demand for this type of service in smaller cities, most migrants head straight for Mexico City. However, in many cases, migrants are forced to live in **spontaneous settlements,** on the edge of Mexico City (Figs 2.24–2.25) (see section 1.7).

Coping with rapid urban growth

Planners in cities such as São Paulo, Bombay and Mexico City face serious problems as a result of rapid urbanisation. One basic problem is an inability to provide adequate housing as the cities expand. During 1995, in Mexico City there was a shortage of 800 000 houses, whilst over 40 per cent of existing homes were in a state of poor repair. Migrating families are thus forced to live in spontaneous settlements. Similarly, industrial workers, although attracted by the city's investment in industry, receive incomes which are too low to afford reasonable quality housing. They too, may be forced to live in spontaneous settlements.

A second problem with which city planners struggle is waste disposal. For example, every day Mexico City generates over 11 000 tonnes of rubbish. Consequently, the collection system is stretched and only three-quarters is removed, while the rest is dumped on open ground, waterways and even on streets. Rubbish clogs the drainage system, which therefore has to be cleared regularly. The city's sewage system needs extensive repairs, especially where it flows into open rivers creating a serious health risk. The Penuco River, in Mexico City, receives 2000 tonnes of untreated waste each day, and much of it flows to farming areas north of the city where it is used to irrigate crops. This leads to the contamination of fruit and vegetables which contain twice the level of lead permitted in neighbouring USA.

Transport in rapidly growing cities is a third problem area. It is difficult for planners to keep pace with the speed of urban expansion. Underground systems, such as the one in Mexico City (Fig. 2.26), are expensive to build – although they are efficient ways of moving people around. Conversely, buses in Mexico City are

Figure 2.26 Zocalo underground station, Mexico City – almost as crowded as the London Underground

old, short of spare parts and add pollution (particularly increasing ozone). The road system of Mexico City is also overloaded by the three million registered vehicles, which add 12 000 tonnes of pollutants to the city's air every day. This leads to a toxic smog surrounding the city. Health authorities state that breathing the air in Mexico City is equivalent to smoking 60 cigarettes a day. The problem is compounded by the fact that most workers live in the eastern parts of the city, but industry is predominantly located in the northern and western zones. Millions of people therefore have to cross the city each day, increasing pollution and leading to grid-lock.

In addition to building the underground system, planners in Mexico City have tried to reduce traffic and air pollution by the *Hoy No Circulan* (No Driving Today)

scheme. Car use is prohibited on a certain day each week according to car registration letters. Unfortunately, the rich simply buy a second or third car and so thwart the scheme's success. Meanwhile, half the newborn children in Mexico City have levels of lead in their blood high enough to impair their physical and mental development.

Attempting to reduce inequalities between families is a fourth major problem which few planners have successfully tackled. For example, the south-western suburbs of Mexico City are occupied by the rich, who live within tight security with surveillance cameras, guards, gates and lights. Here shopping malls have expensive boutiques and restaurants. Yet only a short distance away people have no water, no electricity, no proper homes, no access to social security and often no work. Attempting to deal with such inequalities is a major challenge.

A fifth problem is the difficulty of trying to provide employment in rapidly urbanising areas. Because the government of Mexico is not able to create enough jobs, many people are **unemployed** or **under-employed,** or have to live in the informal sector on very low pay (see sections 1.7, 7.3)

9 Essay: to what extent are the problems created by rapid, recent, urban growth in ELDCs, such as in Mexico, similar to those created by rapid nineteenth-century urban growth in EMDCs, such as in the UK?

Summary

- Cities developed in fertile river areas, from at least 5000 years ago.
- Early cities were small, walled and with marked residential segregation.
- The period 600 BC to AD 600 saw the rapid growth of cities in the Mediterranean region.
- Before the Industrial Revolution, cities across the world both grew and declined at a steady pace.
- Rapid urbanisation first occurred in the nineteenth century in conjunction with large-scale industrial development.
- Early attempts at planned urban development tried to keep green open space and avoid areas of tightly packed housing.
- Post-industrial cities in EMDCs have developed a new urban structure.
- Urbanisation in ELDCs is more recent and rapid than that in EMDCs.
- Natural increase and migration from rural areas cause city growth in ELDCs.
- Rapid urbanisation has created serious problems for planners in many ELDCs.

3 Urban settlement patterns

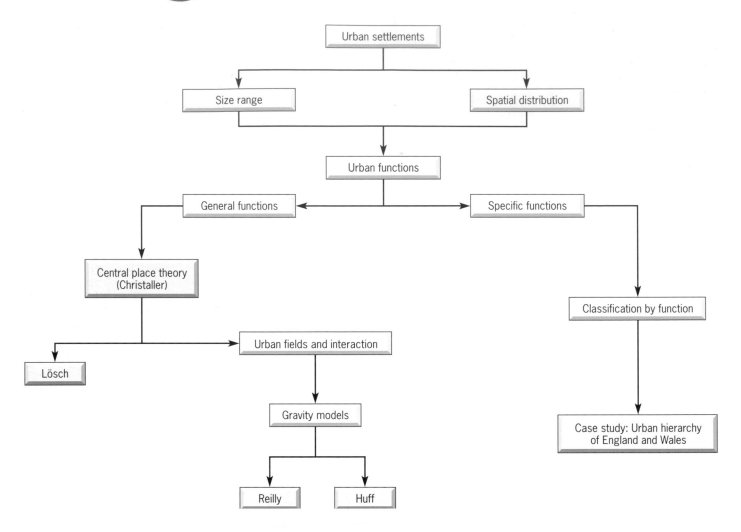

3.1 Introduction

In countries all over the world, towns vary in size from large to small. Also, towns are almost never arranged in a regular pattern. The key questions we need to ask here are:

- Why do such variations in size exist?
- Why is the distribution of urban settlements very irregular?

The answers to both questions are linked to the concept of urban functions – i.e. what urban settlements do. In this context, urban settlements have two types of function: general functions; and specific functions.

General functions
These are functions which all urban settlements provide, such as shops, banks and schools. Such services are provided for people both in the town itself and in the surrounding countryside. The range of services may vary (Figs. 3.1 and 3.2). Urban settlements providing these services are called **central places**.

Specific functions
These are functions which are restricted to a small number of towns. Examples include resource-based functions such as coal mining and port facilities (Fig. 3.3) and large industrial plants such as car factories (Fig. 3.4).

Figure 3.1 Entrance to Queen's Park Hospital, Blackburn, Lancs. Note the area served by the hospital.

Figure 3.2 A school in Hatfield, Hertfordshire

Figure 3.3 Dover: town, castle and ferry terminals

Figure 3.4 Part of the Rover car factory at Cowley, Oxford

Functional linkages

In real life, general functions and specific functions are linked. For example, a town's specific functions may include an electronics industry employing a large workforce. These people will create a demand for general functions, such as shops and restaurants. These facilities in turn will bring more people to the town, helping it to grow. Good facilities and a supply of labour will then attract yet more specialised functions.

3.2 Central place theory: Christaller

Central place theory looks at the general functions of towns and the spacing of towns of different sizes in the landscape. It is based on the work of the German, Walter Christaller, who published his famous book *Central Places in Southern Germany* in 1933.

**Figure 3.5 Caernarfon: castle, town and harbour.
Note the defensive site of the castle and the walls
surrounding the older part of the town**

Christaller realised that in southern Germany (and elsewhere) there are fewer larger towns than smaller ones, and the larger places are further apart than the smaller ones. But why is this? Why are settlements not all the same size? His contribution was to ask a simple question about something ordinary to which the answers are complex. Christaller asked: *Are there laws which determine the number, size and distribution of towns?* By laws, Christaller meant regular relationships.

At the time (1930s), geographers tried to explain the location of towns in terms of the existence of favourable features such as bridging points, defensive sites (Fig. 3.5) and sheltered harbours. However, many towns had grown at sites lacking such advantages. A second approach was to study individual town histories to try to find shared themes and reasons for their size and location. This was an enormous task. A third approach was statistical, classifying and counting all the settlements and analysing the results. However, this was only descriptive and did not explain any of the patterns found.

In developing his theory, Christaller began with a set of basic assumptions which were simple and therefore widely applicable. He then tried to reason what would happen if these assumptions held true. In so doing, he was able to arrive at three basic principles from which his theory grew.

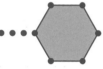

Christaller's central place theory

Basic assumptions

In order to simplify reality, Christaller made six basic assumptions before building his theory. These are:

1 An unbounded, uniform plain in which there is equal ease of transport in all directions and only one form of transport.

2 A population of farmers who depend on others to meet some of their needs, who are evenly distributed and have the same incomes, tastes and demands for goods and services.

3 These goods/services vary by cost and frequency of need. Some goods/services are required more frequently than others. The same good or service costs the same wherever it is available.

4 People get their goods/services from the nearest place where they are available, to minimise transport costs and time taken.

5 Goods/services are provided at central places.

6 The people providing them try to maximise profits by locating as far as possible from other providers of the same goods/services.

Basic principles

There are three basic principles which underlie Christaller's theory:

1 Threshold population

This is the minimum number of people needed to sustain profitably a shop or service. Large stores such as Marks & Spencers and Boots need a much larger threshold population than, for example, a baker's shop. This is one important reason why towns will always vary in size – because their different functions have different thresholds.

?

1 Study the list of goods/places shown below:
- sweets;
- a CD;
- a pair of jeans;
- aftershave or perfume;
- a magazine or newspaper;
- a pair of shoes;
- a restaurant;
- a library;
- a new coat;
- a soft drink;
- a cinema;
- a concert-hall;
- a present for someone else.

a Rank each item in the order of frequency that you buy/visit it.

b Now try to explain the link between the prices of these goods or services and how often you replace them or make a return visit.

c What are the relationships between cost, frequency of use and the distance you are prepared to travel?

2 Study Figure 3.6.

a Put a sheet of tracing paper over the map. Using only evidence from the map, divide the settlements (by their size) into hamlets, villages, small towns (market towns) and medium-sized towns.

b Now study Table 3.1 on page 40 and use it to improve your map in order to distinguish between hamlets, villages, small towns and medium-sized towns.

c Briefly describe the pattern of types of settlement shown on your map.

d Use the data in Table 3.1 to make general comments on the changes in hamlets, villages and towns, particularly as regards growth and decline. Suggest possible reasons for the changes you describe.

e Carry out a nearest neighbour-hood analysis of the villages listed in Table 3.1. What does this analysis reveal about the general pattern of villages shown on the map?

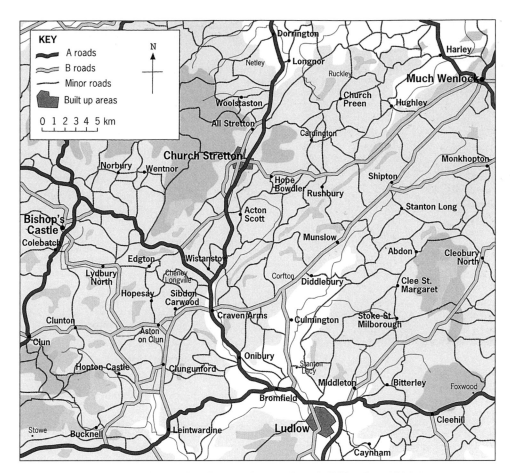

Figure 3.6 Part of south Shropshire (*Source:* Geographers A–Z Map Co., 1966a)

3 Study Figure 3.7. The Menzies chain of shops sells newspapers, greetings cards, videos, books and stationery.

a What is the threshold population for this chain store?

b Describe in detail the general relationship between size of store and catchment area as shown by the curve. For example: At what rate does floor space increase for each extra 100 000 people? At what point does store size tend to become constant?

c Why do you think the curve levels off in catchment areas of over 600 000 people?

d As floor area increases, would you expect the shops
• to offer a greater variety of goods in the same basic range; or
• to become more specialised – e.g. become video and music shops; or
• to combine these two strategies?
Give reasons for your answers.

2 The order of goods

Goods which people buy regularly – e.g. bread and newspapers – are called low-order goods. They have a lower value than high-order goods which people buy only rarely – e.g. furniture, television sets and cameras.

3 The range of a good or service

This is the maximum distance a person is prepared to travel in order to obtain a good or service. People are generally not prepared to travel far to obtain low-order goods, such as a bar of chocolate, but are willing to travel further for high-order goods like computers.

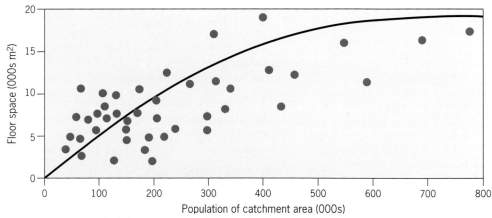

Figure 3.7 Menzies stores: the relationship between store floor space and population of catchment area, 1995 (*Source:* Menzies plc)

Table 3.1 Settlements in part of south Shropshire: population and number of functions, 1966–95 (Sources: 1991 Census; Shropshire County Council Planning Department)

Settlement	Population 1971	Population 1995	Number of functions 1966/1983[a]	Number of functions 1995
Acton Scott	124	109	2	3
Bishops Castle	1199	1619	34	46
Bromfield	316	355	6	6
Cheney Longville	516	508	1	0
Church Stretton	3344	4781	76	78
Cleehill	680	735	25	8
Clee St Margaret	102	136	5	4
Clun	1261	1405	29	14
Clunton	467	500	5	2
Craven Arms	1462	1355	31	28
Culmington	334	533	5	1
Diddlebury	915	505	5	3
Hopesay	360	433	3	2
Hope Bowdler	143	193	2	1
Ludlow	7466	7580	140	168
Lydbury North	528	564	8	8
Much Wenlock	2445	2486	59	75
Munslow	344	403	11	9
Onibury	297	335	6	5
Rushbury	476	500	2	2
Stanton Lacy	352	35	3	0
Winstanslow	607	668	6	1

[a] Number of functions in 1966 for villages and hamlets; 1983 for towns (estimated for Ludlow)

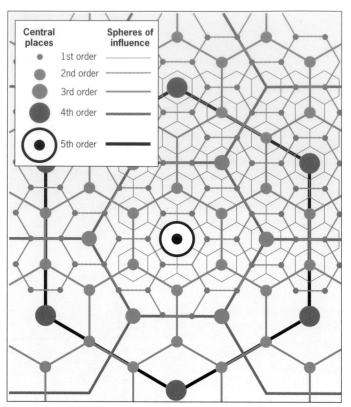

Figure 3.8 Christaller's central places and their spheres of influence (*Source*: Rogers, 1995)

Christaller's model

Christaller combined these ideas to produce a theory in which low-order goods, with a low range and needing low thresholds are sold in small towns. By contrast, high-order goods, with higher ranges and large thresholds are sold only in large towns. The same is true for services. For example, a small town is likely to have a doctor; a larger town will have a hospital as well as general doctors; and a conurbation may have a specialist eye hospital as well as several general hospitals and many general doctors.

Applying this theory to his imaginary unbounded flat plain, Christaller generated a theoretical distribution pattern for settlements of different sizes (Fig. 3.8). This pattern has the following features:

1 Goods and service providers locate in central places, at equal distances from one another. The exact distance is determined by the range of the goods/services. A regular lattice of central places is formed.

2 Each central place is in the centre of the area it serves. Each area (**sphere of influence**) takes the form of a hexagon – the most efficient way of filling space without gaps or overlaps.

3 There is a hierarchy of central places (**urban hierarchy**). First-order places are close together and serve small areas; second-order places are further apart and have larger spheres of influence; third-order places are even further apart and serve even larger areas; and so on (Fig. 3.8).

4 Places within each order will be a constant distance apart.

5 The number of central places in each order always forms a regular pattern, but varies depending on the organising principle.

Although Christaller's data were for southern Germany, his central place theory is based on general assumptions that could – in theory! – apply anywhere. He knew that nowhere in the world was quite like his unbounded plain and that people do not always behave rationally. However, when faced with the complexity and diversity of the world, he had to make these simplifying assumptions in order to answer his basic question.

Several studies in EMDCs were made to see how far Christaller's ideas could be applied in the real world. Professor Berry in Iowa in the 1960s showed that an increase in town size was linked to an increase in the number of functions and in the size of the sphere of influence (trade area) (Fig. 3.9). However, this rather neat pattern is only rarely found.

Figure 3.9 The settlement hierarchy of south-west Iowa, USA, in the 1960s (*After:* Berry, 1977)

Settlement type	Stores	Gas stations	Restaurants	Sphere of influence (sq km)
Hamlets	1 general store	1	1	20
Villages	40+ stores	2+	2+	180
Towns	100+ stores	30+	40+	500

3.3 Central place theory: Lösch

In the 1950s, the German geographer August Lösch attempted to improve Christaller's theory by bringing it closer to reality. He developed Christaller's work to include a series of 'sectors' within each of the original hexagons. There is still a lot of debate amongst geographers as to whether Lösch's continuum or Christaller's tiered system of urban centres is closer to reality.

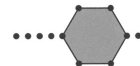

Lösch

In any given area, Lösch expected that there would be some sub-areas with a lot of high-order settlements and others with relatively few. He called these sectors 'city-rich' and 'city-poor' (Fig. 3.10). He thought that if an area lacked the 'correct' number of high-order settlements, we should look at nearby areas which might compensate for this, rather than reject Christaller's ideas completely. Lösch's system has a continuum of settlement sizes from small to large, instead of the distinct tiers or orders of Christaller's earlier model.

?

4 Refer back to Figure 3.6 and Task 2, and the average distance between villages that you calculated.

a On a copy of Figure 3.6, use the average distance as the diameter for a series of circles with their centres on these settlements.

b Now try to explain the areas of overlap in the circles, and the areas where there are gaps between the circles. Refer to both human and physical factors in your explanation.

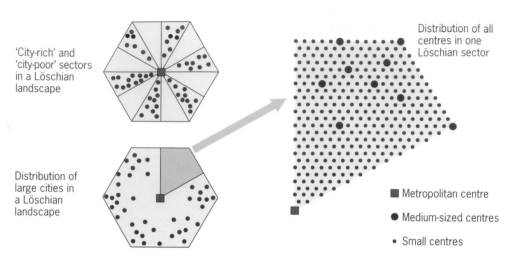

Figure 3.10 Lösch's modification of central place theory
(*Source:* Daniel and Hopkinson, 1991)

3.4 Theory into practice: examining urban fields and interaction

?

5 Essay: What are the main advantages and disadvantages of each of the methods used to investigate the urban field of Wrexham (Fig. 3.13), as shown in Figures 3.11 and 3.12?

Christaller introduced the idea that the influence of a settlement extends for a limited distance over its surrounding area. His theory gave rise to many attempts to calculate and map the extent of spheres of influence, that is **urban fields**. Urban fields can be investigated in two main ways:

• by asking companies in the town about the area to which they deliver goods and services (Fig. 3.11); and
• by asking individuals in rural areas which settlements they use when shopping for day-to-day needs and which for longer term needs (Fig. 3.12).

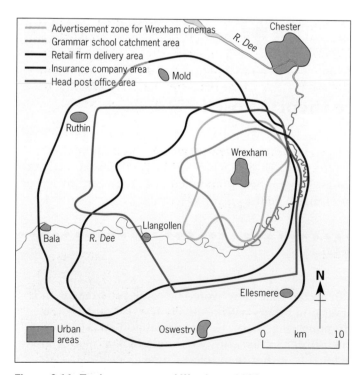

Figure 3.11 Trade areas around Wrexham, 1990
(*Source:* Knapp *et al.*, 1991)

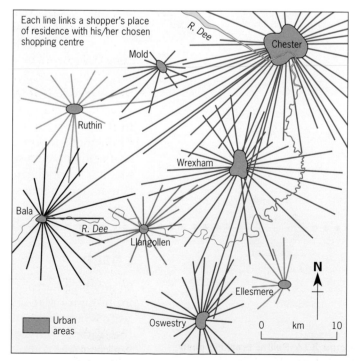

Figure 3.12 Patterns of shopping for longer term needs in the Wrexham area, 1996 (*Source:* Newman College sample survey)

Figure 3.13 Wrexham town centre

Interaction between settlements: gravity models

Geographers also attempted to develop theoretical models to try to calculate the size, shape and extent of spheres of influence. These are known as **gravity models**. For example, Reilly's law of retail gravitation seeks to calculate the point at which the sphere of influence of one town ends and that of another town begins.

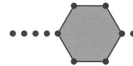

Reilly's law of retail gravitation

Reilly argued that, along a route between two towns A and B, there will be a **breaking point**. People living on one side of the breaking point would shop in town A, whilst people on the other side of the breaking point would shop in town B. Reilly devised a formula to locate the position of this breaking point, based on the assumption that larger towns (as measured by their population size) were likely to attract more shoppers than smaller towns (Fig. 3.14).

The formula is:

$$\text{Distance of breaking point from smaller town B} = \frac{\text{Distance between towns A and B}}{1 + \sqrt{\left(\dfrac{\text{Population A}}{\text{Population B}}\right)}}$$

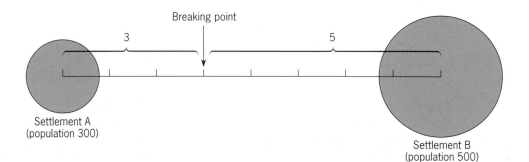

Figure 3.14 Reilly's breaking point between two settlements of different sizes (*Source:* Everson and Fitzgerald, 1969)

6 Refer to Table 3.2.
a Use the distance and population data to work out the position of the breaking points between Luton and each of the other towns, and plot these on a map.
b Describe Luton's sphere of influence as shown on your map.
c Using the data in Table 3.2, rank the towns by retail turnover. Compare these results with those obtained in **a**.

Table 3.2 Towns in the Luton area: population and retail turnover (Source: HMSO, 1995)

Town	Distance from Luton (km)	Population (1994)	Total retail turnover (1991, in £000s)
Luton		180 800	98 972
Bedford	30	137 000	71 284
Letchworth	18	39 870	14 729
Stevenage	21	75 900	47 249
Welwyn Garden City	21	42 490	28 741
St Albans	19	65 000	47 395
Hemel Hempstead	19	76 000	45 792
Dunstable	8	42 000	25 741
Leighton Buzzard	21	25 000	10 952

Gravity models have been criticised for being too simplistic. They assume that the larger the town, the more attractive it will be to shoppers, and that people will always behave in a logical way. This is clearly not always the case – e.g. people may be willing to travel further to an unpolluted pedestrianised shopping centre. Also, some shoppers have cars and can choose where they go; others have to rely on public transport and may be able to get to some towns, but not to others.

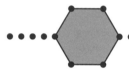

Huff's model

Huff's model attempts to predict the probability of people going to a particular town. Huff argued that the probability (P) of a shopper going to their local town (I) rather than to another is related to:

- the number of shops in their town, compared with those in other towns; and
- the ease with which different towns can be reached.

Huff's formula is:

$$PI = \dfrac{\dfrac{\text{Number of shops in Centre I}}{\text{Distance or travel time to reach them}}}{\dfrac{\text{Total number of shops in whole study area}}{\text{Total distance or travel time to reach them}}}$$

Usefulness of models
Huff's formula allows us to compare towns (usually four or five) or different shopping centres within the same town. It tries to predict which town people are most likely to use for their shopping. However, as with most models it assumes that all people make rational choices based on a very small number of factors. In reality, people do not always make rational choices about where to shop. Also, a wide range of factors may influence their decisions – e.g. fashion, the price and variety of goods, and the opportunity to combine shopping and non-shopping activities.

Models can be useful in highlighting the *expected* behaviour of shoppers. This can be compared with *actual* shopping behaviour, discovered by means of field work, and we can see if the results deviate from the expected pattern. It is at this point that the skill of the geographer comes into play in trying to explain any differences.

3.5 Specific functions of towns

We talk about major urban functions in everyday speech – e.g. when we discuss ports, holiday resorts or manufacturing towns. This approach to classifying towns based on one specific function has no theoretical basis and does not work well in practice. For example, Cambridge is widely known as a university town, but it is also an important centre for hi-tech industry. To accommodate a range of functions, classification systems have had to become more complex. This trend has grown with the use of more sophisticated statistical techniques – e.g. multivariate analysis, a technique which can assess the relative importance of many variables.

The development of the urban hierarchy of England and Wales

This description of the development of the urban hierarchy of England and Wales draws on ideas from both central place theory and the development of special urban functions.

Phase 1: Isolation

Often on the sites of earlier Roman settlements, the Anglo-Saxon boroughs of England and Wales provide an early example of the pattern of towns. In 1086 there were 112 boroughs in England and Wales (Fig. 3.15), of which London was by far the largest, followed by York, Lincoln and Norwich. At this time, transport was both basic and slow, and towns tended to be isolated from one another, each serving a small surrounding area. The development of a structured urban hierarchy from this pattern was primarily the result of the need for an effective system of government.

Phase 2: Interaction

As transport became easier, there was more interaction between towns. During the medieval period, trade grew and new towns were created, filling out the urban system. London remained at the top of the hierarchy, followed by York, Lincoln, Newcastle-upon-Tyne, Bristol and Exeter.

The urban pattern was modified by the creation of an administrative system based on the shires and their county towns. By the eighteenth century, the country was completely covered by the service areas of large provincial capitals – e.g. Bristol, Norwich (Fig. 3.16) and Exeter – within which grew smaller market towns, such as Chipping Sodbury and Chippenham east of Bristol.

Figure 3.15 Wareham, Dorset: the rectangular shape of the earthworks protecting the Saxon planned borough can still clearly be seen

Phase 3: Conurbations

The urban hierarchy changed radically during the late eighteenth and early nineteenth centuries. Even by 1750, the new industrial centres of Manchester, Birmingham, Leeds, Liverpool and Sheffield were emerging and thereby transforming the earlier urban hierarchy (see section 2.5). The growth of these early industrial centres was often evolutionary rather than revolutionary, for many of them had already begun to flourish as a result of the earlier growth in trade.

Figure 3.16 Norwich: the market square, with the castle in the background

Table 3.4 The new urban hierarchy of England and Wales, 1851 (*Source*: Carter, 1983)

Rank	City	Population
1	London	2 363 000
2	Liverpool	375 955
3	Manchester[a]	367 233
4	Birmingham	231 841
5	Leeds	172 270
6	Bristol	137 328
7	Sheffield	135 310
8	Bradford	103 310

[a] Including Salford

Table 3.3 The top 20 provincial towns in England in 1670 and 1750: rank and population size (Source: McInnes, 1980)

Rank	1670 Town	Population	1750 Town	Population
1	Norwich	21 000	Bristol	50 000
2	Bristol	18 000	Norwich	36 000
3	Exeter	12 500	Newcastle-upon-Tyne	29 000
4	Newcastle-upon-Tyne	11 800	Birmingham	23 700
5	York	10 500	Liverpool	22 000
6	Great Yarmouth	9 500	Manchester	18 000
7	Colchester	9 500	Exeter	16 000
8	Worcester	8 500	Plymouth	15 000
9	Ipswich	7 500	Leeds	13 000
10	Canterbury	7 500	Chester	13 000
11	Chester	7 500	Coventry	12 500
12	Plymouth	7 500	Ipswich	12 100
13	Oxford	7 500	Sheffield	12 000
14	Cambridge	7 300	Nottingham	12 000
15	Shrewsbury	7 100	Hull	11 500
16	Salisbury	6 700	York	11 400
17	Coventry	6 500	Worcester	10 300
18	Hull	6 300	Great Yarmouth	10 000
19	Bury St Edmunds	5 500	Sunderland	10 000
20	Manchester	5 500	Portsmouth	10 000

7 Study Table 3.3.
a For 1670 and 1750, decide on a series of size categories for the settlements – e.g. under 10000, 10000–20000, etc. Allocate the towns to these groups, then plot them on two maps, one for each date.
b Describe the patterns of urban size and rank for each date.
c Explain the patterns you have described in relation to central place theory and specific town functions.
d Highlight the main changes in the urban hierarchy between the two dates.
e Attempt to explain the changes you have identified.

Nevertheless, by the 1850s a new urban hierarchy had been formed (Table 3.4). Only Manchester and Bristol occur in both the 1850s list and the 1670 list. Differing from the old county towns servicing their surrounding rural areas, many of the new industrial centres were **urban agglomerations** – such as Birmingham and the Black Country (Fig. 3.17). Such cities grew through the provision of specific functions, often based on resources such as coal which were only located in a few places (see sections 2.5–2.6).

By 1900, however, the pattern was changing again. Most rapid urban growth was then taking place not in city centres, but at the periphery, as industry and population spread outwards. Eventually, this expansion resulted in the formation of **conurbations**, as formerly separate centres merged to form one huge built-up area – e.g. the West Midlands conurbation. By the 1930s, the urban hierarchy of Britain was dominated by these large, industrial conurbations.

Figure 3.17 The Black Country near Wolverhampton, in 1866

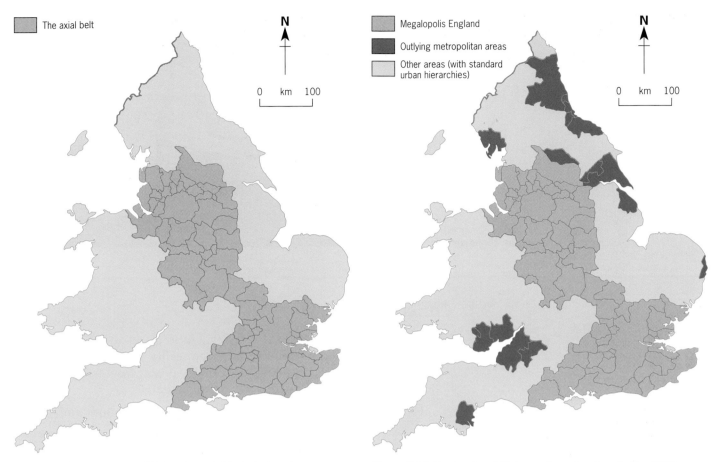

Figure 3.18 England and Wales: the axial belt during the inter-war period (*Source:* Carter, 1990)

Figure 3.19 England and Wales: urban structure in the 1990s (*Source:* Carter, 1990)

Phase 4: The axial belt

Throughout the period between the two world wars (1918–39), traditional heavy industries such as coal mining, steel making and engineering declined. In addition, rail transport became less significant as the more flexible road transport began to grow in importance. The result of these changes was to confirm the dominance of London within the urban hierarchy, which was parallelled by the decline of outlying conurbations such as that in South Wales. At this time, there was a flow of population into the **axial belt** (Fig. 3.18) which stretched from the south-eastern counties, through London and the Midlands, to Merseyside.

Phase 5: Metropolis

The growth of London and south-east England has dominated the UK's post-1945 urban geography. This has been due to several factors, including:

1 the continued decline of traditional heavy industries;

2 the growth of new, footloose industries (not tied to a raw material);

3 the increase in personal mobility;

4 the ever-growing importance of road transport; and

5 the significance of trade links with the rest of the European Union.

In fact, mobility is the dominant theme of this phase – mobility of people, factories, offices and service centres. One consequence of this is that many people's daily lives now routinely take place in more than one locality. For example, an accountant may work in a central London office; her world of work may also include clients in Tokyo and San Francisco; her home may be in a commuter village in Norfolk, where her children may go to the village school; and she may do the family shopping in Norwich.

In order to meet the demands of mobile people, out-of-town shopping centres have developed (see section 7.4) in, or within reach of the prosperous areas of the country. These have contributed to the decline of traditional urban hierarchies. The result has been to reinforce the dominance of the axial belt which has evolved to become a highly complex regional system.

England and Wales may now be thought of as comprising three main types of area (Fig. 3.19):

1 Metropolis England, also known as Megalopolis England – the former axial belt. Although this zone is generally prosperous, the continued dispersal of

population to the outer fringes of the metropolitan areas has resulted in much inner city decline (Fig. 3.20).

2 The outlying conurbations. Here, economic fortunes are more mixed and change is generally taking place more slowly.

3 The remaining area. Here, the pattern is still based on a traditional hierarchy of towns and their spheres of influence.

Figure 3.20 Leeds: inner city decay. Note boarded-up shops and 'For sale' sign

3.6 Conclusion

The study of a complex urban hierarchy like that of England and Wales, past and present, illustrates the complex links between reality and theoretical models such as Christaller's. The question inevitably arises: How useful are such models? In their defence, it is possible to argue that:

• range and threshold do still operate in relation to providing goods and services;

• all towns are central places to some extent; and

• some towns have specific functions and/or features from their past growth which affect their present size and influence.

Summary

• Urban settlements are not uniform in size, but vary from large conurbations to small towns.

• Urban settlements are not located in a random pattern.

• Urban settlements have two main types of function: general (central place) functions and specific functions.

• Central place theory is based on the work of Walter Christaller in Germany in the 1930s and on that of Lösch in the 1950s. Their work has since been considerably modified.

• Christaller's theory is based on the concepts of the order, range and threshold of a good/service.

• Attempts have been made to measure and map the spheres of influence of settlements using gravity and other models.

• Attempts have also been made to classify urban settlements based on their specific functions.

• Hierarchies of urban settlements evolve through time and have identifiable phases.

• Studies of urban hierarchies must include consideration of the impacts of historical development as well as of general and specific functions.

4 The internal structure of cities

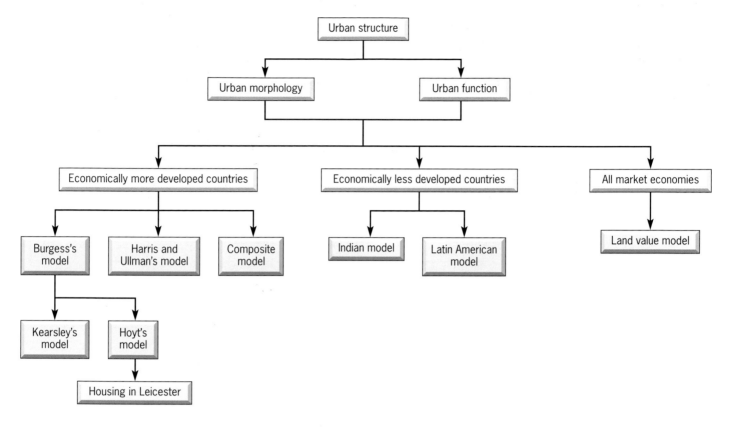

4.1 Introduction

A visit to any city anywhere in the world soon confirms that there are variations in the way land is used (Figs 4.1 and 4.2). Some land is used for industry, some for housing and some for leisure. Although each city has its own unique elements, there are also some basic similarities in patterns of land use between cities. For example, city centres are often dominated by retail and office functions. This chapter examines the nature of the internal structure of towns and cities, and considers some of the theories that have been developed both to describe and to explain their internal structure.

4.2 Urban structure

Urban structure is a combination of form and function. As towns grow, different functions tend to group together in various parts of the town, forming functional zones. These functional zones are generally easy to recognise from maps (Fig. 4.3).

The form, or shape, of a town and the arrangement and layout of its buildings are referred to as its **urban morphology**. Physical factors, such as topography and climate, and human factors, such as ethnic mix (chapter 5) and cultural history (chapter 2) combine to produce a wide range of morphological types.

Geographers have tried for many years both to find and describe patterns of form and function, and to explain the patterns they have identified. In the course of this work, several models have been developed to try to describe and explain the internal structure of towns and cities. The earliest model is that of Burgess.

Figure 4.1 Singapore: high-rise flats

Figure 4.2 Singapore: container port

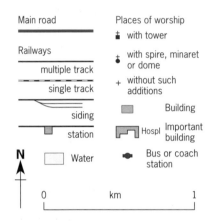

Figure 4.3 Extract from OS 1 : 25000, sheet SO 88/98, Stourbridge

?

1 Study Figure 4.3.

a On a tracing of the map, draw in the main roads, canals and railway lines.

b Now mark and name the town centre. What map evidence did you use to decide on its position?

c Shade in black and name the main industrial zone of the town.

d Shade in red the main areas of terraced housing.

e Shade in green areas of open space including parks and golf courses.

f Shade in yellow the newer suburban areas. What map evidence did you use to identify these areas?

g Now try to explain the location in Stourbridge of: the industrial area; the areas of open space.

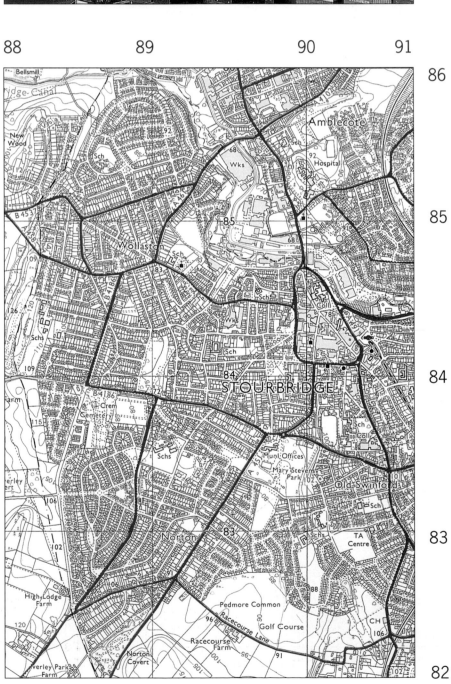

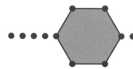

Burgess's concentric zone model, 1924

E. W. Burgess and his associates, working in the USA in the 1920s, developed the concentric zone model (Fig. 4.4) based on research in cities such as Chicago (Fig. 4.5). Burgess adapted ideas used by plant ecologists such as competition and dominance. He assumed that, within a city, people competed for limited space. Only those who could afford them gained the best locations for their homes and their businesses. The poorest groups therefore had least choice and were left with the worst locations. Burgess argued that this led to different zones of the city having different functions. He believed that the morphological and functional zones of a city are arranged concentrically, and that each zone is different in terms of its age and character.

Burgess's urban zones

At the heart of Burgess's city is the **central business district (CBD)** which is the social, commercial and cultural focus. It is the most accessible part of the city because all transport routes start and end here. This zone is dominated by department stores, specialist and variety goods shops, offices, cinemas, theatres and hotels because they can best afford to pay the high property values and rents for these sites.

The **zone in transition** surrounds the CBD. This is an area of mixed land uses. Part of it often consists of car parks or vacant and derelict buildings, poor-quality cafes and areas where slums have been demolished. It may also contain some large, older houses which have been converted to office or light industrial uses.

The **zone of working-class houses** surrounds the transition zone and has some of the older, often terraced, housing areas of the city (Fig. 4.6). Originally, this area housed families who moved out of poorer quality housing in the transition zone, but who still needed to live close to their workplace because of high travel costs.

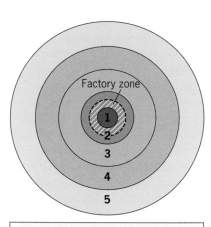

1 ■ Central business district (CBD)
2 ■ Transition zone (wholesale light manufacturing)
3 ■ Low-class residential zone (working men's homes)
4 ■ Medium-class residential zone
5 ☐ High-class residential zone (commuters' homes)

Figure 4.4 Burgess's concentric zone model, 1924 (*Source*: Park et al., 1925)

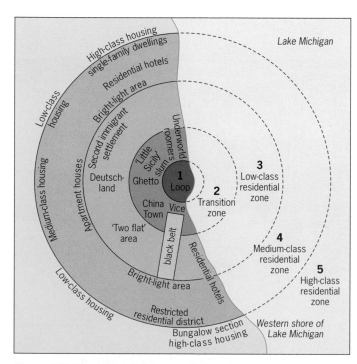

Figure 4.5 Burgess's model as applied to Chicago (*Source*: Park et al., 1925)

Figure 4.6 Nineteenth-century working-class terraced housing in Leeds

Figure 4.7 Part of Glasgow's urban fringe (background)

The **residential zone** is an area of middle-class housing, where terraces have been replaced by semi-detached or detached houses. There will also be some light industry in this zone, often in industrial estates which grew up on the edge of the built-up area. Burgess's model also recognised a **commuter zone** beyond the built-up area. In this zone are dormitory suburbs together with public utilities such as recreational facilities, golf courses, sewage works and power plants. These urban land uses are separated by non-urban uses such as woodland and pasture (Fig. 4.7). Burgess, with another researcher called Park, also recognised that there were parts of the city, within the broad concentric zones, which were occupied by people of similar race, language and socio-economic status. For example, Burgess identified a Chinatown and a Little Sicily in his model of the structure of Chicago (Fig. 4.5). Also, Burgess realised that his model of concentric zones might be altered by factors such as a steep slope or a lake shore (as in Fig. 4.5). He called these factors **opposing features**, and many are physical in character.

Burgess and urban growth

Burgess saw the mechanism of urban growth as being similar to the ecological process of invasion and succession. He thought that immigrants would tend to concentrate in groups in areas of cheaper housing (Fig. 4.8). Over a number of years, the area would expand as more people arrived. In time, as the group prospered, some people would filter outwards into the next zone. In this way, higher-status residential areas came to be occupied by people from different ethnic groups. Once abandoned by the first ethnic group, the cheaper housing in the inner zone would be taken over by a second immigrant group, possibly of different ethnic origin.

This type of pattern has been identified by geographers studying the Brooklyn area of New York (Fig. 4.9).

?

2a Make a list of the factors which might distort the growth of concentric zones around a town.
b Compare your list with others in your group and try to combine your list into groups of factors such as physical, social, political, etc.

Figure 4.8 Immigrants in a tenement flat, Brooklyn, New York, c.1910

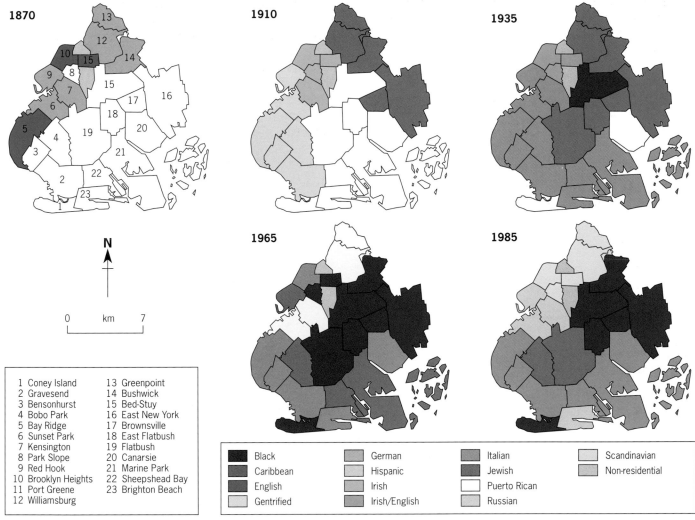

1 Coney Island
2 Gravesend
3 Bensonhurst
4 Bobo Park
5 Bay Ridge
6 Sunset Park
7 Kensington
8 Park Slope
9 Red Hook
10 Brooklyn Heights
11 Port Greene
12 Williamsburg
13 Greenpoint
14 Bushwick
15 Bed-Stuy
16 East New York
17 Brownsville
18 East Flatbush
19 Flatbush
20 Canarsie
21 Marine Park
22 Sheepshead Bay
23 Brighton Beach

Legend:
Black
Caribbean
English
Gentrified
German
Hispanic
Irish
Irish/English
Italian
Jewish
Puerto Rican
Russian
Scandinavian
Non-residential

Figure 4.9 The distribution of ethnic groups in Brooklyn, New York, 1870–1985 (*Source*: Warf, 1990)

3 Study Figure 4.9.
a Describe the pattern of ethnic groups in Brooklyn in 1910.
b List the main changes in the pattern of ethnic groups between 1910 and 1935; 1935 and 1965; and 1965 and 1985.
c How far do you think that the study of Brooklyn supports the ideas of Burgess in terms of: the development of concentric rings; and the process of invasion and succession?

Some criticisms of Burgess's model

The main criticisms of Burgess's model are that:

• The model implies clear-cut boundaries between the zones, but fieldwork has shown that such boundaries are hard to find. In practice, zones merge gradually into each other.

• The model only considers ground-floor use and ignores the height of buildings and uses on other floors.

• Within each zone, there are often quite wide variations. For example, in the residential zones, house types may vary from blocks of multi-storey council flats to large private detached houses.

• Little is said about the location of industry whose position in the urban area has become more significant.

• The model aids the understanding of urban patterns in specific places at specific times, particularly the USA in the 1920s, but is less relevant to other times and other cities, especially those in ELDCs.

Burgess himself recognised that his model would need some modification before it could be applied to other cities in the world. However, his model is important because it was the first attempt to analyse the internal morphology of towns and to suggest a causal process.

Kearsley's model of urban structure, 1983

In recent years, geographers have begun to re-evaluate Burgess's work, and have tried to update it. One of the most important of the new models is that produced by Kearsley in 1983 (Fig. 4.10). Kearsley tried to adapt the Burgess model to include modern aspects of urban change such as inner city decline and decentralisation (the movement of people, shops and offices from the city centre to edge-of-city locations).

Figure 4.10 Kearsley's model of urban structure, 1983 (*Source*: Kearsley, 1983)

4 Study Figure 4.10.
a List the main ways in which Kearsley's model differs from Burgess's model.
b Of the points on your list, which do you think are the result of post-1930 changes in urban geography, and which are the result of the different geographies of UK cities and US cities?

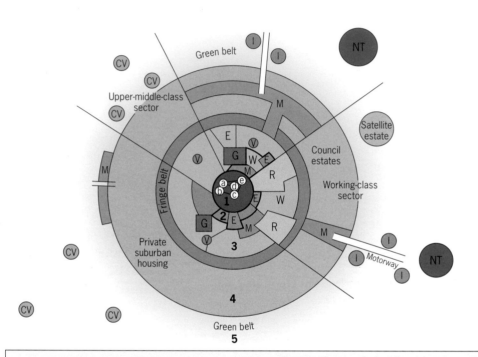

a–e Specialised nodes of activity within the CBD
CV Commuter village
E Ethnic-minority residential area
G Area of gentrification
I Inter-urban commercial/industrial site
M Manufacturing district located on radial and concentric routes or in twilight zone
R Local development scheme
V Encapsulated village
W Area of stable working-class communities

☐ The divide between the inner city and the outer suburbs (often marked by a fringe belt of institutional land uses)
1 Central business zone
2 Transition zone
3 Pre-1918 residential development
4 Post-1918 suburban development
5 Ex-urban commuter zone
NT New Town

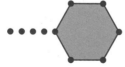

Hoyt's sector model, 1939

Homer Hoyt developed his sector model (Fig. 4.11) as an extension of the Burgess concentric zone model. Hoyt believed that, as the city expanded, residential areas of similar social status would grow outwards from the CBD in a pattern of wedges or sectors. The examples of Boston and Minneapolis in the USA (Figs 4.12–4.13) were used by Hoyt to support his theory. Hoyt agreed with Burgess that high-income groups bought up the 'best' residential land in the city, leaving the poor to live in the least desirable areas such as the transition zone or next to manufacturing industry.

Hoyt argued that sectors developed because some outlying areas had better transport access to the CBD than others. For example, high-class residential areas grew up along suburban railway lines.

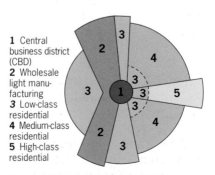

1 Central business district (CBD)
2 Wholesale light manufacturing
3 Low-class residential
4 Medium-class residential
5 High-class residential

Figure 4.11 Hoyt's sector model, 1939 (*After*: Hoyt, 1939)

1900   1915   1936

Boston, Massachusetts

Fashionable residential area

Minneapolis, Minnesota

Figure 4.12 The distribution of fashionable residential areas in Boston and Minneapolis, 1900–36 (*Source*: Hoyt, 1939)

Figure 4.13 Nicollet Avenue, Minneapolis, *c*.1904

Some criticisms of Hoyt's model

The main criticisms of Hoyt's model are that:

- It was based on a study of rents and housing rather than on land use as a whole.
- There is great variation within a sector – for example, in medium-class housing, the range may be from council flats to private semi-detached houses.

Hoyt's model should be seen as complementary to Burgess's model, rather than as competing with it. Hoyt focused on social status and class, and emphasised the importance of transport in urban morphology. He found both these elements to be sectoral. Burgess focused on the distribution of house types which may be more concentric in pattern. Remember also that both models were developed before the growth of car-based suburbs, rapid urban expansion, inner city redevelopment and the migration of shops and offices to the urban periphery (see section 1.5).

Housing and social class in Leicester

N

0   km   200

Leicester

Figure 4.14 Leicester

Research by Pritchard in 1976 examined the development of different types of housing in Leicester (Fig. 4.14) between 1870 and 1938. One of the aims of the research was to examine the usefulness of Hoyt's sector model in relation to different types of housing. Four housing types were identified on the basis of value, size and the socio-economic character of the residents (Fig. 4.15).

The changing distribution of upper-class housing shows a clear sectoral pattern. In 1870, the main area of upper-class housing spread outwards from the CBD in a south-easterly

direction. As the city centre grew and became increasingly congested with factories, workers' houses, traffic, noise and pollution, wealthier merchants and factory owners began to move outwards (Fig. 4.15, 1884 map). The poorer workers had to live within walking distance of their work, but the wealthier citizens had their own horse-drawn carriages – and later the horse-drawn trams – which allowed them to live some distance from their place of work.

Further transport improvements such as the motorised tram and bus service increased the accessibility of the south-eastern part of Leicester and encouraged further high-class house building in the area. By 1911, the high-class housing had reached the city boundary and at that time could not extend further. Between 1911 and 1938, therefore, areas of similar housing quality grew up nearby (Fig. 4.15, 1938 map). These new areas of housing effectively prevented the invasion of lower-class properties.

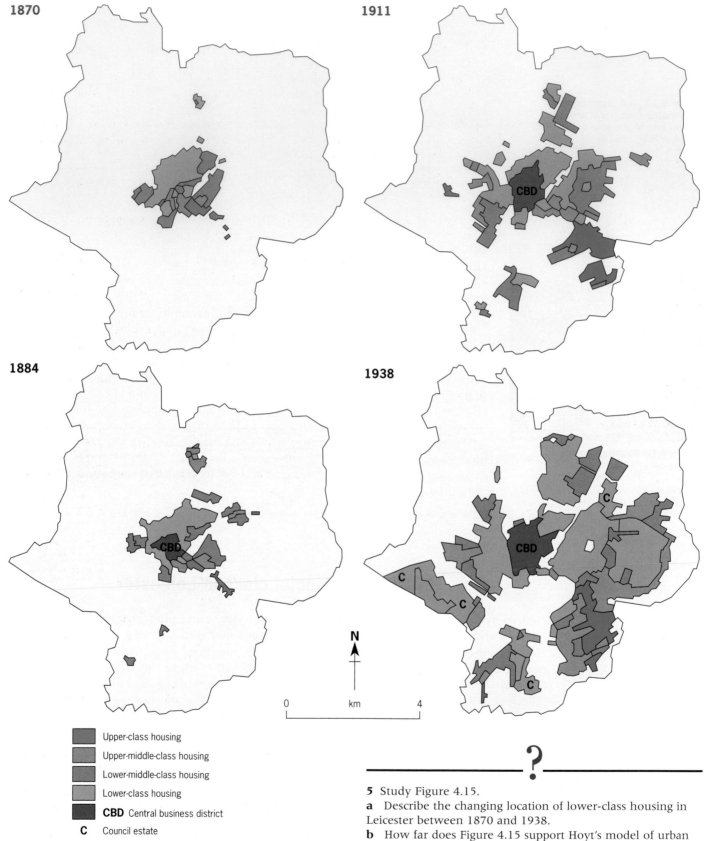

1870

1911

1884

1938

N

0   km   4

     Upper-class housing

     Upper-middle-class housing

     Lower-middle-class housing

     Lower-class housing

CBD   Central business district

C   Council estate

Figure 4.15 The changing social structure of the city of Leicester, 1870–1938 (*Source*: Pritchard, 1976)

?

5 Study Figure 4.15.

a   Describe the changing location of lower-class housing in Leicester between 1870 and 1938.

b   How far does Figure 4.15 support Hoyt's model of urban structure?

c   Which criticisms of the Burgess model can be applied to Hoyt's model?

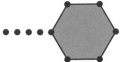

The Harris and Ullman model, 1945

Two geographers, Harris and Ullman, developed a different model in 1945 which challenges the idea of a single, dominant CBD and suggests that a town might grow around a number of different nucleii (Fig. 4.16). Larger cities, they argued, would have more nucleii than small towns. Examples of nucleii include former villages swallowed by city growth and new suburban shopping centres.

In developing their model, Harris and Ullman argued that:

- Some activities tend to locate near each other – e.g. shops, enabling customers to compare goods and prices.

- Some land uses tend to repel others. For example, high value housing is not usually found close to manufacturing industry.

- Some activities can pay higher rents and property prices than others. For example, large shops and offices can afford the high rents of the CBD, so tend to locate there; manufacturing industry cannot afford such high rents and has to locate on cheaper sites (see section 4.4).

Harris and Ullman's model envisages a town without clear-cut zones or sectors, but which grows around nucleii. For example, manufacturing industries may locate along main road and rail routes, while higher-class residential areas may be concentrated away from industrial zones, often on higher ground.

1 ■ Central business district (CBD)
2 ■ Wholesale light manufacturing
3 ■ Low-class residential
4 ■ Medium-class residential
5 ■ High-class residential
6 ■ Heavy manufacturing
7 ■ Outlying business district
8 ■ Residential suburb
9 ■ Industrial suburb

Figure 4.16 Harris and Ullman's multiple nuclei model, 1945 (*After*: Harris and Ullman, 1945)

Figure 4.17 The growth of Amsterdam (*Source*: Hull et al., 1988)

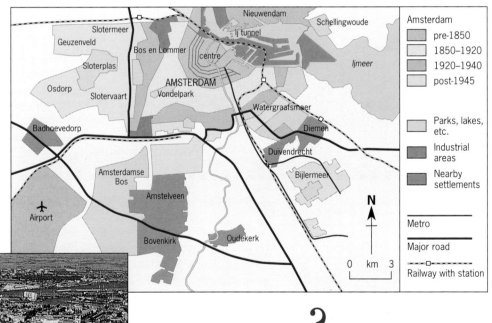

Figure 4.18 Amsterdam, aerial view

?

6 Study Figures 4.17 and 4.18.
a Describe the pattern of Amsterdam's growth from 1850 to the present, including details such as main areas of expansion (with dates) and periods of stability.
b To what extent do you think that Amsterdam fits the Harris and Ullman model of urban structure?
c What problems arise in trying to relate models to real-world cities such as Amsterdam?

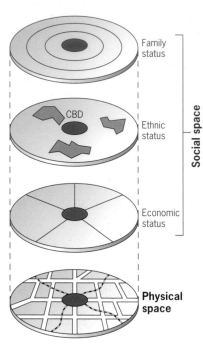

**Figure 4.19 Elements in a city's
residential structure
(Source: Murdie, 1969)**

A composite model

The models of urban structure considered so far are based on studies of cities in capitalist democracies where people usually have some choice over where they live. We can pick out some common elements from these models to create a composite model which may help us to understand aspects of a city's residential structure (Fig. 4.19).

Physical space

The basis of any town or city is the physical geography of its site. Important factors include the presence/absence of a coastline or major river; slope and aspect; and climate. Superimposed on this physical space are the three main dimensions of social space – socio-economic status, family status and ethnic status.

Socio-economic status

Socio-economic status is essentially sectoral in nature. People's choice of home is usually constrained by their income. The rich have greatest choice and seek the most desirable areas; the poor have fewer options.

Family status

Family status is determined by the stage in the life-cycle which people have reached. At each stage, people have different housing needs. For example, on leaving home a young person may seek a rented flat, perhaps in a converted, older house. This house may be located in the inner ring of the city. Later in life, the same person may have a family and seek a larger house with a garden, perhaps located in the suburbs. Thus people live in different parts of the city at different stages in their lives, following a broadly concentric pattern.

Ethnic status

In general, specific ethnic minorities tend to cluster in specific parts of cities, creating a pattern which is neither sectoral nor concentric (section 5.4). For example, Manchester has a large Chinatown; Notting Hill in London has a large West Indian community.

4.3 Models of urban development in ELDCs

All the models considered so far in this chapter have been based on EMDCs (economically more developed countries). The rapid urbanisation in ELDCs (economically less developed countries) has attracted the attention of geographers and planners, who seek to use models to predict future growth trends. At first, geographers tried to adapt the early models of Burgess and others to cities in ELDCs. It quickly became apparent that such models were not always appropriate because:

• Urban growth in ELDCs is much more rapid than it was earlier in the EMDCs.

• Cities in ELDCs are growing in a different way from those in EMDCs. For example, much growth in ELDC cities is directed by government planners.

• The colonial experience of most ELDCs means that their internal structures are different from those of EMDC cities.

Consequently, new models of urban growth have been developed to try to understand the form and function of cities in ELDCs.

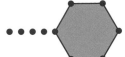

A model of Indian cities

Figure 4.20 shows a simplified, four-stage model of the evolution of the form and functions of an Indian city. In the first, pre-colonial phase, a walled town is located next to an older high-walled fort. Within the town, space was very limited and functions were mixed. Eventually, overcrowding led to residential expansion outside the walls.

When India became part of the British Empire in the eighteenth century (Fig. 4.20, phase 2), a military garrison or cantonment, built on a grid pattern, was established separate from the original city. This was followed by an area known as the 'Civil Lines' for the colonial administrators.

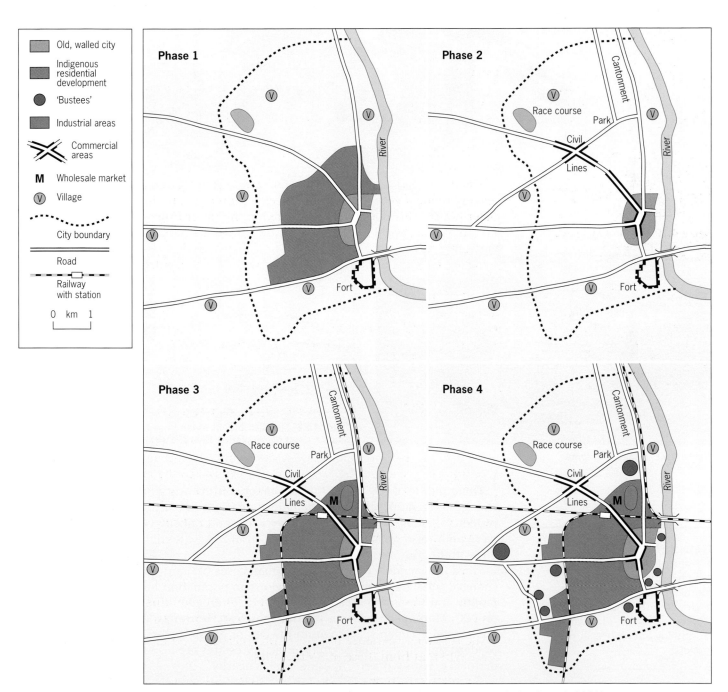

Figure 4.20 An evolutionary model for Indian cities (*After*: Joint Matriculation Board, 1991)

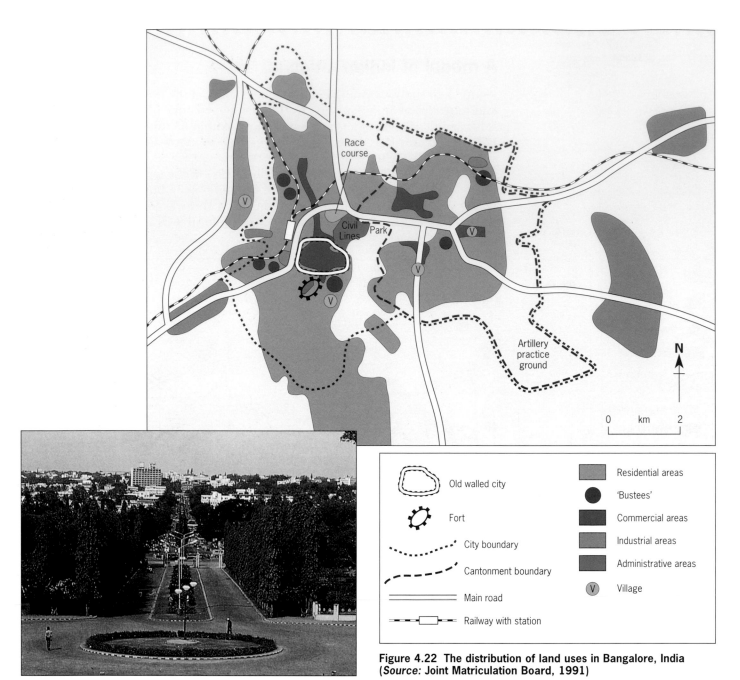

Figure 4.22 The distribution of land uses in Bangalore, India
(*Source:* Joint Matriculation Board, 1991)

Figure 4.21 Bangalore, India

?

7 Study Figure 4.22
a Briefly describe the urban morphology of Bangalore in southern India.
b How far does Bangalore seem to follow the pattern of urban morphology described in the model?

The building of the railways in the nineteenth century brought further changes (Fig. 4.20, phase 3). The railway lines often cut through pre-existing residential areas. New bridges, railway yards and railway workers' housing were built (also on a grid pattern). Industrial zones (textile mills) began to grow up nearby.

Since Independence in 1947, the urban cores of many Indian cities have changed relatively little. However, the urban population has increased very rapidly and the urban area has also grown, often engulfing villages in the process. Many people live in **spontaneous settlements**, called bustees, which are located on open spaces within the city or peripherally (Fig. 4.20, phase 4). Modern industries in large units or factory estates are also located on the periphery, with workers' housing estates nearby.

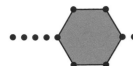

A model of Latin American cities

Cities in Latin America are quite distinct from those in Europe, North America, Africa or Asia. The model of Latin American urban structure (Fig. 4.23) shows the importance of the central CBD, and the presence of a very distinct sector of high-income residences. This sector is often along a main radial road or even a river valley. Around the CBD is the zone of maturity, where older apartment blocks are often deteriorating into slums under the pressure of population growth. Beyond this zone is an area of rapid urban expansion in which new blocks of flats, factories and shopping centres are being built. The outermost zone of squatter settlements, known as favellas, is one of self-constructed housing often lacking services such as water, sewerage and electricity (section 2.8). The disamenity sectors are areas dominated by land uses such as polluting factories which are often located along road or rail routes.

Figure 4.24 shows the distribution of different land uses in Mexico City. With a population of over 24 million, Mexico City is one of the world's largest and fastest growing cities and has extreme housing contrasts (Figs 4.25–4.26).

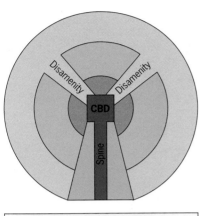

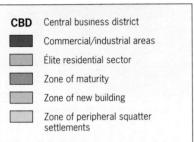

CBD Central business district

Commercial/industrial areas

Élite residential sector

Zone of maturity

Zone of new building

Zone of peripheral squatter settlements

Figure 4.23 A land use model for Latin American cities (*Source*: Robinson, 1995)

8 Study Figure 4.24
a How far do the functional zones of Mexico City seem to follow the pattern shown in Figure 4.23?
b in what ways and for what reasons do the internal structures of cities in ELDCs differ from those in shown models based on EMDCs?

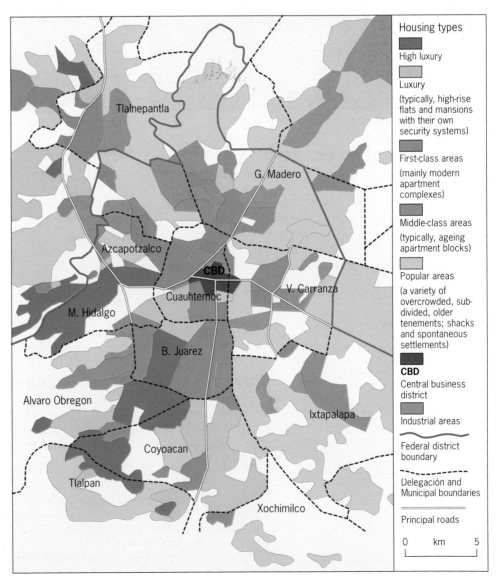

Housing types

High luxury

Luxury
(typically, high-rise flats and mansions with their own security systems)

First-class areas
(mainly modern apartment complexes)

Middle-class areas
(typically, ageing apartment blocks)

Popular areas
(a variety of overcrowded, sub-divided, older tenements; shacks and spontaneous settlements)

CBD
Central business district

Industrial areas

Federal district boundary

Delegación and Municipal boundaries

Principal roads

0   km   5

Figure 4.24 Distribution of land uses in Mexico City (*Source*: Ward, 1990)

Figure 4.25 Mexico City: luxury flats in the centre

Figure 4.26 Mexico City: spontaneous housing on the outskirts

4.4 Land values and urban structure

Most urban models attempt to explain spatial patterns at least partly in terms of land values. In the past, such models would not have been relevant to cities in socialist countries such as the former USSR and the republics of eastern Europe, where land was not sold privately for profit. However, these nations are not now communist-controlled and property is privately owned. In future, therefore, their urban patterns will also be influenced by the market values of land, together with the aims of planning authorities who often have clear ideas how an area should develop.

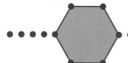

The land value model or bid–rent theory

The land value model, also known as bid–rent theory, is an attempt to theorise the role of locational rent in shaping urban land use patterns. Two basic facts about land values in cities apply wherever a market economy is found:

- First, land values vary from place to place within the urban area. Generally, values are highest in the city centre – the most accessible area – and decline away from it. However, there may also be some secondary high-value 'peaks' (Fig. 4.27). For example, the intersection of a ring road and a major radial route may become a suburban shopping centre.

- Secondly, urban land uses differ in terms of both the type of location they need and the amount of rent they can afford. Each urban land use has a different **bid–rent curve** – that is, the amount of rent it can afford to pay

Figure 4.27 Land value peaks in an urban area (After: Simmons, 1964)

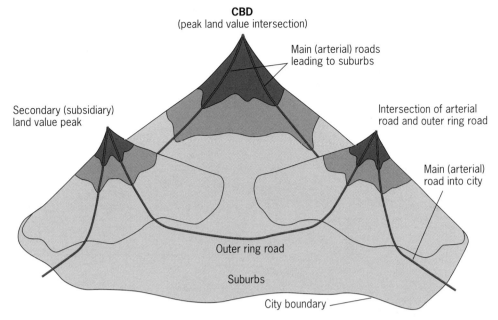

CBD
(peak land value intersection)

Main (arterial) roads
leading to suburbs

Secondary (subsidiary)
land value peak

Intersection of arterial
road and outer ring road

Main (arterial)
road into city

Outer ring road

Suburbs

City boundary

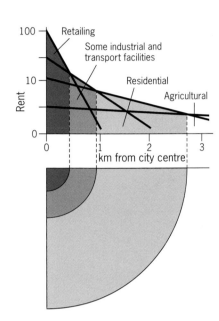

Figure 4.28 The land value or bid–rent model (Source: Fielding, 1975)

(Fig. 4.28). For example, retail shops need to be highly accessible to their customers. In the right location, they can achieve a high turnover relative to their floor area. Thus they can afford to pay high rents for the best central sites.

When these two basic principles are combined, we can see that similar functions come together within cities because they have the same locational needs and can afford the same level of rent. Thus, while retailing and offices cluster in city centres, industry and transport functions tend to locate further out (Fig. 4.28). They still need some accessibility, but cannot afford to pay the highest rents. Housing is even less competitive and so tends to be pushed still further from the city centre. Agriculture, with the lowest bid rent, is found only in the urban fringe and beyond.

Summary

- The internal structure of towns consists of a series of functional and morphological areas.
- Urban morphology varies from city to city but there are some common themes.
- Theoretical models try to explain the internal structure of cities.
- All models have their advantages and disadvantages.
- Different models have been developed for cities in ELDCs.
- Within cities, land values vary with accessibility.
- Different urban functions have different bid rents and different locational requirements.
- Some of the clustering of land uses evident in models can be explained by the operation of land values and bid rents.

5 Social patterns in cities

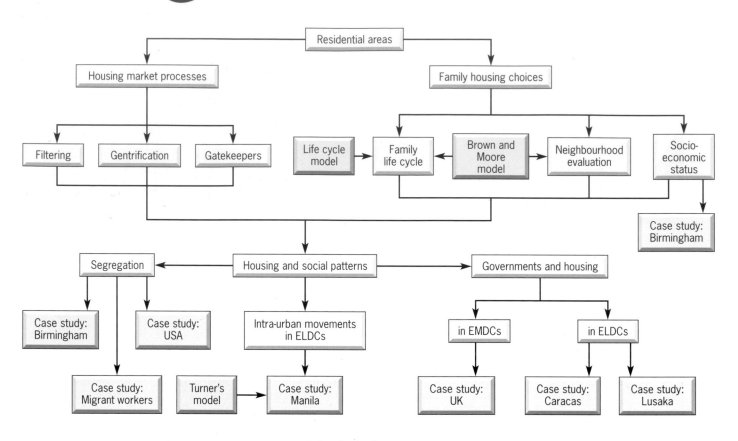

5.1 Residential areas

Housing is by far the largest user of space in cities. It is also one of the most dynamic elements within urban areas. New houses are built; old ones are renovated or decay; and people move house. In general, housing is newer towards the edge of the urban area and older near the centre, with the exception of renewal areas (Chapter 8). We have also seen in Chapter 4 how different types of housing are sometimes located in different sectors of the city. This chapter examines the processes by which different types of urban residential area form and how they may change through time.

There are many different ways to categorise housing – as you will have discovered from Task 1 (see also Figs 5.1, 5.2 and 5.3). The most common are on the basis of age, type (detached, terraced, flat, etc.) and ownership/tenure (council or privately owned). Also, we tend to link house types with particular social groups – e.g. high-income detached housing – even though such identification may tell us very little about the nature of the people living there.

In studying urban residential areas, we seek to understand:

• why people choose to live where they do (although some groups have little or no choice as to where they live); and

• the processes that produce and influence patterns of housing and social space.

5.2 Housing market processes

Housing and social patterns in cities in EMDCs are partly the outcome of a number of general processes that operate to influence individual and family decisions.

1a Work in pairs and choose six categories for mapping different types of housing in your local area.
b Draw a sketch map of the area using a key to show your categories.
c Discuss the reasons for your choice of categories with others in your group. What features did you select in common?

2a In pairs, list the type(s) of housing (in the UK) likely to be occupied by each of the following economic groups: high-income; middle-income; low-income.
b Where do former council houses which have been bought by their owners feature in your list?
c Compare your list with those of other pairs. What similarities and differences are evident?

Figure 5.1 London: terraced housing, Isle of Dogs

Figure 5.2 São Paulo, Brazil: luxury apartment block in the Moema district

Figure 5.3 Manila: part of a spontaneous settlement

?

3 Make a list of the groups of people in cities here and in other countries who do not have any choice in where they live. Be as precise and detailed as you can. For example, many 'poor' people have little choice in where they live, but what are the causes of that poverty (e.g. unemployment, underemployment, family size)?

4 Study Figures 5.1, 5.2 and 5.3 and use them to produce a matrix comparing the three types of housing on the basis of size, building materials and environmental quality of area.

Filtering

An important contribution to the overall pattern is made by **filtering** – the process by which social groups move from one area of housing to another (Fig. 5.4). For example, the construction of new housing on the edge of the urban area (Fig. 5.4b) may encourage wealthier groups to move there. In turn, the housing areas they vacate will be occupied by other groups who may move out from inner parts of the city (Fig. 5.4c). In this way, housing areas change their social character over a period of time.

Gentrification

Gentrification is the process by which older (often rundown) housing areas, usually close to the city centre, become socially desirable and are physically and socially upgraded (Figs 5.4e and 5.5). Professional groups such as teachers, doctors and lawyers are attracted by the character of the housing and its greater accessibility to the centre. These groups begin to move in, renovating the houses. As a result, other property in the area becomes more 'desirable'; house prices rise; and the social composition of the area is changed. An example of gentrification can be found in eastern Edgbaston, close to the centre of Birmingham.

Housing gatekeepers

The choice of where to live in EMDCs is further complicated by the operation of **gatekeepers**. These are institutions and their representatives who in various ways act to limit people's choice.

Figure 5.4 The urban filtering process (*Source:* Burtenshaw, 1983)

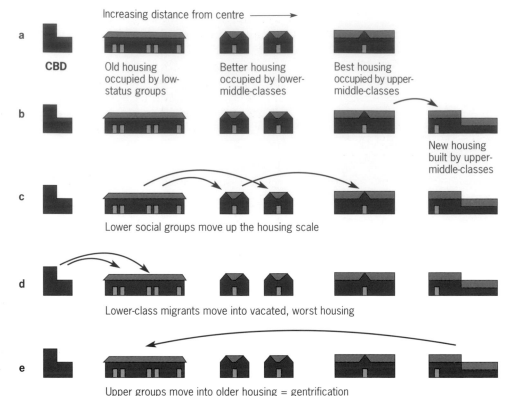

Increasing distance from centre ⟶

a   CBD   Old housing occupied by low-status groups   Better housing occupied by lower-middle-classes   Best housing occupied by upper-middle-classes

b   New housing built by upper-middle-classes

c   Lower social groups move up the housing scale

d   Lower-class migrants move into vacated, worst housing

e   Upper groups move into older housing = gentrification

Figure 5.5 London: gentrified housing, Elgin Crescent, Kensington

Institutions

Banks, building societies and finance companies together with estate agents, solicitors and mortgage brokers, operate in a way that allocates people to housing. The financial institutions lend invested money to prospective house buyers. The prime concern of such financial institutions is to ensure that their investment is safe. They therefore consider the income(s) of the house buyer(s), their age and their family commitments. These socio-economic features will determine how much money they are prepared to lend and over how long a period of time. The financial institutions also consider the value, location, type, age and state of repair of the house or flat to be bought.

Features of the operation of this system in the UK are:

- a tendency to lend most to middle-class, male-headed families;

- a tendency to lend more to white than black or Asian families;

- a tendency to lend more on newer properties;

- the relative neglect of some inner city areas;

- the exclusion of some groups, such as the poor, the elderly, single parents and some ethnic minorities, from house ownership in some parts of some cities.

Council housing

Access to council housing in the UK is controlled by a different set of gatekeepers. Local authority housing managers allocate council housing of a selected type and in a selected area to tenants on the basis of a points system which determines their relative priority. For example, people living in overcrowded conditions or having specific medical needs are all given points and are put on a waiting list, to be given a house or flat when one becomes available. Unfortunately, with little or no council house building recently and with the sale of council houses (which has reduced the local authority housing stock), waiting lists have become longer.

?

5a In the UK, what benefits and problems exist for: people who bought council houses; local authorities who sold council houses; and poorer groups seeking housing?
b In each case, identify the cause(s) of the benefits/problems.

Dominant and muted groups
An alternative way of looking at the various constraints on access to housing in both EMDCs and ELDCs is to distinguish between *dominant groups* and *muted groups*. Dominant groups are those with the money and political power to control the allocation of housing resources. These groups indirectly control the lives of others. The muted groups include ethnic minorities, the poor and single-parent families who are disadvantaged because the city's housing is structured in the interests of the dominant groups.

5.3 Family housing choices

In recent years, geographers have studied how individuals and families choose where to live. From such studies, it is clear that three main groups of factors are responsible for patterns of urban housing choice: the family life cycle; neighbourhood evaluation and socio-economic status.

The family life cycle
The concept of the family life cycle (sometimes abbreviated to life cycle) was developed in relation to people in EMDCs. The basic idea is that people's lives pass through several stages, each with different housing needs. Consequently, people move house to meet these needs. **Intra-urban moves** (within the same city) are usually to different districts or sectors.

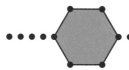

The family life cycle model

In the model (Fig. 5.6), a person moves through six stages during their lifetime. Stage 1 (childhood) is often spent in semi-detached or terraced houses, located in one of the middle zones of the city. In stage 2, the children have grown up and become independent; they may move to a rented room or flat in another area. Setting up home with a partner (stage 3) may mean a move to a larger flat or a small house (either a council-owned or a privately owned starter-home), probably in a different part of the urban area.

In stage 4, an increase in family size (having children) combined with a larger income (often the result of both partners working) leads to a move to a

Table 5.1 Household size in the UK, 1961–91 (*Source:* Census of Population, 1991)

Number of persons	Percentage of all households	
	1961	1991
1	12	25
2	30	29
3	23	17
4	19	18
5	9	7
6	7	4

Figure 5.6 Family life cycle moves in a UK city (*Source:* Burtenshaw, 1983)

Housing age zones
new
old

	1	**2**	**3**	**4**	**5**	**6**
Type	semi-detached	rented room in converted large Victorian house	owned starter home	owned family home	owned family home	owned retirement bungalow
Stage	childhood	pre-child	pre-child/ child rearing	child launching	child launching	post-child/ late life

6 Study Table 5.1.
a Draw a graph to show the main changes in family size between 1961 and 1991.
b Try to explain the changes in family size in relation to general population and social trends.
c What effect might these family-size changes have on the future demand for different types of housing?

larger, often newer house further out in the suburbs. (The model assumes continued employment and family commitments.) In stage 5, children begin to leave home and the parents may move to a smaller house. Finally, when all the children have left and one partner dies, the remaining partner may decide to move to a bungalow or flat which may again be in a different part of the urban area.

Some criticisms of the family life cycle model

This model has several limitations, some of which are similar to those of other models in urban geography:

• it is very generalised;

• few families follow all its stages;

• many families follow none of its stages; and

• it makes many assumptions about families and their lives.

However, the value of the model lies in the link between the demand for different types of housing and the needs of families at different points in their lives.

Neighbourhood evaluation
In any individual or family decision to move house, a personal evaluation of different residential areas takes place – i.e. an assessment is made of their **place utility**. Brown and Moore have included this along with family factors in their housing choice model.

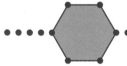

Brown and Moore's model, 1985

Fewer than 10 per cent of the people moving house in the UK move over 80 km; over 50 per cent move less than 10 km – i.e. often within the same city. Understanding their decision-making processes can help us to understand the urban social patterns that result. A model developed by Brown and Moore examines the pressures which cause individuals and families to move.

The decision to move is based on two main groups of factors (Fig. 5.7): internal (to the individual/family) and external. Pressures within one or both groups build up, often causing stress and dissatisfaction with the existing house or flat. If the stress becomes too great, the individual/family may decide to relocate. This starts a search process which continues until a suitable new home is found or the search is abandoned. The model is based on the importance of personal choice, although the factors which may force the individual/family to abandon searching – such as the high cost of housing – may have nothing to do with choice.

7 Make two lists of factors, one internal to a family and one external to a family, which may start the search for a different house or flat.

8 Interview at least five households (parents or other people) who have considered moving house. Get them to explain the reasons for their last move (or non-move). How far do their reasons seem to fit the Brown and Moore model?

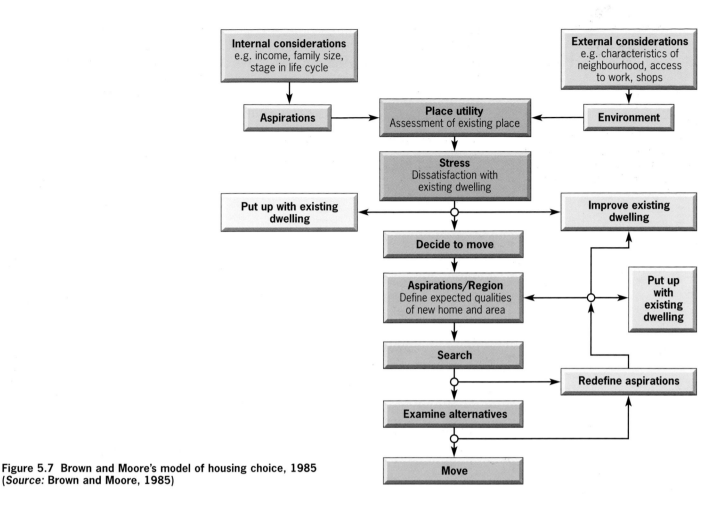

Figure 5.7 Brown and Moore's model of housing choice, 1985
(*Source:* Brown and Moore, 1985)

Socio-economic status

The third set of factors affecting UK urban housing choice is people's income, wealth, education and occupation – known collectively as their **socio-economic status**. A pioneering study by Rex and Moore in Birmingham in the 1980s found a link between the type of house people occupy and their socio-economic group. Based on this, eleven different social housing classes have been identified in British cities:

• outright owners of large houses in desirable locations;

• mortgage payers of large houses in desirable areas;

• outright owners of medium- and small-sized houses;

• mortgage payers of medium- and small-sized houses;

• outright owners of former council houses;

• mortgage payers of former council houses;

• council housing tenants;

• tenants in slum housing owned by councils;

• tenants in privately rented accommodation;

• owners of houses forced to rent rooms to meet mortgage repayments;

• tenants in slum housing privately owned.

House type and socio-economic status in Birmingham

Birmingham (Fig. 5.8) provides a good example of the way in which patterns of housing can be linked to different socio-economic factors.

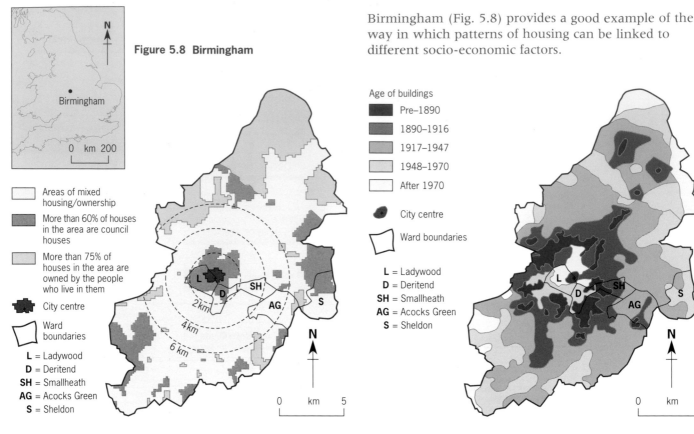

Figure 5.8 Birmingham

Areas of mixed housing/ownership

More than 60% of houses in the area are council houses

More than 75% of houses in the area are owned by the people who live in them

City centre

Ward boundaries

L = Ladywood
D = Deritend
SH = Smallheath
AG = Acocks Green
S = Sheldon

Age of buildings
Pre–1890
1890–1916
1917–1947
1948–1970
After 1970

City centre

Ward boundaries

L = Ladywood
D = Deritend
SH = Smallheath
AG = Acocks Green
S = Sheldon

Figure 5.9 Council-owned and privately owned housing in Birmingham, 1993 (*Sources:* Ellis, 1987 and Birmingham Planning Department, 1993)

Figure 5.10 Age of buildings in Birmingham, 1997 (*Sources:* Ellis, 1987 and Birmingham Planning Department, 1993)

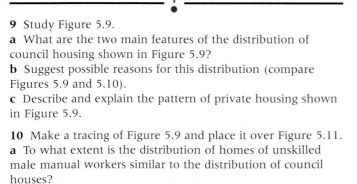

?

9 Study Figure 5.9.
a What are the two main features of the distribution of council housing shown in Figure 5.9?
b Suggest possible reasons for this distribution (compare Figures 5.9 and 5.10).
c Describe and explain the pattern of private housing shown in Figure 5.9.

10 Make a tracing of Figure 5.9 and place it over Figure 5.11.
a To what extent is the distribution of homes of unskilled male manual workers similar to the distribution of council houses?
b What other factors might influence where unskilled manual workers live?
c To what extent is the distribution of homes of male employers, managers and professional people similar to the distribution of private housing?
d List the factors which might influence where employers, managers and professional people live.

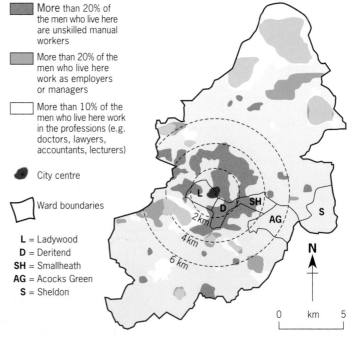

More than 20% of the men who live here are unskilled manual workers

More than 20% of the men who live here work as employers or managers

More than 10% of the men who live here work in the professions (e.g. doctors, lawyers, accountants, lecturers)

City centre

Ward boundaries

L = Ladywood
D = Deritend
SH = Smallheath
AG = Acocks Green
S = Sheldon

Figure 5.11 Some socio-economic groups in Birmingham, 1993 (*Sources:* Ellis, 1987 and Birmingham Planning Department, 1993)

Table 5.2 Social conditions in eastern Birmingham, 1997 (*Source:* Birmingham City Council, 1999)

	Ladywood	Deritend	Smallheath	Acocks Green	Sheldon
Percentage of people who are					
Children under 16	23	32	31	19	6
Pensioners	22	9	13	22	21
Unemployed males	25	33	29	16	14
Unemployed females	16	12	12	8	6
Born outside the UK	21	36	40	11	6
Percentage of families living in the ward with					
Over 3 children	7	22	24	6	5
Only 1 adult	27	13	4	5	7
No car	67	59	57	46	32

11 Study Figure 5.12, which is a transect across Birmingham from Ladywood, an area close to the city centre, eastwards to Sheldon, a suburb built in the early 1960s on the outskirts of the city.

a Use Table 5.2 to draw a similar diagram to show changes in social conditions along the same transect.

b Use Figure 5.12 and your diagram to write a brief report on the variations in population density, home ownership, home renting and social conditions found in: Ladywood, Deritend, Smallheath, Acocks Green and Sheldon.

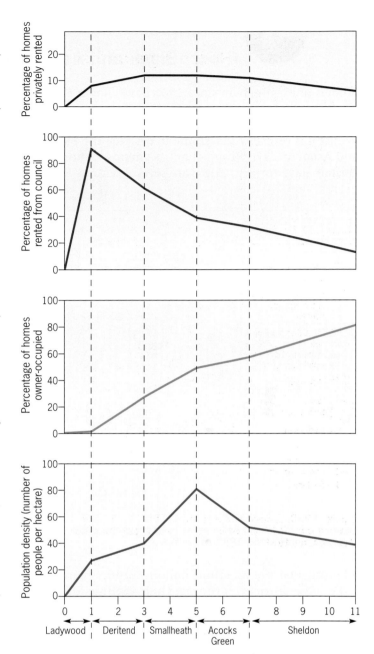

Figure 5.12 Housing conditions in a transect through central-eastern Birmingham, 1998 (Source: City of Birmingham, 1999)

5.4 Housing and social patterns

Housing market processes, family factors and people's assessment of different urban neighbourhoods all combine to determine housing choices and, eventually, create social patterns in cities. The remaining sections explore some of these patterns in EMDCs and ELDCs.

Social segregation

The greatest degree of social segregation is often experienced by ethnic minority groups within cities. Conditions of almost total segregation result in single-group areas known as **ghettos**. The term ghetto derives from the district of Geto in medieval Venice which was reserved for Jews.

Black and Asian areas in Birmingham

Studies of Birmingham since 1961 have shown a tendency for the black and Asian communities to concentrate in particular parts of the city (Fig. 5.13). Whilst it is probably inaccurate to describe the black and Asian areas in Birmingham as ghettos, definite clusters have formed. There are several reasons for this.

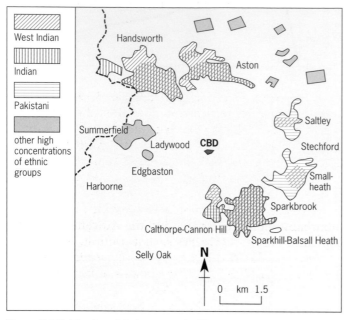

Figure 5.13 Black and Asian areas in Birmingham, 1996 (*Sources:* Burtenshaw, 1983 and authors)

- For members of an ethnic minority group, living in the same district can **reduce their feelings of isolation** and provide a sense of community and security.

- In some cases, living in an ethnic cluster is a **defensive reaction** related to a fear of conflict with surrounding groups.

- **Avoidance of outside contact** is sometimes another reason for ethnic clustering. Residents can support each other and establish their own shops, services and places of worship to serve their community's needs (Fig. 5.14).

- **Preservation of identity** and **promotion of cultural heritage** are also important reasons for clustering. Groups with their own language, religion and social organisation often have a strong wish to remain distinctive.

- Finally, some authors have written about the **attack function** as a reason for ethnic concentration. A group can plan and carry out activities that promote solidarity and help to ensure survival in a possibly hostile environment. These activities can be peaceful, such as protests against racial discrimination.

Recent trends in ethnic minorities in UK cities

Recent research on ethnic groups living in UK cities found that most minority groups had arrived in the UK at about the same time after the Second World War, and they all faced similar problems of discrimination. However, over time these ethnic groups have developed significant differences in terms of where they live in cities and the types of housing they occupy.

Indian families tend to live in suburban, often semi-detached locations where they are owner-occupiers, often in white-collar jobs. Pakistani families are most liable to have blue-collar jobs and to live in terraced housing as owner-occupiers. Bangladeshi families tend to work in blue-collar jobs and to live in council housing and inner-city terraced houses. Afro-Caribbean families tend to work in blue-collar jobs, and many live in council housing, but they are much more widely spread across areas of cities than the Bangladeshi or Pakistani families. The research also argues that we should not underestimate the continuing power of discrimination in producing these patterns, but adds that ethnic cultural values are also important in understanding the distribution patterns. For example, ethnic minorities with a South Asian background tend to live in male-dominated, nuclear families; there tend to be

Figure 5.14 Central Mosque, Birmingham

few lone parents with children. By contrast, Afro-Caribbean families tend to be female-dominated. Marriage, in this context, is a middle-class institution often adopted after the rearing of a family. So there are many single female-headed households amongst the Afro-Caribbean ethnic groups.

The result of these processes is that ethnic segregation in UK cities by the year 2000 had produced a much more complicated picture than the inner-city stereotype of the 1960s. It is true that the overall picture shows a pattern of economic disadvantage for minority groups, who continue to struggle with discrimination and racial harassment. However, there has been some modest improvement in incomes for

?

12 Compare Figure 5.13 with Figures 5.9, 5.10 and 5.11.
a To what extent do the distributions of black and Asian groups in Birmingham relate to: housing types; age of buildings; patterns of employment?
b What other information would you need in order to explain more fully the location of Birmingham's black and Asian populations?

some groups. There has also been some decentralisation from inner-city areas to suburban (but not rural) areas. In general, pattern of Afro-Caribbean families in UK cities showed less segregation by 2000 than in 1960. Pakistani and Bangladeshi families, in contrast, showed a continuing trend for segregation either in areas of owner-occupied or council housing. Indian families tended to be less segregated in 2000 than in 1960.

Hence patterns of ethnic minorities in UK cities had changed significantly between 1960 and 2000. These differences varied from group to group, and were the result of social, economic and political factors.

Ghettos in the USA

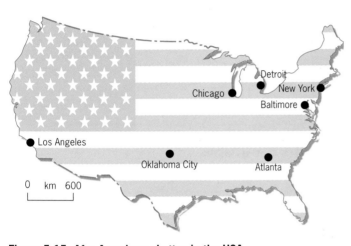

Figure 5.15 Afro-American ghettos in the USA

Afro-American ghettos in the USA (Fig. 5.15) are larger and used to be more clearly defined than those in the UK. They also exhibit a much greater degree of recent change, as the example of Oklahoma City illustrates. Ghettos were recognisable in the 1920s in cities such as Atlanta, Baltimore, Chicago and New York, and soon developed in most other US cities.

More recently, population growth has led to a suburbanisation process amongst the African-American population of most US cities such as Detroit, Atlanta and Los Angeles. Much of this suburbanisation takes the form of **spillover** – i.e. the gradual outward spread of the ghetto in a sectoral fashion.

In other cities, areas that were once separate poorer towns and villages beyond the urban fringe, have been

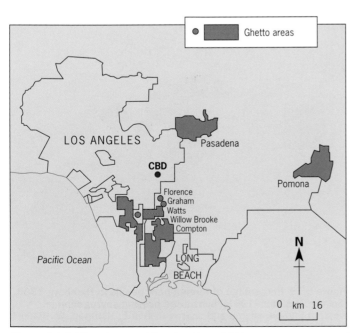

Figure 5.16 The ghettos of Los Angeles, 1983
(*Source:* Burtenshaw, 1983)

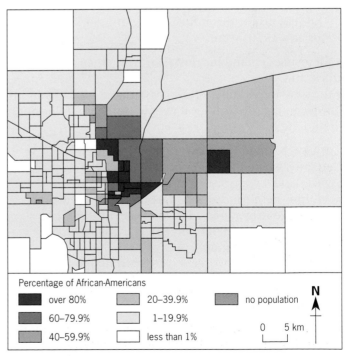

Figure 5.17 The distribution of African-Americans in Oklahoma City, 1990 (*Source:* Knox, 1995)

swallowed up by the spread of the city. As a result, these areas have become African-American suburbs.

In yet other cases, **leapfrogging** has taken place, involving the colonisation of a white suburb by African-American families. In the case of Los Angeles, the core of the ghetto was Watts, and African-Americans have leapfrogged to Compton, Willow Brooke, Florence and Graham (Fig. 5.16).

---

13 Study Figures 5.17 and 5.18.

a Describe the distribution of African-Americans in Oklahoma City in 1990.

b How far does this distribution reflect: spillover; swallowed towns; leapfrogging?

c What income levels are associated with the main African-American clusters?

Figure 5.18 Average family incomes in Oklahoma City, 1990 (*Source:* Knox, 1995)

Median family income ($)
- 55000–80000
- 45000–55000
- 35000–45000
- 25000–35000
- 15000–25000
- less than 15000

N

0   5 km

Migrant workers in European cities

The social geography of European cities has changed greatly in the last 40 years, with the arrival of thousands of migrant workers, mostly from the poorer areas of the Mediterranean. By 1998, there were some 20 million migrant workers living in European cities, half of whom were young adult males who migrated to find work and the other half, the families who came with them.

The reasons for this influx of migrant workers in the 1960s and 1970s were:

• the rising demand for unskilled workers in European cities; and
• the growing number of unpleasant and menial jobs in European cities which local people were very reluctant to undertake.

By 1975, there were two million foreign workers in Germany, 1.5 million in France, and 500,000 in Switzerland.

Within these countries, most of the migrant workers live in large urban areas. For instance, in 1990, two million of the six million foreigners living in France lived in the Paris region.

Because migrant workers were recruited to low-skill, low-wage jobs, they are now clustered in the most run-down neighbourhoods. Migrant workers want cheap housing, but the fact that they are concentrated in camps, factory hostels, immigrant hostels, shanty towns or inner city areas is reinforced by discrimination.

In spatial terms, there is a consistent pattern across European cities, from Serbs, Croats and Turks in

- Fewer than 5% foreign
- More than 20% foreign
- More than 40% foreign

Figure 5.19 Percentage of foreign-born people in Hamburg 1986. (*Source:* Huttman (1991) 'Subsidised housing segregation in Western Europe, stigma and segregation in E. Huttman, W. Blauu and J. Saltman (eds) *Urban Housing Segregation of Minorities in Western Europe and the United States*, Duke University Press, Durban, Fig. 6.2, p.132)

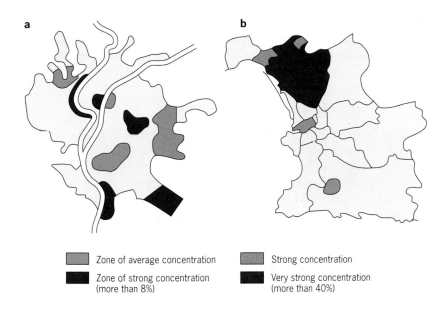

Zone of average concentration

Zone of strong concentration (more than 8%)

Strong concentration

Very strong concentration (more than 40%)

Figure 5.20 Foreign born populations in 1982 in a) Lyons b) Marseilles (*Source*: Huttman (1991) *op. cit.* Figs. 7.3 and 7.4 pp148–9)

Duisburg, Frankfurt and Cologne, to the Algerians, Tunisians and Italians in Paris. The location of foreign-born people in Hamburg (Fig. 5.19) is typical of the pattern of migrant workers in other European cities, where the priority for migrant workers is to live in cheap accommodation close to their jobs.

In some cities, such as Lyons and Marseilles (Fig. 5.20) a second pattern has developed. This is the result of allocating migrant workers to dilapidated public housing estates on the edge of the urban area.

The results of this economic, social and political polarisation are that many of second- and third-generation migrant workers feel cut off from the rest of society, as well as feeling excluded and discriminated against. Unless the city authorities take rapid measures to improve living conditions in these areas, serious social and political conflict seems inevitable.

Intra-urban movement in ELDCs

Patterns of intra-urban movement in ELDCs like the Philippines are different from those in EMDCs such as the UK. One of the main factors generating intra-urban movements in ELDCs is **migration** from the countryside. The regular influx of newcomers in search of a better quality of life combines with high rates of natural increase to create intense pressures on available housing. A model of the movements of migrants within cities was produced by John Turner, an American geographer writing in the 1970s.

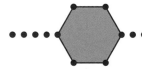

Turner's model, 1974

Turner's model (Fig. 5.21) identifies the three main stages that urban migrants pass through following their arrival in the city in search of work.

Bridgeheaders

The first move to the city is often made by only one (usually male) member of a family. Turner called this person a 'bridgeheader'. The bridgeheader's main priority is to find work (Fig. 5.21); he is prepared to tolerate very poor housing conditions, often in overcrowded tenements, so long as they are close to his place of employment. At first, bridgeheaders often stay with relatives or friends from the same village who have already moved to the city. Thus the already very overcrowded slums close to city centres and industrial estates become even more overcrowded.

Consolidators

Eventually, the bridgeheaders find better paid and more secure jobs and become what Turner calls 'consolidators'. They can afford to travel to work, so

Proximity to employment

Security (e.g. legal tenure of land)

Access to amenities (e.g. more space, schools, shops)

Figure 5.21 Turner's model, 1974: the changing priorities of low-income families in ELDCs (*Source*: Drakakis-Smith, 1987)

their need for proximity to employment declines (Fig. 5.21). Often they are joined by their families and start to search for a larger living space near better facilities. For poor people in ELDCs, this means moving to a **spontaneous settlement** (a shanty town) where they can build their own home from scrap materials.

Status-seekers

In the third stage of Turner's model, the consolidators continue to prosper as more members of the family find work. Children often work selling water, shining shoes or helping to sort and sell rubbish. As the family's income grows, they seek to improve their situation and become status-seekers. They may move to another, better, area (often another spontaneous settlement) where services such as water, electricity or sewage disposal are available. Status-seekers also try to build more permanent houses of brick or concrete, and try to buy the land on which they live (Fig. 5.21).

Manila: housing for the poor and the rich

Figure 5.22 The Philippines

Figure 5.23 Two contrasting images of Manila

Housing for the poor in Manila

The Philippines has a population of over 67 million, spread over a series of islands in the Pacific (Fig. 5.22). Seven million people live in the capital Manila (Fig. 5.23) where the population is increasing by over 1000 per week as more people arrive from the countryside.

In Manila, bridgeheaders often move at first into overcrowded slum areas like Intramuros close to the Old City and harbour (Fig. 5.24). When they become consolidators, they move with their families to a spontaneous settlement. The consolidators main area in Manila is Smokey Mountain (Figs 5.24, 5.25 and 5.26). Smokey Mountain is built on top of Manila's rubbish dump which spills out into North Manila Bay.

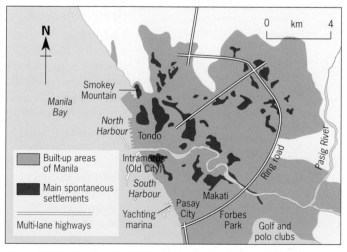

Figure 5.24 Manila, the Philippines (*Source:* **Drakakis-Smith, 1987**)

Figure 5.25 Smokey Mountain, Manila

Figure 5.26 A home in Smokey Mountain, Manila

Figure 5.27 Spontaneous housing, Tondo, Manila

Figure 5.28 Relocation housing in Tondo, Manila, for people from Smokey Mountain

Figure 5.29 High-rise luxury apartments near the yacht harbour, Roxas Boulevard, Manila

Figure 5.30 Shopping plaza in the Makati commercial area, Manila

Over 10 000 people in Smokey Mountain earn a living by sorting through and selling rubbish. Conditions here are difficult with no domestic water, electricity or sewerage systems. Smokey Mountain is an illegal settlement in that the people do not own the land, but at least there is space to build houses and scrap materials with which to build them.

When entering the status-seeker stage, families often move from areas like Smokey Mountain to other settlements such as Tondo (Figs 5.27 and 5.28) where conditions are better. Tondo is a mixed area with street markets and some modern buildings as well as the spontaneous settlement. Here some houses have water and electricity (legally or illegally), though drainage is still a problem and most sewage and rubbish is dumped in rivers and streams. However, local people are proud of the efforts they have made to improve their houses and the area.

In ELDCs, poorer people in cities like Manila have to balance a range of conflicting priorities:

• proximity to a job;

• cheap rent; and

• access to amenities (water, electricity).

These choices govern the type of accommodation that is available and its location, and result in the evolution of distinctly different social areas.

Housing for the rich in Manila

The wealthiest parts of Manila lie to the south of the Pasig River (Fig. 5.24). Few of the people living in spontaneous settlements ever become rich enough to live in areas like these (Fig. 5.29). Places like Pasay City have luxury, air-conditioned apartments, with

swimming pools; families have two or more cars. Such developments also include shopping plazas and expensive hotels (Fig. 5.30), surrounded by high fences and patrolled by private security guards.

14a Produce a matrix to show the housing conditions at each stage in the life cycle of a family following Turner's model.
b How do the conflicting priorities of the poor in cities in ELDCs compare with those of the poor in cities in EMDCs?

15a Draw a diagram similar to Figure 5.6 to show intra-urban movements in Manila.
b Describe and explain the pattern of housing moves shown on your diagram.

16a Draw a diagram similar to Figure 5.7 to show housing choice in Manila.
b What are the main differences between your diagram and Figure 5.7?

5.5 Governments and housing

Government involvement in the provision of housing varies from country to country and, frequently, from region to region within a country. The case study of local authority housing in the UK illustrates a type of local government housing provision found in several European EMDCs.

Local authority housing in the UK

Figure 5.31 The UK

In the UK (Fig 5.31), a substantial part of the housing stock has been built and is owned by local authorities (councils). Studies suggest that the housing choices of council tenants are very different from those of mortgage-holding owner-occupiers (sections 5.2 and 5.3).

A study of council tenants in London showed that many wanted to move but were unable to do so. About 44 per cent wanted to move from the inner estates to areas nearer the edge of the city. Many requests were from families wanting to move from multi-storey blocks of flats to houses. However, a study in Newcastle-upon-Tyne showed that council tenants there were requesting moves away from the suburbs and towards the centre. Their reasons included poor service provision in the suburbs and high travel costs to the city centre.

Tenants on the west side of Newcastle upon Tyne tended to request moves only on that side of the city and people from eastern estates remained firmly on their side of the city. This tendency to select from only one sector of a city is also found among owner-occupiers considering moves.

Local authority house ownership also affects social patterns in UK cities in other ways. For example, some council estates – including the Manor estate in Sheffield and Meanwood in Leeds – have gained reputations for crime and violence. These reputations are sometimes unjustified, but exist in the public mind and serve to dissuade some tenants from moving to these estates and to persuade others to try and leave.

In some areas, local authorities have deliberately tried to create a mix of social groups on estates by introducing tenants from a wide range of backgrounds. This happened in the Harborne area of Birmingham during the 1930s when people being rehoused from inner city slum clearance schemes were mixed with tenants who were often older and who had been on the council waiting list for several years.

In the past, local authorities were required to provide homes for people who could prove that they were homeless. The rising number of homeless people in the 1980s and 1990s created huge pressures on the stock of local authority homes, with the result that parts of some estates, especially the less desirable ones, gained many formerly homeless families. In the 1980s in Birmingham, for example, there was a large inflow of these families to some of the unpopular multi-storey blocks of flats in inner city areas such as Lee Bank and Highgate.

During the 1980s and early 1990s, the government encouraged council tenants to buy their houses and flats. Many families took up this offer on estates all over the UK, but the take-up rate varied greatly from estate to estate. In Birmingham, for example, many council tenants in Harborne bought their homes, but in Nechells and Ladywood very few did so.

Another feature of the 1980s and 1990s has been the growing importance of housing associations, rather than local authorities, as owners and developers of rented housing (Fig. 5.32). Central government encouraged the growth of housing associations as a

means of quickly providing additional rented accommodation without increasing the influence of local authorities. Housing associations affect urban social patterns by their choice of the type of tenant they think suitable for their schemes. In general, groups such as the unemployed, the homeless and ethnic minorities are under-represented in schemes run by housing associations.

Figure 5.32 The Bismillah, a former silver factory in Birmingham's Jewellery Quarter, converted in 1995 by the Focus housing association to provide 150 homes for single people.

In most ELDCs, the rapid increase in urban population has caused severe housing provision problems. The informal sector has responded by building spontaneous settlements, as we have seen in the case of Manila. In some countries, including Venezuela, there have been massive official efforts to build extra houses and flats.

Ranchos and rehousing in Caracas, Venezuela

Figure 5.33 Caracas

In 1920, Caracas, the capital of Venezuela, (Fig. 5.33) had a population of 92 000 people. With the export of oil from the 1920s onwards, the city grew to 600 000 in 1948; to 2.0 million in 1962; and 3.2 million in 1995. Most incoming migrants settled in spontaneous settlements called *ranchos*, many of which lacked the potential for upgrading due to their site characteristics (Fig. 5.34). In an attempt to get rid of the *ranchos* in the 1950s, the city government of Caracas used some of its oil revenues to finance the construction of 97 blocks of 15-storey flats into which people were compulsorily relocated (Fig. 5.35). The aim

was to provide people with an improved environment, in which health problems would decrease.

Unfortunately, the scheme was not a success, mainly because too many people arrived from the countryside. Some people from the *ranchos* were rehoused, but the provision of housing attracted even more migrants from the countryside and the high-rise blocks of flats themselves became extremely overcrowded. Other problems included non-payment of rents and a failure to maintain the blocks of flats. As a result, large areas of Caracas now require improvement.

17 Study Figure 5.34 and write a report on the redevelopment problems posed by the *ranchos* in Caracas, pointing out the differing nature of the problems from zone to zone and giving your suggested list of zones for priority action, with the reasons for your decisions.

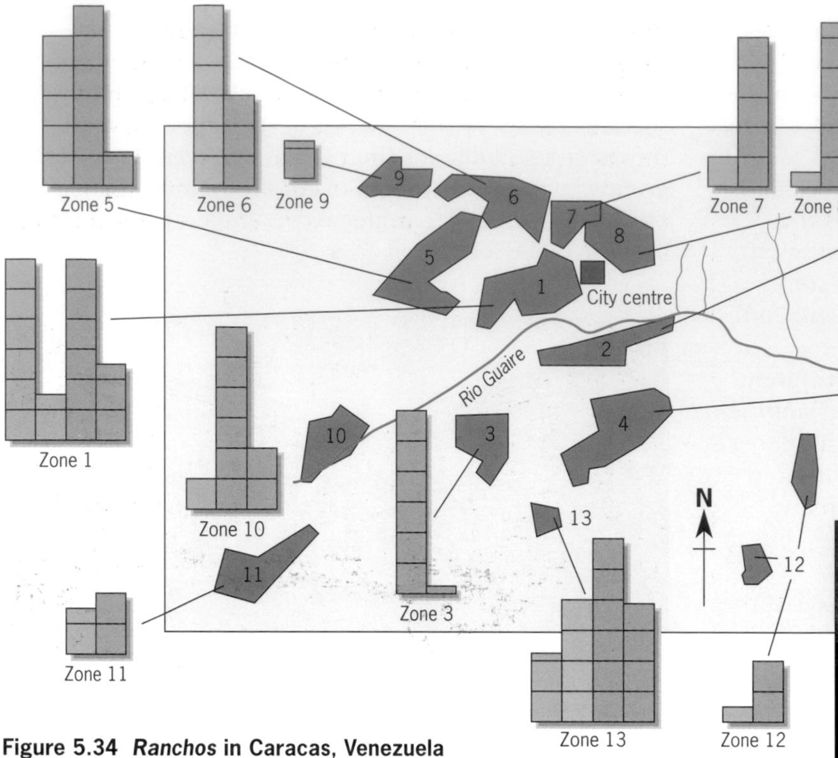

Possibilities for improvement
(one square = 250 *rancho* homes)

Little danger in topographic situation; can be improved

Street alignments irregular; very little improvement possible

Complete relocation necessary; no improvement possible

Ranchos

0   km   2

Zone 5   Zone 6   Zone 9   9   6   7   Zone 7   Zone 8   Zone 2

5   8

1   City centre

Rio Guaire   2

Zone 1   10   3   4   Zone 4

Zone 10   13   N   12

11   Zone 3   Zone 13   Zone 12

Zone 11

Figure 5.34 *Ranchos* in Caracas, Venezuela
(*Source:* Flint, 1987)

Figure 5.35 A new office block and low-rent flats, Caracas

Most ELDC governments do not have the finance to undertake massive new housing provision. Instead, accepting the reality of spontaneous settlements, they have taken steps to try to improve conditions within them. In Zambia, for example, the government has been trying to upgrade some of the settlements by means of aided self-help schemes and by **site-and-services schemes**.

Contrasts in Lusaka, Zambia

Figure 5.36 Zambia

Lusaka (Fig. 5.36), now the capital of Zambia, was originally no more than a railway siding. It grew slowly as an administrative and commercial focus for the central part of the country. In the 1920s, the authorities decided to move the capital from Livingstone to Lusaka, a process that was completed in 1931. The resulting urban structure (Fig. 5.37) is a mix of a gracious planned capital city (never completed) superimposed on a sprawling town segregated economically, socially and spatially by race (Fig. 5.38).

New government buildings were planned in an administrative district separate from the commercial centre and the railway depot. The white administrators occupied handsome houses with spacious gardens and servants' quarters in government suburban housing areas well away from industry and commerce (Fig. 5.37). Privately owned vehicles, company cars or government cars were available for journeys to the centre. Beyond the second-class and third-class residential districts of the colonial capital, incoming migrants found open space in which to camp and then build flimsy homes in what became spontaneous settlements (Fig. 5.37).

After independence, the government houses were taken over by the rich African élite and by the staff of foreign embassies. A high-income residential area also

afford – is the supermarket in the affluent neighbouring area of Kabulonga (Table 5.3).

Since the 1970s, attempts have been made by the Zambian government, the World Bank and several NGOs (non-governmental organisations) to improve conditions in some of the spontaneous settlements, including Kalingalinga, by installing electricity, a clean

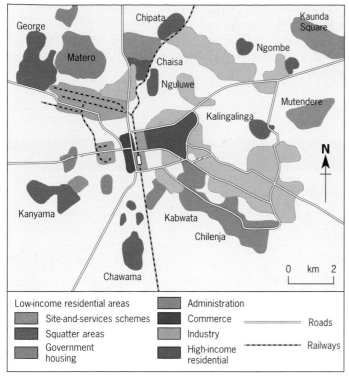

Figure 5.37 The urban structure of Lusaka, Zambia (*Source:* **Waugh, 1987**)

Low-income residential areas
- Site-and-services schemes
- Squatter areas
- Government housing

- Administration
- Commerce
- Industry
- High-income residential

Roads

Railways

Figure 5.38 A general view of Lusaka, Zambia

became established near the city centre with easy access to shops and other central facilities, including government buildings and greatest police protection. As migrants continued to flood into the capital, the size and number of spontaneous settlements increased. Extreme poverty and extreme affluence existed – and still exist – side-by-side within the city. For residents of low-income Kalingalinga, for example, the closest grocery shop – most of whose goods they cannot

18a Work in pairs to make a list of measures to reduce the inequalities between families living in Kabulonga and in Kalingalinga. Divide your list into measures relating to: income; employment; housing; other.
b Compare your list with those of other pairs in the group. To what extent do you all: agree; disagree?

Table 5.3 Lifestyles in Kabulonga and Kalingalinga in the mid-1980s (*Source:* Burdette, 1988)

Kabulonga	Kalingalinga
High-income, low-density	Low-income, high-density
House: large, with gardens and servants; surrounded by tall concrete walls; bars on windows; night-watchman may be employed.	House: a shack or small dwelling; outside water taps dry up in the dry season; sewage facilities are poor; dust/mud paths and narrow streets.
Occupation of male head of household: lawyer, civil servant, banker, politician, merchant.	Occupation of male and female members of household: many are unemployed; those who are employed or have a few possessions are preyed upon by thieves; employment ranges from manual labour (rubbish collection, street sweepers, house servants, night-watchmen) to badly paid low-level white-collar jobs (clerks, shop assistants, nurses).
Wife: probably does not work; goes shopping in suburban shopping centres (safer than the city centre); visits female friends and relatives; ferries the children to school and to visit friends in similar houses.	
Children: attend private and/or public schools (if they are not at boarding school in the UK or Zimbabwe); travel by car with their mother; otherwise kept at home for their safety.	Children: attend local schools, shabby and overcrowded but popular (education is one of the few hopes for people to get out of the area).
Vehicles: large Mercedes or Peugeot for commuting to work (and as a status symbol); Isuzu or Datsun pick-up truck for visiting rural investments; saloon car for the wife.	Vehicles: none; public transport (buses) available along main roads; access to city centre poor.
In the evening: the husband changes into a leisure suit; watches TV; drinks imported beers and spirits; his Western-style meal is cooked by the servants, but served to him by his wife; afterwards he visits élite bars and hotels to socialise. His family remains at home and watches TV until bedtime (it is thought too dangerous for them to go out at night).	In the evening: women bring home water for cooking and washing; meals are of traditional maize dishes with vegetables; local beer is cheap; unemployed youths hang around in the dirt streets, still wearing their old school uniforms.

water supply and sewage disposal facilities. The provision of these services encourages residents to begin other improvements to their homes and to the local area. Schemes of this type are known as **aided self-help schemes**. Site-and-services schemes are also being undertaken – the infrastructure is provided for a whole new area, and people can obtain a plot for a low rent and build their own house. This is a relatively cheap yet effective way for governments to help people to help themselves.

Summary

- Housing in cities creates a wide variety of social patterns.
- Different criteria can be used to describe housing (e.g. age of buildings, socio-economic factors); they all have advantages and disadvantages.
- People's choice of where to live in cities is affected by a range of factors (e.g. income, position in the family life cycle).
- Urban social patterns are constantly changing as a result of processes such as gentrification and filtering.
- Gatekeepers affect urban social patterns through their control of access to housing.
- Governments affect the availability of housing in a variety of ways (e.g. the provision of council housing, aided self-help and site-and-services schemes).
- Social segregation within urban areas has arisen for a variety of reasons and has created distinctive areas and ghettos.
- Patterns of intra-urban movement in ELDCs are related to migration, population growth and household income.

6 Patterns of inequality

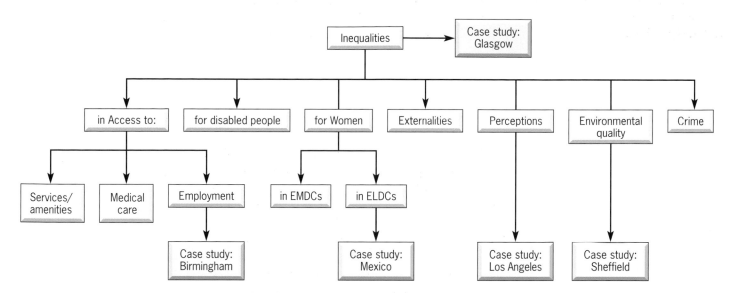

6.1 Introduction

There are many different types of inequality in cities and this chapter examines some of them. One group of inequalities arises from variations in the access of different individuals and groups within cities to services and amenities – for example, shops, health care, education and open space. The study of this type of inequality has a spatial dimension which geographers have sought to discover and explain. A second group of inequalities arises from spatial variations in features – for example, population density, income and employment levels. These are features whose distributions we can map and analyse to investigate some of their main causes and effects.

Glasgow: patterns of deprivation

Glasgow is a large European city which underwent substantial industrial decline in the 1970s and 1980s, before experiencing urban redevelopment and regeneration in the 1990s. In the 1980s, researchers were trying to define what **deprivation** in Glasgow meant. They used data from the census enumeration districts in order to identify nine deprivation indicators which were: housing amenities (e.g. inside toilet and bath), degree of overcrowding, proportion of vacant dwellings, child density (children as a proportion of all persons living above ground floor level), percentage of population unemployed, percentage in low-income occupations, percentage of disabled/permanently sick persons, percentage of single-parent families and percentage of large households. The census data were then used to compute an overall index of deprivation for the different areas of the city (Fig. 6.1).

Deprivation in urban areas has many facets, from unemployment to poverty and illness, but usually concentrations of deprivation can be mapped in most

cities. The researchers in Glasgow found that multiple deprivation – i.e. families suffering from several different types of deprivation – was to be found in many parts of the city. There were some pockets of deprivation in the old, inner-city, tenement (flats) areas such as Parkhead and Bridgeton, but the main focus of deprivation was in the newer council estates often on the edge of the urban area such as Easterhouse and Drumchapel (Fig. 6.1).

1a Suggest possible reasons why levels of multiple deprivation in the council estates of Glasgow were higher than in the inner-city areas.
b What other indicators could have been used to measure deprivation?
c How might the indicators in the Glasgow study be weighted to reflect their relative importance?

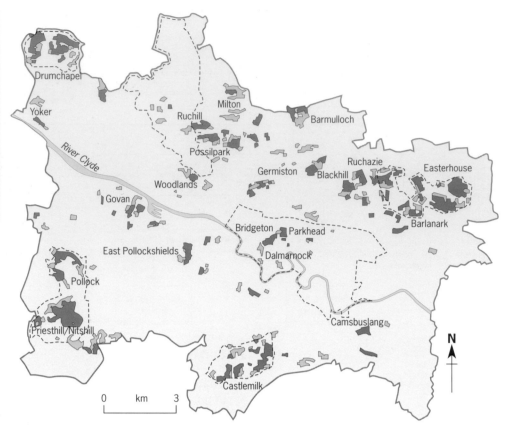

■ Worst 0–10% of Census Enumeration
Districts

■ Worst 10.1–20% of Census Enumeration
Districts

- - - - - District Council Priority Area boundaries

**Figure 6.1 Patterns of social
deprivation in Glasgow, 1981
(*Source*: Rae, 1983)**

2 Figure 6.2 illustrates the sort of
case that can be made against a
potential disamenity. In addition to
groups like Friends of the Earth,
the most vocal groups in protests
are often local house-owners and
local people with school-age
children.
a Write your own report for a
newspaper with the title 'City
incinerator: a big bonus', putting
the other side of the case and
stressing the potential benefits of
the incinerator.
b Why do you think that local
house-owners and local people
with school-age children tend to be
the most vocal protesters?
c Which disamenities do you think
would unite all ages and genders
against them? (Hint: think about
new road schemes and similar
developments.)

6.2 Access to services and amenities

In every large city, there are a great variety and number of services – elements
that meet people's basic needs (e.g. shops, schools and hospitals) – and
amenities – facilities which improve the quality of the environment (e.g.
parks, playgrounds and golf courses). These services and amenities are found in
specific locations within cities.

There are also **disamenities** in cities – that is, features that many people do
not want to be near, such as an air-polluting incinerator. However, not all
urban features are easy to classify. For example, a busy public park may be
regarded as a major disamenity by those nearby residents who dislike noise.
However, others may see the park as a major amenity and might wish to live
as close to it as possible.

City incinerator a 'disaster' – claim

BIRMINGHAM Friends of the Earth have
released a report which they claim exposes the
potential dangers involved in the proposed new
incineration plant at Tysley.

The group fears that the incinerator, which
will turn household waste into energy, could
become a gigantic white elephant within years,
as well as an environmental disaster for decades
to come.

They claim the furnace could emit dangerous
toxic compounds into the atmosphere, increasing

air pollution across the West Midlands and
working against the growing international
campaign to counter the causes of global warming.
The group also fears tens of thousands of tonnes
of highly toxic ash will be produced and dumped
in a landfill site, which could become a serious
environmental hazard for many years.

Financial problems also bother the group,
which is concerned that the new waste-to-energy
process set to provide 25 megawatts of power
per year, will jeopardise the recycling industry.

Figure 6.2 City incinerator a 'disaster'? (The Birmingham News, 11 February 1994)

Figure 6.3 A busy non-pedestrianised shopping centre in Hemel Hempstead, Herts

Figure 6.4 Outside a London nightclub

Figure 6.5 People's preferred residential distance from public facilities (*Source*: Smith, 1980)

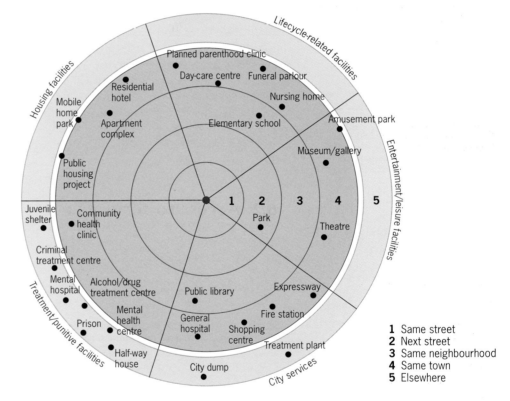

1 Same street
2 Next street
3 Same neighbourhood
4 Same town
5 Elsewhere

3a Study Figures 6.3 and 6.4. Working in pairs, make a list of the advantages and disadvantages of living near each of these urban features.
b Why might these urban features lead to conflict between groups in cities?

4 Study Figure 6.5.
a Into which five groups are the public facilities divided?
b Which public facilities do people ideally want to see in their local area (i.e. in the same street, next street or same neighbourhood)?
c Make a list of the facilities that people wanted 'Elsewhere' and suggest possible reasons for their choices.

5a Ask any three people (in your group/at home) how close they would ideally like to live to each of the facilities shown in Figure 6.5 (i.e. same street, next street, same neighbourhood, same town or elsewhere).
b Draw a diagram to show the main differences between their answers.
c How do you explain these?

One result of the distribution of services/amenities and disamenities in a city, is that there is competition and conflict to live either close to or away from them. The competition and conflict take place at the level of different housing markets. For example, more affluent housing areas try to 'capture' as many services and amenities as possible in order to have easy access to them. Studies of cities in Europe and the USA led to the development of a model of people's preferred residential distance from particular public facilities (Fig. 6.5).

6.3 Patterns of accessibility to medical care

The pattern of accessibility to medical care facilities is a good example of the way in which the location of services can affect the quality of neighbourhood life. In parts of cities where a large percentage of the population are still without access to private transport, the distance from home to the doctor's

Figure 6.6 Doctor's surgery in a large Victorian house

?

6a Refer back to Figures 5.9, 5.10, 5.11 and 5.12 to try to explain the patterns of accessibility shown in Figure 6.7.
b How far does the evidence of Figure 6.7 support the idea of an inverse care law?
c What other factors might influence accessibility to medical care? Group your factors into those related to people (income, car ownership, etc.) and those related to the area (number of 'problem' residents, etc.).

---

surgery is critical. In the USA and in the UK, it has been found that 0.75 km (pram-pushing distance) is the upper distance limit of walking for mothers with school-age children. Access to medical services in the UK is related to:

• distance from the surgery;
• access to a car; and
• the quality of public transport.

For example, single parents on low incomes, living in high-rise flats with no car, often have extremely poor access to medical facilities.

The location of general practitioner (GP) surgeries in the UK tends to make the problem of accessibility noticeably worse for some groups of the population. In most UK cities, GP surgeries are often concentrated in older, middle-class or higher socio-economic areas (Fig. 6.6). This pattern is reinforced by two factors. First, family doctors tend to live and work in well established, high-status areas, where they can earn extra income from private patients. Secondly, many council-house estates were built without suitable premises for surgeries.

The net result of these factors is an uneven distribution of medical resources. This is often referred to as the **inverse care law**, in which the availability of medical services is inversely proportional to the needs of the population. Figure 6.7 uses an index to measure accessibility to GP surgeries in Birmingham. The index takes account of the relative size and location of GP services, together with local levels of car ownership and the relative speed of public and private transport. Scores of over 100 on the index indicate that a neighbourhood has good access to primary medical services.

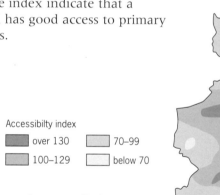

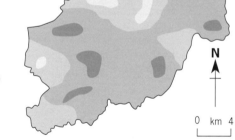

Accessibilty index

■ over 130   ▨ 70–99
▨ 100–129   □ below 70

N

0   km   4

Figure 6.7 Access to primary medical care in Birmingham, 1995 (*Source*: authors' research)

6.4 Access to employment

Access to local employment varies greatly within cities and is affected by many factors. Some of these are discussed next.

Qualifications and skills
In general, people with more qualifications and/or a variety of skills are more likely to find employment than those without these advantages. However, in times of economic recession – such as the mid-1990s – there is a general shortage of employment opportunities and many school-leavers and graduates in the UK are unable to obtain jobs (Fig. 6.8). When applying for lower-paid posts, e.g. as office cleaners or waiters in hotels, graduates are often thought to be overqualified. Therefore qualifications alone do not guarantee employment.

The range of local employment opportunities
This varies from place to place, and also changes through time. For example, in the 1980s and 1990s, various UK cities saw the closure of many steelworks, shipyards and engineering works. Those changes greatly reduced the available

Figure 6.8 Outside a JobCentre in the UK

employment opportunities. Workers from such factories often found it hard to find jobs because their particular skills were no longer required. Since then, some people have retrained and have found other employment (e.g. in the financial services sector) or have started up their own businesses (e.g. computer software).

Access to transport and the employer's location

These are two further factors affecting access to employment. Although in 1998 there were 32m cars in the UK, over 30 per cent of families still had no access to their own transport. The mobility of these families is therefore dependent on public transport, which tends to be radial in pattern – from the suburbs to the city centre. Therefore, travelling from home in one suburb to a potential employer in another suburb can be both time-consuming and expensive, especially for low-income people. The UK trend in, and since, the 1990s has been for many new employers, especially in offices and shops, to locate away from city centres, in suburban or edge-of-city locations. This often adds to the problem of access to employment for low-income groups without private transport.

Social factors

The age, gender, ethnic status and relative ability or disability of the individual seeking work are all factors affecting access to employment. Despite legislation, recent surveys suggest that discrimination on the basis of gender, ethnic status, disability and age still persists in the UK. Some companies and organisations operate a policy of positive discrimination designed to recruit people from disadvantaged groups, but some still do not.

Access to employment in Birmingham

In Birmingham, the 1991 Census gave the average level of male unemployment as 17 per cent. However, such average figures can conceal great differences (Fig. 6.9). In 1995, the male unemployment rate amongst ethnic minorities was 25 per cent or more.

Figure 6.9 Male unemployment rates in Birmingham, 1993 (*Source*: Birmingham Economic Information Centre)

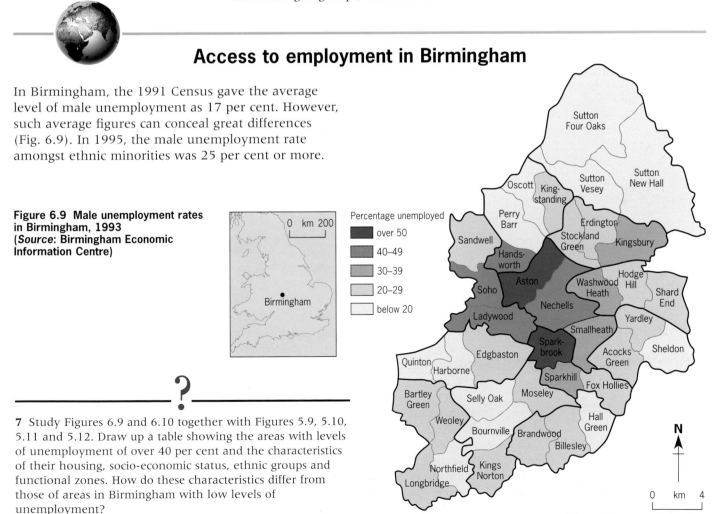

7 Study Figures 6.9 and 6.10 together with Figures 5.9, 5.10, 5.11 and 5.12. Draw up a table showing the areas with levels of unemployment of over 40 per cent and the characteristics of their housing, socio-economic status, ethnic groups and functional zones. How do these characteristics differ from those of areas in Birmingham with low levels of unemployment?

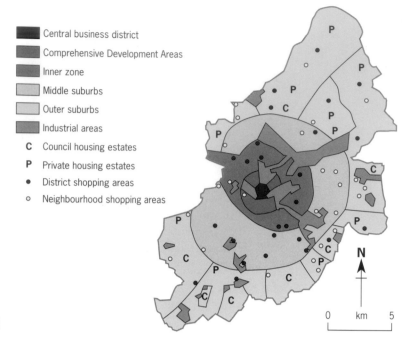

Figure 6.10 Functional areas of Birmingham (Based on: Ellis, 1987)

Legend:
- Central business district
- Comprehensive Development Areas
- Inner zone
- Middle suburbs
- Outer suburbs
- Industrial areas
- C Council housing estates
- P Private housing estates
- ● District shopping areas
- ○ Neighbourhood shopping areas

6.5 Access for people with disabilities

Most writers on urban geography assume that people are able-bodied and this, it is argued, is **ableist geography**. In other words, for a long time geographers ignored people with disabilities, as did urban planners and developers. As a result, cities often present many barriers to access and mobility. Typical problems include steep steps, high curbs, the absence of wheelchair ramps, narrow doors and an absence of information in Braille. Worse still, lifts for disabled people are often sited in unattractive locations (e.g. next to the kitchens), badly signposted and with buttons that are inaccessible.

Public transport is an additional challenge for people with disabilities. The introduction of buses with easy access and 'ring & ride' schemes has helped some people to overcome some of the transport challenges, but cost remains a key issue.

The development of shopmobility schemes in the UK makes an important contribution to enabling people with disabilities to reach shops and other urban services. Shopmobility schemes provide a range of powered and manual wheelchairs and electrical scooters for loan to mobility-impaired people. The first scheme was established in Milton Keynes in 1978; by 1996, 144 schemes were operating throughout the UK (Fig. 6.11). Shopmobility schemes should ideally be centrally located, with reserved parking spaces and close to public transport terminii. As retailing has changed, so too shopmobility has responded to the changes, so that although most schemes are town centre based, some have been incorporated in out-of-town shopping centres, such as Merry Hill in the West Midlands and Meadowhall in Sheffield.

Shopmobility benefits a town's economy. A survey in 1994 showed that people with disabilities spent £47 per trip to the city centres. In 1993, in Redditch, 123 000 shopmobility clients spent an estimated £1.3 million in the town's shops.

Access to urban shops and services for people with disabilities is an important and growing issue. Between 1991 and 2036, the number of people in the UK aged 70 or over will rise from 6.3 million to 8.6 million. Many of these people will suffer mobility and other impairments. Geographers and planners need to study this issue in detail as a matter of urgency.

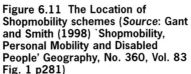

Figure 6.11 The Location of Shopmobility schemes (*Source*: Gant and Smith (1998) `Shopmobility, Personal Mobility and Disabled People' Geography, No. 360, Vol. 83 Fig. 1 p281)

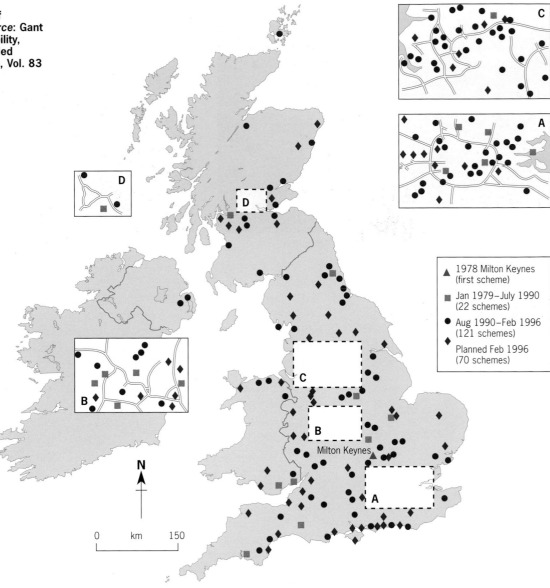

6.6 Women in cities in EMDCs

Within cities, women often have special problems in obtaining access to services and amenities. In part, this is due to the **decentralisation** – of people, shops, services and some jobs – that has taken place in cities in EMDCs in the last 20 years. Employers (e.g. retailers) and planners now tend to make location decisions assuming perfect mobility – i.e. they assume that everyone has access to a car or good public transport. One outcome has been the rapid growth of shopping malls in suburban and edge-of-city locations (Fig. 6.12). Americans now spend more time in shopping malls than anywhere else, apart from their homes and workplaces (Fig. 6.13). But increased personal mobility favours:

• the middle classes;
• the middle-aged; and
• men.

These groups are more able to afford cars than other groups in society. Even in relatively affluent parts of US cities, 6 out of 10 women do not have access to cars because they do not have priority over other household users (e.g. partner, children).

?

8a Make a study of a nearby shopping centre and town centre to assess the degree to which it is 'friendly' towards people with disabilities. Map the location of parking spaces for disabled people, and of stores with ramps, wide doors, separate wheelchair access, lifts etc. Mark the location of 'problem areas', such as high curbs, steep steps, lack of access etc.
b Write a report on how the area you have surveyed could be improved to make it more accommodating for people with disabilities.

Figure 6.12 An edge-of-city shopping mall, Edmonton, Canada

Figure 6.13 Interior of an indoor shopping mall, Washington, DC, USA

9a To what extent do you think that women in the UK experience problems of access to services and amenities similar to those of women in the USA? In what ways are women in UK cities: better off; worse off?

b How far do you agree that women in the UK are trapped in certain types of job in particular urban locations?

10a How might the patterns shown in Figure 6.14 be changed by an increase in the number of women working from home using computers, faxes, etc.?

b How might changes in attitudes towards women (Fig. 6.14) have impacts on: urban transport patterns; urban structure?

11a What are the effects of low-paid, unskilled jobs on one-parent families?

b What might be done to improve the position of women in this situation?

Gender roles

In the relatively affluent suburbs of US cities, women with access to a car still have other problems related to their gender roles. Society allocates customary gender roles to both men and women. In the case of women, gender roles restrict their access to services and amenities. For example, American women with cars are expected to:

- be home-makers;
- provide breakfast for the family;
- drive the children to school;
- prepare lunch;
- pick up the children from school;
- take the children to sports or leisure activities;
- prepare dinner; and
- be available at home to accept deliveries, supervise repairs or care for sick children.

Fulfilling all these roles is very time-consuming, especially if the woman is pursuing a fulltime career. Consequently, the time remaining in which women can obtain access to services and amenities is extremely limited. They often have to go shopping late at night, or negotiate flexi-time at work in order to be available to collect young children from school.

Such problems are even greater for women who do not have access to a car. In the USA, women who are poor, who are old and who are single parents usually have extremely limited access to services and amenities. No wonder many women feel trapped in cities.

Access to employment

In both US and UK cities, employment for women tends to be concentrated in certain types of job, often within the service sector. Such jobs may be in financial services (e.g. insurance and banking), retailing, or in health and educational services. Also, these types of employment are located in particular parts of cities. For example, financial services are often concentrated in the CBD or in office parks, whilst retail services may be located in a suburban hypermarket. The result, as Paul Knox (2000 p.165) says, is that 'Women in US cities are trapped, economically, socially, culturally and ecologically'.

Figure 6.14 shows how the structure of US and UK cities reflects a basic division between places of production (workplaces) and places of reproduction (mainly the suburbs). This basic division discriminates against women who are forced to move between the different parts of the city much more than men. Women without access to a car are particularly hard hit by this structure.

6.7 Women in cities in ELDCs

The increase in female employment opportunities in cities in ELDCs is creating issues of women's access to services and amenities similar to those in EMDCs. However, the patterns vary greatly between ELDCs. For example, in the Caribbean and Latin America, there are more women than men in cities. This is the result of large-scale migration from the countryside in search of higher living standards and better access to services. The demand in the Caribbean and Latin America for women to work is so great that more women migrate than men. By contrast, in Africa and parts of Asia, men are more numerous in cities. This reflects social and religious views which oppose women working anywhere other than in the home.

The work of women in ELDCs varies enormously. In most countries, women have the usual heavy domestic roles of child rearing, food preparation, cleaning and clothes washing, as well as earning a living.

In many ELDCs, women work in their home on tasks such as sewing labels on garments or preparing food for sale on the street. This pattern of working from home is growing, both because it is more convenient for women and also because it is very profitable for the people who organise the women workers. These organisers pay very low wages, and if women are unable to work they receive no pay. The organisers can also withhold work, or play individuals off against each other as another means of keeping wages low.

Jobs outside the home include working as servants and in hotels, shops and restaurants. In parts of Asia and Latin America, including Mexico, women are also employed in factories producing a wide range of goods from clothes and cigarettes to electronic and electrical apparatus.

Figure 6.14 US/UK urban structure and women

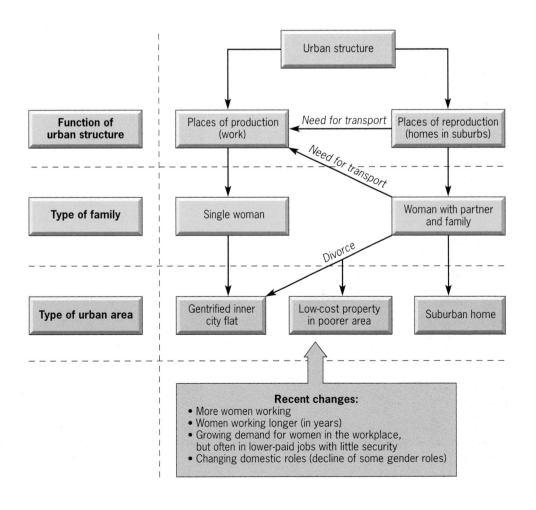

Maria del Rosario Garcia in Matamoros, Mexico

Figure 6.15 Maria del Rosario Garcia

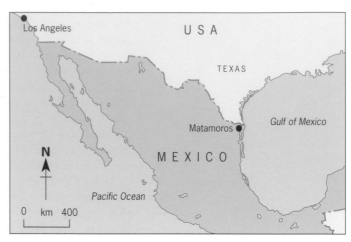

Figure 6.16 The USA–Mexico border

Maria (Fig. 6.15) is 42 years old and a single parent, living in the Mexican border town of Matamoros (Figs 6.16 and 6.17). Maria used to work for Kemet, a US electronics components manufacturer, but she was sacked just 2 days before completing 20 years' service which would have entitled her to a payment of several million pesos. The practice of sacking workers just before they become entitled to pension or other rights is common among US transnational companies operating in Mexico. Maria used to earn $60 a week – a tenth of what employees in Texas get for doing the same work.

Cheap labour and proximity to US markets have made the 2400-km Mexican border zone attractive to the 23 500 US companies that have located there in the last 27 years. Household names – including General Motors and toy-makers Fisher King – have opened factories in Mexico where they employ half a million

workers, most of whom are young women. These companies now provide Mexico's second-biggest source of foreign exchange.

However, for women like Maria there is a price to be paid for their country's improved balance of payments. Maria can only afford to live in a tiny house made of blocks, with a corrugated iron roof. Her children have to play barefoot in the polluted mud rivers that serve as streets. Despite these conditions, Maria's children (Maria, 8, and Juan, 2) are dressed in freshly washed clothes as she fights to maintain standards.

Women like Maria are employed in factories because they have greater manual dexterity than men, and are willing to work long hours for low wages. Maria used to rise at 4 a.m. to arrive at the factory for the 6 a.m. shift. In the 8-hour day, she had only one break of 10 minutes and one of 20 minutes. The company advertises for 'Women older than 17, younger than 30, with a minimum of a primary school education and a maximum of a secondary school education, willing to work all shifts'. Now that Maria has been fired, she and her children are in real danger of starving as she struggles to find another job.

12 Write a short report for the UN Committee on Women, pointing out the range of problems faced by women such as Maria in gaining access to services.
13a How could conditions for women like Maria in Matamoros be improved by: the Mexican government; the US government?
b What would be the main problems in trying to introduce these measures?

Figure 6.17 A shanty town in Matamoros, Mexico

6.8 Homosexuality and the city

Urban areas have had a great impact on the development of homosexuality and vice versa. Cities provide greater anonymity and a wider tolerance of alternative lifestyles compared to the hostility directed towards gay and lesbian people in many rural areas. In the period before 1967, when homosexuality was a crime in the UK and USA, secret bars and clubs in cities provided meeting places. These bars facilitated meetings for sex, enabled news and gossip to be exchanged and provided a place for new entrants to be introduced to the gay world. The bars were clustered in particular sections of cities, often close to red light areas. Many had bells or lights to warn customers not to stand too close to persons of the same sex when there was a police raid. Other sites in urban areas associated with gay and lesbian activity were 'cottages' (usually public toilets), or areas of public parkland that enabled cruising and sexual liaisons.

It is important to remember that lesbianism was never a criminal offence; therefore the impact on clustering in urban areas was never as pronounced as that for gay men.

Post-1960

Since the 1960s, there have been major changes in the nature and location of gay and lesbian spaces in cities. These changes reflect broader social and political changes in society. There is now, arguably, greater tolerance towards homosexual activity, although the extent of this tolerance should not be exaggerated. Recent studies show continued high rates of physical assault on gays and lesbians. However, despite this, gays and lesbians have become more overt and vocal in making clear their political demands (Fig. 6.18). Following the formation of the Gay Liberation Front in 1971 in New York, selected areas of cities have developed distinctive residential characters – they are composed largely of gay people and gay lifestyles are displayed explicitly.

Gay people have played a leading role in the gentrification of some inner-city areas such as Islington in London or the Castro district of San Francisco. One reason for the rapid growth of the gay and lesbian areas in San Francisco was the fact that many people serving in the US armed forces were discharged in San Francisco, and chose to remain there rather than face intolerance and possible persecution at home. A study of Amsterdam in 1995 noted that 3000 of the 25 000 jobs in the tourist industry of the city depended on gay tourism, and the city authorities actively promote the gay area.

The impact of male homosexuality on urban areas has received more research than that of lesbianism, often because lesbian subcultures are smaller

Figure 6.18 Gay Liberation March San Francisco, 1978

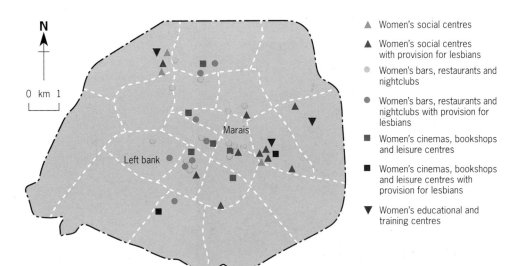

Figure 6.19 Lesbian facilities, Paris, France. (*Source*: Winchester & White (1988). Fig.1, p.48 'The location of marginalised groups in the inner city', Environment and Planning D: Society and Space 6, 37-54)

▲ Women's social centres

▲ Women's social centres with provision for lesbians

● Women's bars, restaurants and nightclubs

● Women's bars, restaurants and nightclubs with provision for lesbians

■ Women's cinemas, bookshops and leisure centres

■ Women's cinemas, bookshops and leisure centres with provision for lesbians

▼ Women's educational and training centres

N

0 km 1

Marais

Left bank

Figure 6.20 Gay and social venues in Brighton in the 1990s
(*Adapted from*: Wright, 1999, 'Sexuality, communality and urban space,' Unpublished PhD thesis, Dept of Geography, University of Southampton Fig. 5.6 p. 182 P. Knot and S. Pinch (2000) *Urban Social Geography*, Prentice Hall, London. P321

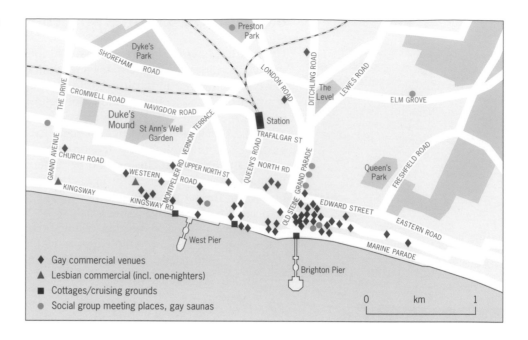

and less visible. However, maps of lesbian areas in Paris (Fig. 6.19) do show the extent to which clustering does take place. Many lesbian areas are squats or housing co-operatives or housing associations, and are attempts to create safe areas for women at risk from violence. In that sense not all areas marked on the map are strictly for lesbians. Often women have fewer financial resources than men and they face the threat of male violence. Therefore, lesbians often locate in relatively cheap housing, which may have an 'underground' quality.

Geographical studies which have identified gay and lesbian area in cities have been criticised on a number of grounds:

• many gay and lesbian people do not live in the clusters shown on maps;
• not all the people shown in a cluster on a map are gay or lesbian;
• the work on mapping gay ghettos ignores the fact that many gay men and lesbians hide their identities at certain times to avoid persecution or discrimination.

Other geographers have argued that the identification and mapping of gay or lesbian enclaves in cities has only served to sustain the idea that gay lifestyles are something separate, different and deviant. The development of HIV and Aids in the population generally meant that gay enclaves took on a new role as points for healthcare services and support networks.

14 Study pages 93 and 94, then write a brief summary of the influence that gay and lesbian groups have had on the urban geography of cities in EMDCs.

The pink pound

Another change in gay urban spaces has been the commercialisation of the areas as people have tried to exploit the high incomes of some gay households. As a result, the Soho area of London, Manchester's Canal Street, and areas of Brighton (Fig. 6.20) have developed bars, clubs and shops catering specifically for gays. This has also raised the profile of gay lifestyles, but in fact these developments cater only for the young and wealthy in the gay community. Those gays who are older and poorer tend to be excluded from such developments, so even within gay communities there will be sub-groups with unequal access to urban resources.

Figure 6.21 Gay Pride march, New York, USA

?

15 Study Figures 6.22 and 6.23. The Dell is a soccer stadium.
a Tabulate the main similarities and differences in the distribution of noise nuisance and parked car nuisance around the Dell.
b Draw a map to show the main similarities and differences listed in your table.

6.9 Urban externalities

The results of activities by an individual, group or institution which affect the welfare of others are known as **externalities**. For example, the presence of a factory causing air or water pollution is a **negative externality**; a well-kept public park is a **positive externality** to most of the local residents. In general, those households with the greatest wealth, most power and best knowledge are able to gain the benefits of positive externalities. Such households are also more able to fend off activities such as new road schemes which generate negative externalities.

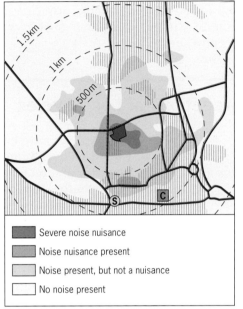

⬤	Station
C	City centre
◢	The Dell
▥	Non-residential areas

■ Severe noise nuisance	
■ Noise nuisance present	
▨ Noise present, but not a nuisance	
☐ No noise present	

Figure 6.22 Noise nuisance around The Dell, Southampton (*Source*: Humphries *et al.*, 1983)

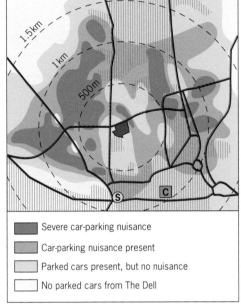

■ Severe car-parking nuisance	
■ Car-parking nuisance present	
▨ Parked cars present, but no nuisance	
☐ No parked cars from The Dell	

Figure 6.23 Car parking nuisance around The Dell, Southampton (*Source*: Humphries *et al.*, 1983)

?

16 Study Figure 6.24. The features shown tend to generate positive externalities.
a Describe and suggest reasons for the distribution of cinemas and theatres in Birmingham.
b How far does the map support the idea that the size and number of public open spaces decreases with increasing distance from the centre?

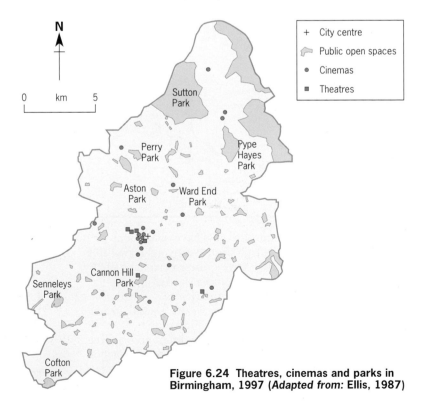

Figure 6.24 Theatres, cinemas and parks in Birmingham, 1997 (*Adapted from:* Ellis, 1987)

6.10 Perceptions of urban areas

People in a city have very different perceptions of it. For example, some people have a very good idea of the location of different parts of the city relative to each other. Other people have only a vague idea about the city as a whole, but have a detailed knowledge of their local area. People's perceptions of an area are often known as **mental maps**.

Mental maps are an important source of information about how people classify and use urban space. We can discover which buildings they notice; which shops they like; which streets they use. People's perceptions of different residential neighbourhoods are also important: we can learn how people perceive areas – as, for example, attractive/unattractive, exciting/relaxing, alarming/reassuring, bright/drab. Such reactions are often reflected in people's choices of where to live.

Perceptions of Los Angeles

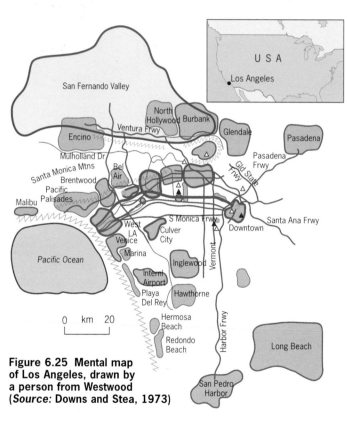

Figure 6.25 Mental map of Los Angeles, drawn by a person from Westwood (*Source:* Downs and Stea, 1973)

Los Angeles is an example of a city that has grown and sprawled over a huge area. Much of its industrial, housing and retailing development has taken place in the suburbs. The result is a huge urban agglomeration linked by motorways, with many different focal points which have often formed around suburban shopping and entertainment centres.

Perceptions of the city as a whole

In Los Angeles, a study of different people's perceptions of the urban environment shows that different socio-economic groups have different mental maps. For example, Figure 6.25 is a sketch map of Los Angeles drawn by a person living in Westwood, a white, upper socio-economic class area near Beverly Hills. Many people in such groups have a detailed mental map of the entire Los Angeles basin. By contrast, Figure 6.26 was drawn by a person living in Avalon, a mainly black, lower socio-economic class area. Here, the mental map is dominated by a small part of the conurbation, namely the grid iron pattern of the city centre.

?

17 Study Figures 6.25 and 6.26. Possible explanations for the differences are: that the person from Westwood is probably wealthier and may therefore have greater personal mobility; and that the person from Avalon has a shorter journey to work and therefore knows less of the city.
a In what other ways might greater wealth lead to greater familiarity with a wider part of the conurbation?
b What other factors might explain the differences between the maps? Think about education, exposure to information sources, etc.

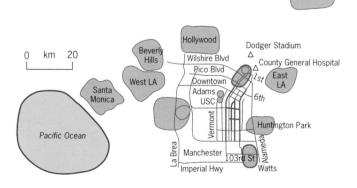

Figure 6.26 Mental map of Los Angeles, drawn by a person from Avalon (*Source*: Downs and Stea, 1973)

Perceptions of different neighbourhoods

In Los Angeles in the 1940s and 1950s, some suburban centres such as Hollywood gained popularity among the wealthy with the expansion of the film industry. Later, areas of high-income housing expanded in areas such as Bel Air and Beverly Hills (Fig. 6.27). Then, in the 1960s and 1970s, beach communities such as Malibu, Santa Monica and Redondo Beach became fashionable.

A survey in Los Angeles in the 1970s asked people to indicate the three neighbourhoods in which they would most like to live, bearing in mind their existing family income. The results (Fig. 6.28) clearly show the popularity of Beverly Hills and Santa Monica, and also a preference for areas on the east side of Los Angeles, such as Arcadia. Although, in some other surveys, these areas have been perceived as less desirable, it is possible that some people find them attractive because of their nearness to the countryside.

Figure 6.27 High-income housing in Beverly Hills, Los Angeles

?

18 Carry out a class survey of a sample of people in yournearest town or city, including different types of people in your sample – for example, people in different age, income and ethnic groups and people from different parts of the urban area.

a Ask each person to draw their own sketch map of the city (or part of it, if it is very large) to show its different neighbourhoods.

b In class, display the maps and consider how far they vary with the person's: age; gender; location in the urban area; wealth; and ethnicity.

c Which parts of the city do all the sample include? Why is this do you think?

19a Ask a sample of people in your nearest town or city to identify the three areas in which they would most like to live, bearing in mind their existing family income. Use the data to draw a map of the most popular areas (similar to Fig. 6.28).

b Try to explain the pattern shown on your map. What are the popular areas like? What features do they have in common?

c Try to explain the pattern of least popular areas. What features do these areas share? Are they the most industrialised areas? Are they areas with high crime rates?

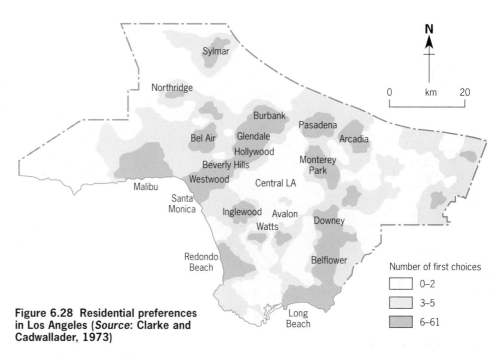

Figure 6.28 Residential preferences in Los Angeles (*Source*: Clarke and Cadwallader, 1973)

6.11 Environmental quality

The condition of streets and buildings, as well as other factors contributing to environmental quality such as amount of green space, is of great interest to geographers, town planners and community groups. Everyone agrees that the quality of urban environments varies from place to place, but problems arise when people try to define exactly what 'environmental quality' means.

Most studies have measured the quality of residential environments by using field surveys. These surveys involve using a scoring system to allocate points to

Table 6.1 Part of an environmental quality assessment schedule (*Source*: Duncan, 1971)

	Penalty points	Maximum
Traffic:		
Normal residential traffic	0	
Above normal residential traffic	3	6
Large amount industrial and through traffic	6	
Visual quality:		
Higher standard than environment	0	
Same standard as environment	1	3
Lower standard than environment	3	
Access to public open space:		
Park/public open space within 5 min walk	0	
No park/public open space within 5 min walk	3	3
Access to shops and primary schools:		
Primary school and shops within 5 min walk	0	
Primary school, but no shops in 5 min walk	2	
Shops, but no primary school in 5 min walk	5	7
No primary school or shops in 5 min walk	7	
Access to public transport to major centres:		
Less than 3 min walk	0	3
More than 3 min walk	3	
Landscape quality:		
Mature, good quality, abundant landscape	0	
Immature, insufficient amounts	2	5
Total or almost total lack of landscape	5	
Air pollution:		
Negligible	0	
Light	3	9
Heavy	9	
Privacy:		
No overlooking on either side	0	
Overlooking on one side	2	5
Overlooking on both sides	5	
Noise:		
Normal residential standard	0	
Above residential, but not industrial/commercial, e.g. main street, standard	5	5

Figure 6.29 Rush hour traffic in a London street

Figure 6.30 Athens

individual buildings, groups of buildings or urban spaces. An example is shown in Table 6.1. Methods of this type are generally used to survey small parts of urban areas, but by using sampling techniques they can be used to cover much larger areas.

All such surveys are necessarily subjective, and are based on the ideas and values of the people who designed the questions. Also, it is necessary to bear in mind that income may influence how people see an area. For example, the less well-off, with more urgent needs to satisfy such as earning enough to feed a family, may not worry much about many aspects of environmental quality. The better-off, having satisfied their own material needs, may be very sensitive to environmental factors such as the appearance of houses, streets and gardens.

The main factors which seem to influence people's levels of satisfaction with a neighbourhood are:

- traffic volumes;
- street cleanliness and maintenance;
- access to open space;
- anti-social behaviour, e.g. vandalism.
- accessibility within the city as a whole;
- social interaction;
- presence/absence of local facilities;
- degree of landscaping (trees, verges);

?

20 Study Figures 6.29 and 6.30.
a Which area do you think has the higher environmental quality?
b What criteria did you use to reach your decision?
c What other criteria might you have used?

Environmental quality in Sheffield

?

21 Study Figure 6.31.

a Use the map and the transect to summarise the main features of the areas of high quality environment in Sheffield in 1976 (for example, distance from the city centre, house ownership type, age of buildings and presence or absence of industry).

b How might the pattern of environmental quality in Sheffield have changed since 1976?

22 As a group, carry out an assessment of the variations in environmental quality in your local town/city.

a Decide which characteristics to use to assess environmental quality.

b Divide the area into relatively small blocks between members of the group.

c Use a large-scale map to decide on either a series of random sampling points, or a series of systematic sampling points.

d Carry out your survey, allocating penalty points to the different sample sites.

e Draw a map of the patterns of environmental quality, thinking carefully about the categories of penalty points you will use, e.g. 0–20, 21–30, 31–40, etc.

f Try to explain the patterns on your map, especially in relation to age/condition of buildings, pollution sources and presence/absence of industry.

A study of Sheffield shows how 'penalty points' can be awarded to different parts of the urban area. The survey gave up to 100 penalty points to areas depending on the quality of certain aspects of the environment, namely:

- the visual quality of houses, streets and gardens;

- the degree to which traffic and pedestrians were separated;

- the degree of access to public open space; and

- the presence or absence of street furniture, especially bus shelters, post boxes and street lights.

The resulting map (Fig. 6.31) shows large variations in environmental quality in Sheffield.

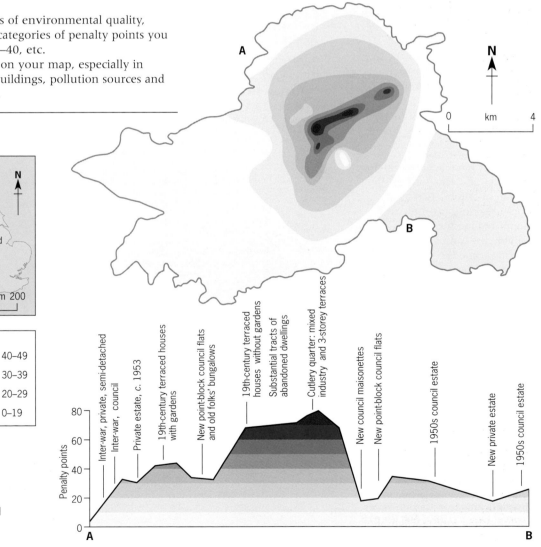

Figure 6.31 Variations in environmental quality, Sheffield (*Source*: Knox, 1976)

Table 6.2 City size and crime rates in the USA, 1991 (*Source*: Knox, 2000)

City size (millions)	Number of reported crimes per 100000 population
6	4972
4–6	4527
2–4	3697
1–2	3921
0.75–1	3257
0.5–0.75	2654
0.25–0.5	2567
<0.25	915

?

23a For a part of a town or city close to you, obtain from the local police force data for a period of 1–3 months for the location of: burglaries; muggings.
b Draw a dot map for each type of crime and describe the resulting patterns.
c How could the areas affected most by these crimes be changed to reduce their incidence?

24a What have been the main responses and reactions to the growth of crimes such as housebreaking, car theft and shoplifting by: the police; individuals; companies; and neighbourhoods?
b To what extent do you think that increased protection and prevention of crime in one area merely displace the crime to another part of the city?

6.12 Urban crime

Crime statistics for American cities show that the rising crime rates are linked to city size (Table 6.2). The largest US cities have the highest crime rates. Theories which have been put forward to explain patterns of crime in EMDCs fall into two groups:

1 Structural theories see crime as being based in inequalities generated by the economic system. Thus crime is viewed as one way in which poorer groups try to get their share of material goods.

2 Ecological theories stress the importance of the neighbourhood, especially the nature of its social groups which may be influences for good or bad.
   However, most writers do agree that crime is a symptom of poverty and deprivation rather than a cause. Studies have concentrated on two main aspects of crime: the location of the crimes; and the location of the criminals.

The location of crimes

Different parts of the urban area are likely to be the scenes of different types of crime. For example, shoplifting tends to be concentrated in the CBD, regional shopping centres and shopping malls. In contrast, patterns of housebreaking and vandalism are likely to be concentrated in inner city areas.

The location of the criminals

In EMDCs, the location of criminals is seen to be linked to 'problem' housing estates, as the example of Cardiff illustrates (Fig. 6.32). In the UK, these are often council estates in the urban fringe or in the most deprived parts of the inner city. However, it would be wrong to relate all crime to poverty, and all criminals to public housing areas. Some types of crime, such as fraud, are more likely to be committed by people who live in the wealthier parts of cities. In the USA, the study of crime has developed the **routine activities theory**.

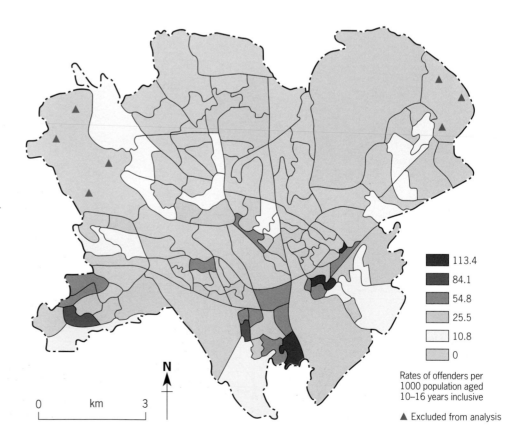

Figure 6.32 Juvenile delinquency: Offenders homes in Cardiff, Wales (*Source*: Evans (1980) Fig. 25 p18. Geographical Perspectives on Juvenile Delinquency, Gower, Westmead, Farnborough)

■	113.4
■	84.1
■	54.8
■	25.5
□	10.8
■	0

Rates of offenders per 1000 population aged 10–16 years inclusive

▲ Excluded from analysis

N

0   km   3

25a Study Figure 6.33. What percentage of the burglaries in this area took place in houses with some form of open space or derelict land behind them?

b What other factors can you suggest to explain the pattern of burglaries shown on the map? Other features of the urban environment which can be very important in crime rates include:
• visibility – are there large areas of alleyways or other zones which are 'hidden'.
• control of property – for example are there caretakers at the entrance to tall blocks of flats? Are there local people with responsibility to oversee play areas and open spaces?
• residential density – research has shown that high residential densities are often linked to high rates of crime.
• state of physical repair – areas of run down housing, empty factories and derelict land are often areas associated with crime.

In this case the characteristics of the population of part of a city bring together the three bases of crime:

• the presence of a motivated offender

• a suitable target

• the absence of a capable guardian.

This means that some areas of cities, by virtue of the characteristics of their population, tend to provide more opportunities for crime than others. However, population characteristics are only one part of the analysis. The physical nature of the urban environment is the second key factor. At this scale, the importance of areas where accessibility for criminals is easy, such as places where there are fields, or open space behind houses, can create significant blackspots for crime. For example analysis of burglary in part of Newcastle-under-Lyme (Fig. 6.33) identified those households most affected, in relation to the surrounding land use.

One geographer, David Herbert, has produced a framework (Fig. 6.34) which tries to bring together features of the population of an area, such as poverty, levels of education etc., with features of the built environment, such as overcrowded housing. Herbert argued that there is a cycle of disadvantage which affects people on low incomes. This poverty means that families often have to live in sub-standard housing, possibly overcrowded and with few facilities. Families in such areas may therefore have a weak educational background, making it harder to acquire high level occupational skills. This in turn may help to perpetuate the poverty of families in the area. This was Herbert's idea of a **cycle of poverty**, linked to a **cycle of disadvantage**. He felt that the poverty, lack of occupational skills, and weak educational background tended to create an impersonal social environment, in which there were few community values. Herbert felt that this created the conditions in which deviant behaviour could flourish.

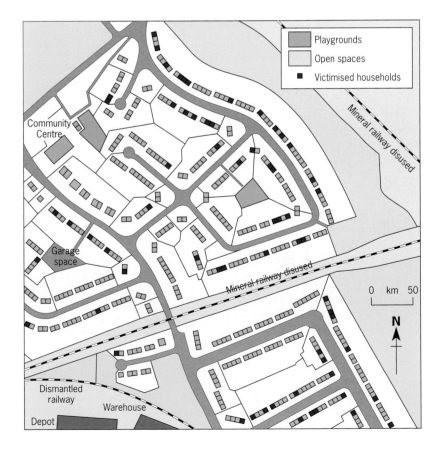

Women and violent crime

Geographers have made a significant contribution to research into women's fear of violent crime. Studies have shown that women fear strangers in public places. However, the research shows that women are more likely to be raped or attacked by men they have known, so they are at much greater risk in their own homes or in semi-private places rather than in public places. This does not mean, however, that women's fear of strangers in public places is irrational. The media are full of reports of violent sexual crime which exaggerates the risks of some types of behaviour, but ignores the risks of other types. Planners therefore need to take account of both the reality of violent incidence and the perception of this, when planning urban spaces.

Figure 6.33 Distribution of burglary victims in Newcastle-under-Lyme, Evans and Oulds (1984), Fig. 5, p349. 'Geographical aspects of the incidence of residential burglary in Newcastle-under-Lyme, UK' (*Source:* Tijdschrift voor Economische en Sociale Geografie, 75, 344–355)

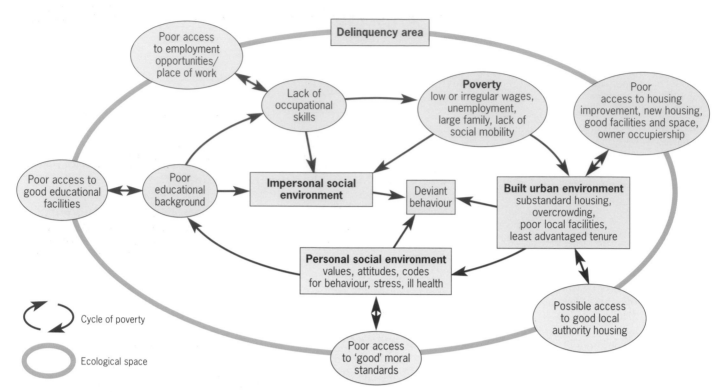

Figure 6.34 Crime and the cycle of disadvantage (*Source*: Herbert (1992) p47 'Neighbourhood incivilities and the study of crime in place' Area, 25, 45–54.)

26a Study Figure 6.34. Outline as many places as possible in the diagram where the cycle of poverty and disadvantage could be broken, e.g. by building new houses in disadvantaged areas. In each case outline who could make the change e.g. local authorities, individuals, community groups.
b Re-draw Figure 6.34 with your changes to show how the cycle of disadvantage could become the cycle of cumulative advantage.

Summary

- There are different types of spatial inequality in cities; in particular, there are variations in access to services and amenities; and variations in the spatial distribution of features such as income and employment.

- Deprivation is a multi-faceted problem with many interlocking causes.

- Access to services (e.g. medical care) varies with many factors (e.g. age, gender, personal mobility).

- Gay and lesbian groups have had an impact on the geography of urban areas in EMDCs.

- Access to employment is related to both personal factors (e.g. qualifications, mobility) and urban features (e.g. the location of employment opportunities).

- Women do not have equality of access to services and amenities in most of the world's cities.

- People have very different perceptions of the urban area in which they live. These perceptions are related to many factors (e.g. age, socio-economic status, location of workplace).

- Environmental quality varies within urban areas in relation to many factors (e.g. open space, traffic, presence/absence of factories).

- Structural and ecological theories have been developed to try to explain patterns of urban crime, but their explanations are only partial.

7 The economic base of the city

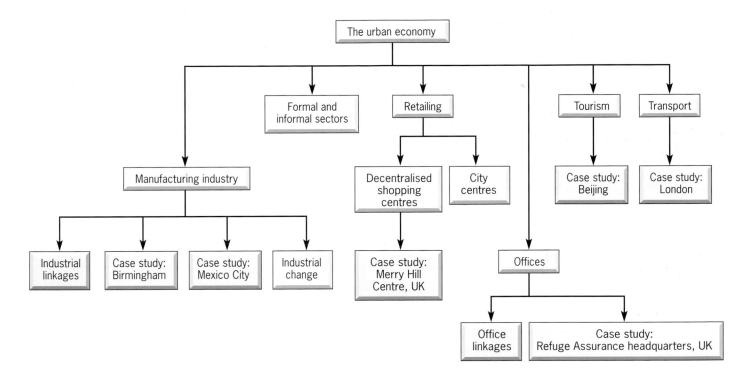

7.1 Introduction

Most of the people who migrated to cities all over the world in the last 50 years did so in search of better employment opportunities. People born and growing up in cities also see the urban area as the focus of employment. Cities have always provided a wide range of employment opportunities (Figs 7.1–7.4).

However, over time, urban employment opportunities have shown great changes in terms of:

- their location within urban areas;
- the number of jobs provided;
- the range of opportunities available;
- the size of establishments involved;
- the type of equipment used;
- the degree of skill(s) required; and
- the gender of employees.

This chapter examines some of these changes and their significance for urban growth, form, functions, transport and pollution.

7.2 The changing location of manufacturing industry

Manufacturing industry originally grew up in or close to the centre of most cities in both EMDCs and ELDCs. The present day distinction between home, shop and workplace was often absent. Products such as shoes, clothing, metal goods and jewellery were made mainly in small workshops, often in the craftsman's home, and customers called there to make their purchases. Early concentrations of some industries occurred in response to a common need – e.g. for a supply of water for power or other purposes. Eventually, however,

Figure 7.1 A street vendor selling water in Calcutta, India

Figure 7.2 Working in the Stock Exchange, Tokyo, Japan

Figure 7.3 Working in a modern office (*above right*)

Figure 7.4 Working in the Honda motorcycle assembly plant, Manáus, Brazil (*right*)

the CBD became the focus for retailing, administration and service industries; separate residential areas were established; and manufacturing industries relocated from the centre to other parts of the urban area.

Over time also, products became more numerous and more sophisticated. After the beginning of the Industrial Revolution in the late eighteenth century, many manufacturing industries required large sites suitable for buildings containing specialist machinery (e.g. cotton mills). An increasing number of firms began to specialise in the manufacture of **components** for use by other firms in the assembly of complex final products (e.g. TV sets; aircraft). Today, a complex web of **linkages** exists between firms in many manufacturing industries in cities around the world.

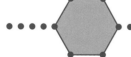

Industrial linkages

There are two main types of linkage between firms: **backward linkages** and **forward linkages**. The links are made up of flows of one or more of the following: materials, information, money and personnel. The main material linkages of a manufacturing plant are shown in Figure 7.5.

Backward linkages
Backward linkages exist between the factory and the suppliers of the materials and services required to make its product. Suppliers of materials include firms supplying raw materials (e.g. timber), processed materials (e.g. steel),

Figure 7.5 The main material linkages of a manufacturing plant (*Adapted from:* Healey and Ilberry, 1990)

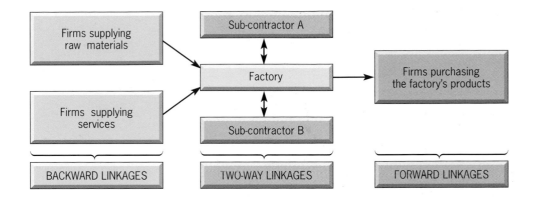

machinery (e.g. lathes) and other equipment (e.g. computers). Suppliers of services include firms of consultants, accountants, lawyers, advertisers, cleaners and maintenance staff.

Forward linkages

Forward linkages are those linkages that exist between the factory and the purchasers of its product. Sometimes the purchaser will be a domestic consumer, but often it will be another manufacturer for whom its product is a material input. For example, in the late nineteenth century and the first half of the twentieth century, many firms in Walsall in the West Midlands specialised in the manufacture of locks and door furniture (door handles, etc.). Their forward linkages included those with wholesale suppliers to the building trade, for whom they made end-products, and motor vehicle manufacturers, for whom they made components.

Two-way linkages

In some industries, parts of the production process may be sub-contracted out from the main factory to other (usually smaller) firms specialising in a particular skill. For example, manufactured metal components may be sent out for machining or for welding, before being returned to the original factory, eventually to become part of a final product. In such a case, both forward and backward linkages exist between the firms involved.

Information-flow linkages between firms are also typically two-way and are of vital importance to some industries, including hi-tech industries which tend to form spatial clusters and develop strong local-area linkages, often choosing to locate in hi-tech science parks (e.g. in Cambridge).

The changing location of manufacturing industry in Birmingham, UK

Pre-1860

Pre-1860, Birmingham's five main industries were making: guns; jewellery; buttons; steel items (e.g. tools); and brass items (e.g. pipes for locomotives and steam engines). Manufacture took place in workshops, in small factories and people's homes, all tightly packed together. The city centre was the focus for the gun quarter and the jewellery quarter (Fig. 7.6), while the button and brass industries were in the eastern industrial district.

1860–1914 Decentralisation

As the range, sophistication and size of machinery increased, factories in Birmingham grew larger, especially in the gun trade. New industries also developed, including the making of bicycles (based on

1 Study Figure 7.6, then list the main changes to the built-up area of Birmingham between 1828 and 1859.

2 Study Figures 7.6 and 7.7.
a List the main changes in the location of industry in Birmingham between 1859 and 1914.
b Suggest possible reasons for these changes.

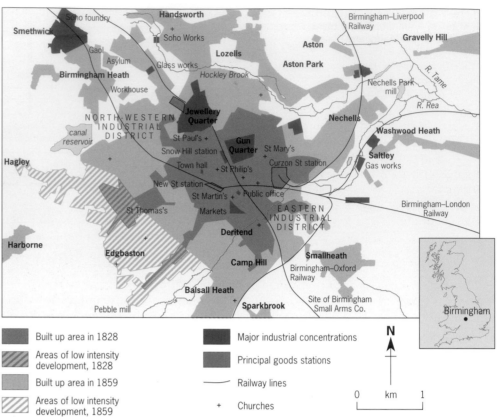

Figure 7.6 The urban structure of Birmingham in 1859 (*Source:* British Association, 1950)

▨ Built up area in 1828	▨ Major industrial concentrations
▨ Areas of low intensity development, 1828	▨ Principal goods stations
▨ Built up area in 1859	— Railway lines
▨ Areas of low intensity development, 1859	+ Churches

N

0 km 1

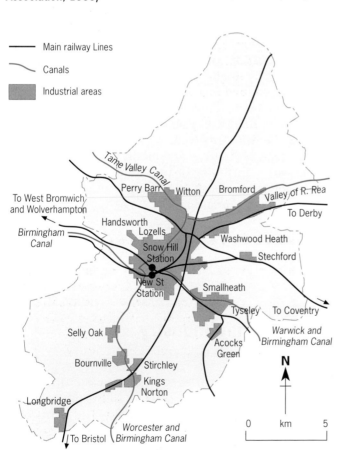

Figure 7.7 Industrial zones in Birmingham in 1914 (*Source:* British Association, 1950)

metal tubes formerly used for gun barrels); electrical goods; cars and chocolate.

The new industries all needed large sites for their factories. As a result, manufacturing industry began to **decentralise** – that is, move away from the city centre to the suburbs. In this, the factories were following a trend established a few years earlier when richer people began to move into new houses built on cheap, spacious outlying sites. This movement of people to the suburbs has been called the **first wave of decentralisation**. The movement of factories (and employment in factories) to suburban sites is sometimes called the **second wave of decentralisation**. Cadbury's, for example, moved to Bournville from the city centre in 1879.

In Birmingham four main industrial zones had emerged by 1914 (Fig. 7.7):

• in the south-east, along the Warwick canal;
• in the north-east, on the former flood plain of the River Rea;
• in the south-west, in Selly Oak and Bournville;
• in the north-west, along the Birmingham canal.

In all these zones, there was space to build large new factories and land was cheaper than in the city centre. In 1906 Herbert Austin had bought the site of a former printing works at Longbridge and began to assemble cars in what was then a very rural suburb.

1914–70

Industrial growth in Birmingham between 1914 and 1970 became concentrated around the car and motorcycle industries and an extensive network of linkages developed. Suppliers of components (e.g. tyres, windscreens, brakes, batteries, seats) mostly located in new factories in suburbs such as Stechford and Acocks Green, often in purpose-built **industrial estates**. Their forward linkages were with the main assembly plants, such as Rover's Longbridge works (Fig. 7.8). Other manufacturing industries such as food processing and electrical goods also located in suburbs 8–10 km from the city centre. The redevelopment of the inner city in the 1960s and 1970s led to the closure of many of the remaining central workshops.

Post-1970

Manufacturing industry in Birmingham declined dramatically during the 1970s and 1980s. First the motorcycle industry declined; and then the car industry contracted. The tightly linked industrial structure disintegrated and many suppliers of components were forced to close down. Some derelict areas were created, especially in the older areas close to the city centre and in the Tame valley. Birmingham lost 160 000 jobs in manufacturing industry between 1981 and 1995.

Some new industrial development has occurred, however, mainly on edge-of-city **greenfield sites**. The Birmingham Business Park, located to the east of the city, between the M6 and the M42, is one example of industrial revival. The site provides relatively cheap land, space for expansion and motorway proximity,

Figure 7.8 Aerial view of Longbridge, Birmingham

attracting a wide variety of firms (e.g. computer assembly). There has also been some limited industrial revival in inner city areas such as the Aston Science Park, a joint venture by the University and the city. Of the more traditional industries that survived into the twenty-first century, some – such as Rover – were taken over on several occasions.

Manufacturing industry in Mexico City

Pre-1940

Mexico City (Fig. 7.9) grew slowly from its foundation (section 2.4) until 1940 by which time – although it was a **primate city** – it covered an area of only 50 sq km. Together with an industrial sector to the north-west, the city centre was the main focus of industrial employment, with a large number of small workshops producing a wide range of goods, from gold and jewellery to pots, pans and weapons. Other manufacturing industries, included textiles, clothing, food processing, drink and tobacco manufacture.

The population of Mexico City grew from 600 000 in 1900 to 1.7m in 1941. Many of its industries developed to meet the needs of the city itself, since it was the nation's capital and its largest single market, especially for goods such as food and textiles. Also, it had the largest concentration of labour in the country.

Post-1940

The growth of Mexico City since 1940 has been rapid, both in terms of people and of industry. The spur for industrial growth was World War II (1939–45), when the supply of imported manufactured goods was disrupted. After the war, Mexico began a programme of industrial development which was encouraged by its initial advantages and by new factors such as the high

Figure 7.9 Mexico City

duties on imported manufactured goods, the discovery of petroleum and the development in the 1960s of the oil refining and chemicals industries on the Gulf coast.

Large numbers of new manufacturing firms have brought investment and new technology to Mexico (Figs 7.10–7.11), making everything from textiles to electrical products, jewellery, ceramics, electronic equipment and cars. Many of the new firms are branches of transnational companies (e.g. IBM and Ford), attracted by Mexico's low wages, non-unionised labour and relative lack of environmental controls. By 1998, over one-third of all Mexico's exports derived from transnational companies who created 1.4 million new manufacturing jobs in Mexico City between 1980

and 1998. The large new factories are located mainly in the north-western and north-eastern suburbs (Fig. 7.12), where advantages include space, cheap land and government-sponsored industrial estates. Expansion to the north-east was made possible by the draining of Lake Texcoco.

Mexico City now has 50 per cent of the country's total industrial output and 55 per cent of its total industrial employment. Firms established there have access to a labour force of 7m people, to government headquarters, to finance and to export markets; they have the best infrastructure in Mexico (water supply, electricity and telecommunications); and they are at the hub of the nation's communications network.

Figure 7.10 Inside the Volkswagen car assembly plant in Mexico

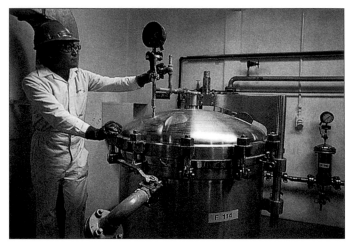

Figure 7.11 Inside a Glaxo pharmaceuticals plant in Mexico

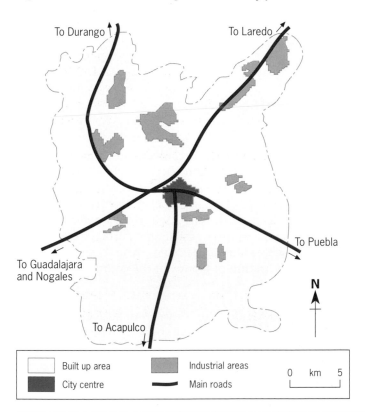

Built up area

City centre

Industrial areas

Main roads

0 km 5

Figure 7.12 Industrial areas in Mexico City, _c_.1990 (_Source:_ Ward, 1990)

?

3 Why does Mexico City dominate the location of Mexico's manufacturing industry?

4 Why did most manufacturing industry originally grow up in the centres of cities like Birmingham and Mexico City?

5 Make a list of the 'push' and 'pull' factors which encouraged industries to move out to the suburbs from central Birmingham and central Mexico City.

6 Contrast the post-1980 changes in manufacturing industry in Birmingham and Mexico City, using the following headings: product changes; employment changes; location changes.

Analysing industrial change

One method of anyalsing change in urban manufacturing industry is to use a framework which focuses on the births, deaths and transfers of firms:

- **Births** occur when firms that are new locate in an area.

- **Transfers** occur when firms move from one area to another. There are two main types of transfer: those involving the closure of the previous premises; and those involving expansion of an existing factory by creating a new branch factory.

- **Deaths** occur when firms close down.

Using this framework shows, for example, that during 1981–95 the decline of industry in Birmingham was caused mostly by the death of firms (85 per cent of the total job losses of 160 000), rather than by the transfer of firms from the area (15 per cent of the total). Underlying causes of the high death rate of firms include the fact that industry had been dominated by small firms which tend to collapse more quickly than larger firms in harsh economic times; and the large number of firms in declining industries rather than in the growth sectors.

?

7 Why is it important for planners dealing with manufacturing industry in cities like Birmingham to be aware of the relative importance of births, deaths and transfers?

7.3 Formal and informal economic sectors

Geographers have classified employment opportunities in cities in different ways. Many geographers distinguish between the **formal sector** of employment and the **informal sector** (sometimes also called the **petty commodity sector**). Jobs in the formal sector are usually permanent, often with set hours of work and levels of pay, and sometimes with the provision of pensions and social security rights. Most, but not all, jobs in cities in EMDCs are of this type. Jobs in the informal sector include activities such as selling water and food or cleaning shoes (Fig. 7.13), and are often undertaken by individuals who are unable to find formal-sector jobs. A much higher proportion of jobs in cities in ELDCs are of this type. The main contrasts between the two sectors are shown in Table 7.1. An example of the informal sector in practice is shown in Figure 7.14.

The value of the distinction between the formal and informal sectors has been questioned by some geographers, including Drakakis-Smith (1987). For example, many jobs like selling water or entertaining are found in both the formal and the informal sectors. Also, many individuals work in more than one sector – for example, a woman may work in the formal sector (part-time in a

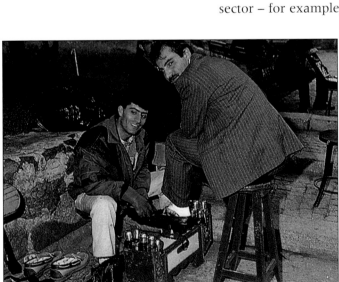

Figure 7.13 A shoe cleaner in Istanbul, Turkey

Table 7.1 Characteristics of formal and informal sectors

Formal	Informal
Difficult to get a job	Easy to start working
Overseas inputs are common	Local inputs are usual
Corporate factory	Carried on from home
Capital-intensive	Labour-intensive
Large-scale	Small-scale
Imported technologies are used	Local, small-scale, technologies used
Formal skills are needed (e.g. education)	Formal skills are not needed
Pay/income varies	Pay/income often small
Employment usually by a company or government department	Usually self-employed
Employees pay tax	Do not pay tax

INFORMAL-SECTOR ACTIVITIES in Jakarta are centred around pondoks – a sort of lodging house specially for migrant traders. The *pondok* is run by a tauke who is a cross between a landlady and an entrepreneur.

In the *pondok*, run by a lady called Ibu Mus, the residents/workers all come from the same village and specialise in ice-cream making. The building is made of bamboo and various scavenged materials and measures only 24 m² but is home for some 15 people.

Life in the Mus household begins at 4 a.m. when Ibu Mus and her husband Pok Manto receive the day's delivery of ice... After the ice has been loaded into the cold storage, they divide up the ice-cream ingredients (for each trader). The rest of the *pondok* awake and begin to descend the rickety ladder down to the ground... It is about 7 a.m. when they start to rotate their buckets of ice-cream and they sit there twisting and turning for the next 3 hours or so.

Ibu Mus turns to her own work after she has finished weighing out the ice-cream ingredients. She carefully pours a variety of herbal medicines that she has prepared the previous evening into 13 well-washed Johnnie Walker bottles... and by 6.30 a.m. sets out to sell them. Ibu Sajum, Manto's sister-in-law, usually returns from market at the time Ibu Mus sets out on her rounds and begins to dice and cook the vast quantity of food she has brought back from market.

At about 10 a.m. the ice-cream is ready, each trader tastes his product and makes any final adjustments that are necessary. When the product is ready, the ice-cream bucket is carefully lifted into a cart and surrounded by a fresh combination of salt and ice. Then one by one, the traders stride into the kitchen, strip and wash themselves, and then change into clean singlets and shorts and sit down to the breakfast that Sajum has prepared.

Sajum has also cooked a vast amount of fried savouries and titbits which she now neatly arranges on trays. Then she too changes into a traditional village *sarong* and *kebaja*, and sets off to sell her savouries. Soon everyone else follows suit. One by one, the ice-cream traders manoeuvre their carts out of the narrow door of the *pondok*.

The traders from Mus's *pondok* respect one another's territory and do not steal customers from each other. But, of course, they compete with the ice-cream sellers from other pondoks. Sajum's customers were buying their regular meal but the demand for ice-cream varies with the weather and the taste of the traders' ice-cream. The trader have invested a lot of money and labour into their ice-cream. As it is perishable and cannot be refrozen, they cannot afford to return to the *pondok* until their stocks have been completely sold.

As Sajum and the ice-cream traders are beginning their rounds, Ibu Mus's is drawing to an end. She too follows a constant route and in most places has regular customers for her herbal medicines which promise to combat a variety of ills ranging from infertility to unfaithfulness. By noon, Ibu Mus returns home. She empties out and thoroughly washes her 13 Johnnie Walker bottles and stands them upside down to dry. Then she sits down to a meal which Sajum has left for her. When she has finished eating, Mus sets off for market. She returns with food for the evening meal which she prepares and cooks so that a meal will be ready whenever the ice-cream traders return. When that is done, she sets off for the market again, this time to buy all the ingredients for the next day's ice-cream trade.

From 6 p.m. onwards the ice-cream traders begin to return. They look exhausted as they push their way through the door of the *pondok* and park the empty carts inside. They had started work at 7 a.m. and if business is slow, it might be 9 p.m. or later before they begin to make their way back home. Each trader unloads and cleans his cart and then silently consumes the meal Ibu Mus has prepared before climbing up into the attic and going off to sleep. They have neither time nor the energy for socialising. The next day's ice will be delivered in a few hours time and their work will begin all over again.

Figure 7.14 Earning a living in the informal sector (*Source:* Drakakis-Smith, 1987)

factory), in the informal sector (cooking food at home for members of her family to sell on the streets) and in the domestic sector (cleaning her house).

It can be argued that distinguishing between formal and informal sectors is a crude process whose main benefit has been to focus attention on the positive values and contribution to the urban economy of the poor. The poor in cities in both EMDCs and ELDCs exist at little cost to the city authorities. They feed, clothe and house themselves and also provide an on-the-spot supply of cheap labour.

?

8a Write a report for a newspaper outlining the main disadvantages of working in the informal sector in cities like Jakarta.

b Why are more and more people in both EMDCs and ELDCs seeking employment in the informal sector? (Think about disadvantages of the formal sector and advantages of the informal sector.)

7.4 **Retailing**

In most cities, retailing located initially in the city centre and has remained there. However, city-centre shops are now increasingly threatened by decentralisation, to the extent that geographers have described retailing as the **third wave** in the decentralisation process.

Figure 7.15 A 1930s shopping parade in Hatfield, Hertfordshire

Decentralised shopping centres

Neighbourhood shopping centres

In EMDCs such as the UK, shopping provision spread dramatically outwards from city centres during the period 1919–39. New private and council estates were designed and built with their own small shopping centres – often a row of 20–30 shops, on a main road, but set back with their own service road in front (Figs 7.15–7.16). This pattern continued after World War II (i.e. after 1945). Today, small centres cater for local needs and sell low-order convenience goods, such as milk, newspapers, cigarettes and sweets.

During redevelopment in the 1960s and 1970s, many shops in inner-city areas, especially corner shops, closed permanently. However, some rows of shops did survive along the main radial routes through these areas (Fig. 7.16).

District shopping centres

District shopping centres are larger groups of 60–70 shops. They are often located at points where ring roads cross the main radial routes (Fig. 7.16).

Retail warehouse parks and superstores

More recently, retail warehouse parks have developed along main roads, usually on the edge of the urban area where land is cheaper and there is space for expansion (Fig. 7.16). Similarly, hypermarkets and superstores have grown up, often on greenfield sites in the urban fringe close to motorways and main roads.

Figure 7.16 Typical locations of shopping centres in a UK city or large town

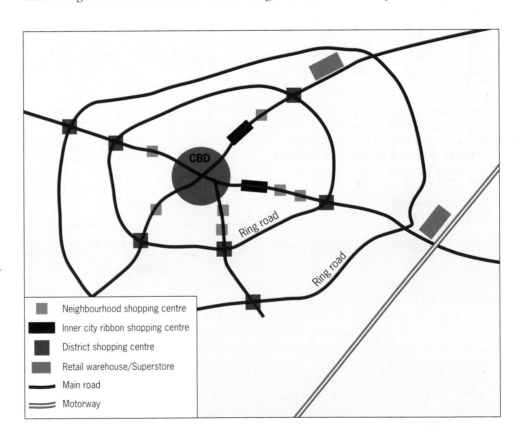

Neighbourhood shopping centre
Inner city ribbon shopping centre
District shopping centre
Retail warehouse/Superstore
Main road
Motorway

?

9a Make a map of the distribution of different types of shopping centre in a town near you. Think carefully about the categories you intend to use, especially to distinguish between neighbourhood and higher-order centres.
b Make a list of recent changes in the shopping centre by: questioning shoppers and shopkeepers; consulting maps (e.g. Goad plans); consulting the local newspaper and library.
c Describe each of the changes; explain the reasons for it; and discuss its effects.

Out-of-town shopping centres

In addition to superstores, new **out-of-town shopping centres** have been built – for example, the Meadowhall Centre outside Sheffield and the Merry Hill Centre near Dudley in the West Midlands. These large developments are indoor centres with over 100 shops, surrounded by huge car parks (Fig. 7.17). Their main features include the separation of pedestrians from

Figure 7.17 Merry Hill shopping centre

traffic (for safety), separate delivery access, an air-conditioned environment, a landscaped setting, large car parks and access to major roads. The centres also contain a range of cafés and restaurants, together with entertainment facilities such as cinemas, in order to promote themselves as 'family-day-out destinations'.

The number and size of out-of-town centres grew dramatically in the 1980s and early 1990s (Fig. 7.18), so that by 1998 they contained 28 per cent of all UK shopping space, and took 20 per cent of all retail sales (only 5 per cent in 1982). They accounted for 71 per cent of all the new retail space built between 1974 and 1998 and have contributed substantially to the decline of retailing in some town centres.

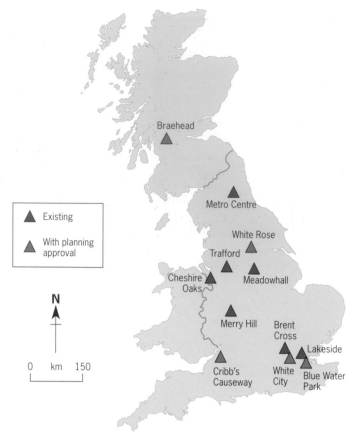

Figure 7.18 Out-of-town shopping centres in the UK, 1997 (*Based on:* Guy, 1994)

?

10 Which features of out-of-town shopping centres are evident in Figure 7.17?

The growth and impact of the Merry Hill Centre, Dudley

The Merry Hill Centre

The Merry Hill Centre (Figs 7.17–7.18) was built between 1984 and 1990 on the site of a former steelworks in the West Midlands; it lies 10 km west of Birmingham and 4 km south of Dudley town centre. It is Europe's largest indoor shopping centre with 135 000 sq m of floor space and a turnover in excess of £350m. There are 260 shops on two levels (Fig. 7.19), including large stores such as Boots, Marks & Spencer and Debenhams as well as specialist shops. Surrounding the centre are car parks with 10 000 free places and coach parks. The centre attracts 50 000 people per day during the week and 72 000 at weekends. It employs 5000 people, many of whom have part-time jobs.

Travel-time lines in the surrounding district show the regional catchment area of the centre (Fig. 7.20).

Due to its location in the heart of the West Midlands conurbation, a total of 1.3m people live within 15–30 minutes' drive and another 1.3m live within 30–45 minutes' drive of Merry Hill. For many of these people, Merry Hill is a popular attraction. For many nearby residents, however, the negative externalities (section 6.7) are considerable (Fig. 7.21).

The impact on retailing in nearby towns

The shopping centres in the nearby towns of Dudley, Brierley Hill and Stourbridge are more traditional. They are located in a series of city-centre streets, some of which are pedestrianised. Each of the centres has a small pedestrianised mall built in the 1980s, and a traditional market. All suffer from problems such as: traffic hazards, lack of free parking and exposure to the elements.

Figure. 7.19 Part of the interior of Merry Hill shopping centre

Merry Hill moaners

I DIDN'T know whether to be annoyed or amused when I read the letter praising the Merry Hill Centre and attacking the 'moaners'. Well, I'm one of the moaners and proud of it.

It is very easy to like the Merry Hill if you don't have to live by it, and I'm sure J Brown loves spending a couple of hours wandering the malls and then returning to his nice residential street in Halesowen.

Unfortunately, those of us who live near the centre don't have a choice. Seven days a week the main roads are jammed, with fumes spewing from cars and lorries. Side streets are used as rat-runs by people trying to avoid the jams.

J Brown says people have a choice – well, I beg to differ. Since the opening of the Merry Hill virtually all the major stores in the surrounding towns have closed down. My shopping choice, unless I travel some distance, has closed down.

If those who want the extension built are so keen, why not buy a house nearby and see how much fun the Merry Hill can be.

Quarry Bank resident

REGARDING the letter from J Brown, of Halesowen, about the development of Merry Hill.

I think J Brown should come and live in Quarry Bank right next to 'Merry Hell'.

He does not live on its doorstep. We can't get out of our homes for car fumes. We were here before the Richardson Bros decided to build it in a built-up area.

Come on Quarry Bankers, say something now before we need a helicopter to get out of our houses.

**Mrs Irene Jones
Quarry Bank**

Figure 7.21 'Merry Hill moaners'
(*Adapted from: The Chronicle*, Stourbridge)

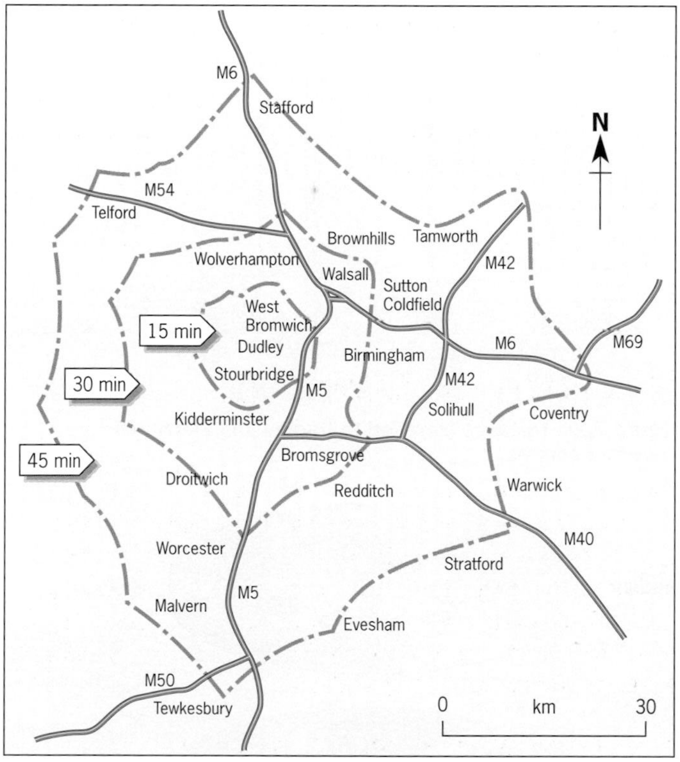

Figure 7.22 Boarded-up shops in Dudley

Figure 7.20 Travel-times to Merry Hill shopping centre
(*Source*: Tyre, 1993)

The growing popularity of Merry Hill has caused serious problems in all three towns. The worst affected has been Dudley where between 1989 and 1998 there was a 27 per cent fall in retail employment and a 74 per cent reduction in retail trade. Large stores such as Littlewoods, Currys and Marks & Spencer closed, many simply moving to Merry Hill. In 1985, Dudley had 190 shops; by 1998, it had only 127. The result is that Dudley town centre has many empty, boarded-up shops (Fig. 7.22). The process generates a downward spiral (Fig. 7.23) in that as shops close, fewer shopping attractions remain; the number of shoppers then declines, making the centre even less attractive to potential new shops.

?

11 Which features of out-of-town shopping centres are evident in Figure 7.19?

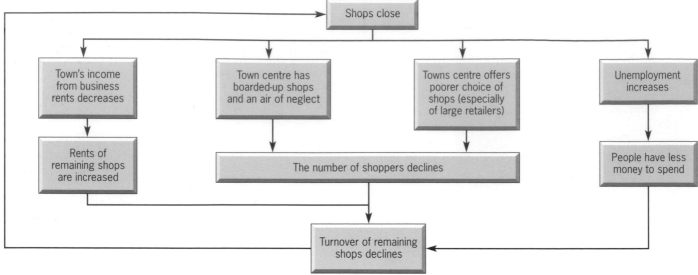

Figure 7.23 The downward spiral of shop closures

Many shops in Stourbridge also closed, reducing its market share of **comparison-goods** shopping by 46 per cent between 1989 and 1998. Brierley Hill, despite being the closest to Merry Hill, has actually been least affected. This is because it was always a lower-order centre with few large supermarkets, multiple stores or department stores. Its smaller shops, selling convenience goods, are not in direct competition with the larger stores of Merry Hill.

Shopping in Dudley and Merry Hill: a comparison

A recent survey of shoppers in Dudley and Merry Hill compared the two centres. Shoppers travelled further to visit Merry Hill (Fig. 7.24); and their main mode of transport was different (Fig. 7.25). The frequency with which they visited the two centres was also different (Fig. 7.26), as were their objectives (Fig. 7.27).

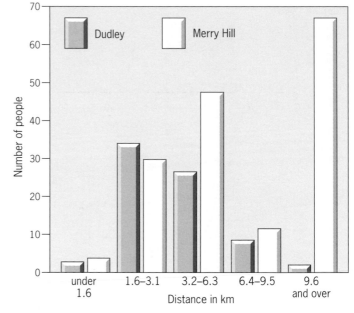

Figure 7.24 Distance travelled to Dudley and Merry Hill shopping centres

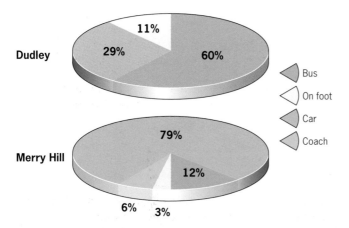

Figure 7.25 Method of transport to Dudley and Merry Hill shopping centres

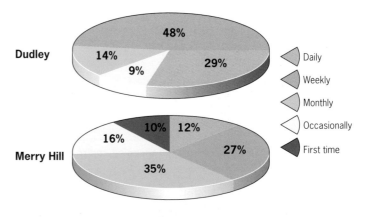

Figure 7.26 Frequency of visits to Dudley and Merry Hill shopping centres

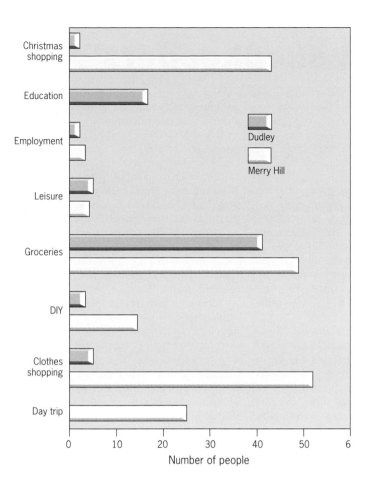

Number of people

12a Suggest ways in which the downward spiral of shopping closures (Fig. 7.23) might be reversed. Group your measures into those to be taken by: the local council; shopkeepers.
b Draw a diagram similar to Figure 7.23 to show the upward spiral of growth at Merry Hill as more shops have been opened.
c What problems might arise for Merry Hill itself as a result of its rapid growth?

13a Draw up a table for the Merry Hill and Dudley shopping centres showing: their advantages and disadvantages for shoppers; distance travelled by shoppers; methods of travel used; frequency of visits; reasons for visits.
b Try to explain the differences you have listed.

Figure 7.27 Reasons for visiting Dudley and Merry Hill shopping centres

City centres fight back

During the early 1990s, the increase in out-of-town shopping centres all over the UK was widely criticised because of their adverse impact on town centres (Fig. 7.29). By 1994, the UK government was attempting to slow the trend by imposing strict planning regulations on new developments. The aims were to:

- restore 'high-quality life' to traditional town centres;
- encourage town centres to improve their facilities (e.g. parking, security, protection from the elements and pedestrianisation);
- reduce dependency on the car;
- utilise 150 000 acres of derelict land in or near city centres;
- reduce traffic congestion in edge-of-city areas; and
- reduce air pollution near out-of-town centres.

As a result, city centres like Birmingham have been pressing ahead with pedestrianisation schemes, together with projects to redevelop and remodel some older areas (Fig. 7.28). These projects have been combined with improvements to public transport, especially the growth of bus lanes and the light railway project. The focus of all these projects is to re-establish the attraction and competitiveness of city-centre shopping.

7.5 Offices

In the past, manufacturing industry was often the main employer in cities, but now service industries, located in offices, have become the dominant employers. Service industries, including transport, education, health, research, administration and finance, were the fastest-growing employment sectors in

Figure 7.28 Centenary Way, in central Birmingham

'Nation of redundant shopkeepers'

BRITAIN will become a nation of redundant shopkeepers unless the growth of out-of-town shopping centres is halted, the chairman of the Commons environment select committee said yesterday.

A report by the committee says that during the 1980s development policies allowed too many superstores and other large retail developments to be built in places which were inappropriate on environmental, heritage and social grounds.

The committee chairman, Barry Field, said the policy 'has turned too many of our town centres into shopping deserts. All too often, we are inclined to deplore the death of once vibrant town and village centres, while enjoying for ourselves the convenience of out-of-town shopping. We all mourn the loss of 'our' corner shop, but if we don't use we lose it.'

The committee recommends significant changes to government planning guidance and says effective public transport must be developed.

Government guidance to local authorities has already changed this year, with superstores now unacceptable if they could cause 'demonstrable harm' to nearby town centres.

The committee recommends that the guidance should be amended to say superstores are best built in or on the edges of town centres unless there are very strong reasons to the contrary. It suggests a new booklet should be issued setting out conditions for permission so that developers, local authorities and planning inspectors all work to the same rules.

The committee points out that 24 per cent of the population do not have use of a car. Problems are caused for these people by 'planning creep', where out-of-town centres offer more and more services such as chemists' shops and post offices. This threatens the continuation of such services in town centres, which are more easily reached by the poor and elderly who need them most.

Some 89 town managers have been appointed to help to revitalise local centres, but most do not have the resources or status to succeed. Restrictions on the compulsory purchase powers of local authorities make it difficult for the necessary public and private partnerships to be developed. The committee urges the Government to give local authorities more freedom and to find ways of financing town centre revitalisation.

The report also tackles 'planning gain' –inducements such as public open space or road improvements offered by developers to get planning permission. The committee says that 'if a development is fundamentally unacceptable in planning terms, then no associated planning gain can be allowed to render it acceptable'.

Figure 7.29 'Nation of redundant shopkeepers' (Adapted from: The Guardian, 2 November 1994)

cities all over the world in the 1980s and 1990s (Fig. 7.30). Offices are places where information is handled, rather than goods and products; they are equipped with telephones, fax machines, computers and video-conferencing facilities. Offices are also important elements of the landscape, especially in city centres where office blocks often dwarf older buildings.

There are four main types of offices:

- Head offices: these exercise overall control of a company and plan and manage its affairs.

- Government offices: in the UK, both central and local government are big users of office space. Central government offices are concentrated in Westminster, London, but there are also regional offices of central government in other major cities such as Manchester, Birmingham and Leeds. Local government departments (e.g. education and housing) also need office

Figure 7.30 The growth in employment in services in UK cities, 1861–1997 (Updated from: Daniels, 1987) (below)

Figure 7.31 Rajpath Government Buildings, Delhi, India (below, right)

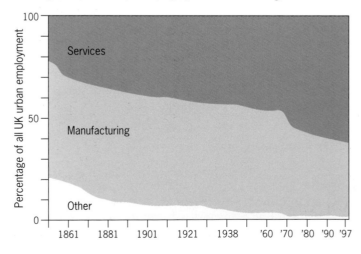

?

14a Using the Thompson Local Directory or YellowPages, count the number of solicitors, insurance agents and travel agents in each place covered by the directory.
b From the Census (or another source), find the population of each place.
c Draw three scattergraphs to show the relationship between size of place and number of solicitors, insurance agents and travel agents. You may need to use logarithmic graph paper in order to show a wide range of values.
d Describe the pattern shown by your graphs, in particular the relationship between population size and number of services.
e Why do some places have one of the office functions, but not the others?

15 Study Table 7.2.
a For all five cities together, count the number of times each of the following reasons is mentioned:
• importance of contacts and communications (both within and between companies, including access to services, amenities, other institutions and decision-makers);
• premises/rents/lease;
• staff recruitment;
• transport;
• space (e.g. to expand);
• other factors (including prestige, parking and tradition).
b Place the reasons in rank order by number of times mentioned.
c Why are the city centres the best locations for offices with these needs?

space – often in city centres. In ELDCs, central governments occupy huge amounts of office space in cities – e.g. Delhi (Fig. 7.31) and Mexico City.

• Commercial offices: these provide services (e.g. insurance, banking and advertising) for other members of the business community.

• Service-providers: these are public or private offices providing a service to individuals (e.g. job centres, estate agents, betting shops and solicitors).

The growing demand for offices

Centralisation

During the last 30 years, there has been a big increase in the demand for office space in cities all over the world. Reasons for this included:

• The increase in the size of many companies as a result of expansion and mergers. This created a demand for new headquarters offices. World cities such as London, New York, Paris, Tokyo and Sydney were particularly popular locations for these headquarters.

• The growth of new or expanding companies seeking larger premises.

• The growth in service industries generally in the 1980s, especially the financial sector (banking and insurance).

• The growth in employment in central and local government, especially in cities like Los Angeles, Calcutta, Bombay and Cairo.

As a result, thousands of office blocks were built in city centres in both EMDCs and ELDCs. City centres provide an environment with a range of easy and personal contacts that are particularly important for decision-makers in headquarters. Surveys show that many managers spend 20 hours or more per week exchanging information with other personnel. Large cities also have international airports and other facilities for the international business person. Many firms also like the prestige associated with an address in a capital city.

Table 7.2 Office location in five city centres: reasons given for choice of central location (in order of importance) (*Source:* Alexander, 1979)

London	Sydney	Dublin	Toronto	Wellington
Contact with external organisations	Availability of premises	Suitable environment	Concentration of decision-makers	Access to contacts
Tradition	Customer/client	Proximity to accessibility	Prestige, visibility services	Availability of parking
Communication with rest of UK	Proximity to public transport	Proximity to customers	Amenities	Staffing
Prestige	Rent	Adequate floor area	Access to public transport	Access to customers/clients
Internal communications	Prestige		Staff availability	Convenience
Contact with government and institutions	Option to renew lease	Low rental	Availability of services	Prestige, visibility, tradition
Contact between head office and associates	Possibility for expansion	Adequate car parking	Proximity to special institutions and government	Contact with government
Supply of staff	Staff availability			Access to special services
Central location	Ease of executive parking			Economic factors
Central to operating area	Access to associated businesses			

Office linkages

The connections between similar or related office functions, such as banking and insurance, are known as **linkages**. The strength of such linkages between offices helps to explain their attraction to city-centre locations. There are five main types of office linkage:

1 **Information linkages** exist between offices. These are the all-important contacts between offices, all of whom have to exchange increasing volumes of information by telephone, fax, e-mail or person-to-person meetings.

2 **Complementary linkages** exist when offices interact (e.g. when an insurance company uses an advertising agency).

3 **Competitive linkages** exist between offices that are competing for the same business. They feel the need to locate near each other to keep an eye on the competition.

4 **Ancillary linkages** form between offices and other businesses that provide services for the office workers (e.g. cafes, restaurants).

5 **Supply linkages** develop when a concentration of offices grows big enough to attract companies supplying equipment (e.g. stationery, computers).

Decentralisation

In the late 1970s and early 1980s, city centres became less attractive places for office activities. Reasons for this included:

- The rising cost of office rents, reflecting high central land values.
- The difficulty and cost of expanding a city centre office on its existing site.
- Growing traffic congestion on roads and public transport systems, resulting in long journey times for staff and clients.
- The difficulty of finding parking places in city centres.
- The high cost of city centre parking.
- Rising staff costs, resulting from competition between offices for staff.

As a result, offices, like population, employment and retailing, began to decentralise from the 1970s onwards. This is sometimes referred to as the **fourth wave of decentralisation**. Many new offices were built in suburban or edge-of-city locations. In addition, some new office developments have taken place in inner-city areas as part of urban regeneration programmes (e.g. London Docklands and Salford Quays).

Refuge Assurance headquarters relocate to Wilmslow, Cheshire

In 1987, the Refuge Assurance Company decided to sell its traditional headquarters building (Fig. 7.32) in the centre of Manchester and relocate to a new, purpose-built headquarters (Fig. 7.33) on a greenfield site in Wilmslow. The main reasons for the move were:

- The Manchester building was a nineteenth-century construction of 31 000 sq m lacking important modern features such as IT conduits and air conditioning.

- The traditional layout of the old building (many small, separate offices) was no longer appropriate for modern working practices.

- The old building had no car park and employees working late felt threatened when having to walk along darkened streets to their cars.

- Expansion on the city centre site would have been difficult and very expensive.

Figure 7.32 The old Refuge Assurance building, central Manchester, in 1960

Figure 7.33 The new Refuge Assurance building, Wilmslow, in 1990

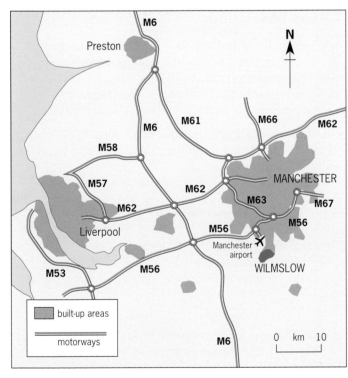

Figure 7.34 Manchester and Wilmslow

- City centre business rates were rising rapidly.

- The new building was purpose-built and included air conditioning, central heating, IT facilities and building security.

- There was space for car parking immediately around the new building.

- Employees complained of the length of time taken to commute to the old building; the new building is very accessible by main road and close to the motorway network (Fig. 7.34), which makes commuting by car easier.

Not everyone at the company has been happy about the move. Some staff used to visit city centre shops during their lunch break at the old site, but can no longer do so. Employees living on the north side of the Manchester conurbation now have a much longer journey to work.

16 Tabulate the main costs and benefits to employees and the company in the move by Refuge Assurance out of central Manchester to Wilmslow.

17a Carry out a survey of offices in your nearest city. Where are the main office clusters?
b Use a questionnaire (see Appendix A) to find out the differences that exist between offices in the city centre and those in the suburbs in terms of their: floor size; type of work; numbers of staff and type of building.

7.6 Tourism

Planners see cities not only as places in which to work, shop and live, but also, increasingly, as places for recreation and tourism. **Recreation** is a short-term activity, usually taking up to a day and involving trips from home (e.g. visiting an ancient castle, a modern shopping centre, a museum, night club or restaurant). **Tourism** is a longer-term activity normally involving a stay away from home.

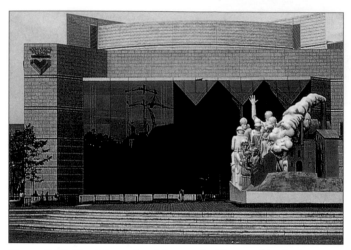

Figure 7.35 The International Convention Centre, Birmingham

Figure 7.36 Kuala Lumpur: main railway station and Pusat Islam Hotel

Cities can be both day-trip destinations and the locations of stays involving several days. In EMDCs, cities such as Bath, London, Edinburgh, Paris and Vienna have all flourished as centres of tourism. In ELDCs, Mexico City is one of the main tourist centres, together with Bangkok and Rio de Janeiro.

Tourism is important to the economic wellbeing of cities in many ways:

* It fosters the development of hotels and conference centres (Figs 7.35–7.36).
* It creates a wide range of employment (e.g. building hotels, work in hotels and restaurants, street-selling, taxi-driving).
* It brings an influx of spending to the city, often involving much-needed foreign exchange.
* It allows the development of specialist shops often selling very high-value goods (e.g. jewellery, designer clothing).
* It creates a demand for artifacts (e.g. handicrafts, T-shirts, models of the Eiffel Tower) that provide employment for the people who make and sell them.
* It stimulates improvements in communications, especially airports and roads.

Tourist attractions

Tourist attractions in cities take different forms. Historic monuments such as the Acropolis in Athens (see Fig. 2.6), the Tower of London or the Grand Palace in Bangkok (Fig. 7.37) are popular places to visit. Museums such as the Louvre in Paris or the Kunsthistorisches Museum in Vienna also attract some tourists, as do world-famous art galleries such as the Prado in Madrid or the Metropolitan in New York. Conference centres serve to attract increasing numbers of business visitors to cities and some cities, like Birmingham, have built major new facilities to develop this trade. Theatres, night clubs and entertainments generally also provide additional tourist attractions.

Problems aggravated by tourism

Large numbers of visitors arriving in working cities can add to problems that already exist. The most obvious examples are traffic congestion and air

Figure 7.37 Wat Phra Kaew (the Grand Palace), Bangkok

pollution. Tourist traffic increases the number of coaches, taxis and cars in the streets and their exhausts add to the atmospheric pollution. This has added to pollution in Mexico City, for example, now visited by 2m tourists a year.

Other problems aggravated by urban tourism include the difficulty and cost of parking, the litter problem, wearing away or damaging historic buildings and sites, and creating overcrowding in cafes, bars and restaurants. Overcrowding on public transport systems is also made worse by tourists – for example, on London's red buses and Underground railway and on Hong Kong's trams and MTR system.

Tourism in Beijing, China

Figure 7.38 Beijing

During the last decade, Beijing (Fig. 7.38) has become an increasingly popular tourist destination. In part, this is due to the government's policy of promoting international tourism as a way of obtaining much-needed foreign exchange; it also reflects the desire of many international tourists for 'new' and more exotic locations to visit. Almost all tours to China visit Beijing and most start or end there (Fig. 7.39).

Tourist attractions

The historic core of Beijing (Fig. 7.40) consists of the old walled city, within which is the Forbidden City of China's former emperors and their Imperial Palace (Fig. 7.41). Also within the old city are several large public buildings, the Mausoleum of Mao Zedong (the former communist leader) and assembly areas such as

Figure 7.39 Beijing Central Railway Station

the huge Tian'anmen Square (Fig. 7.42). This is the area in which tourists spend most time, visiting the Palace, museums, parks, squares and temples.

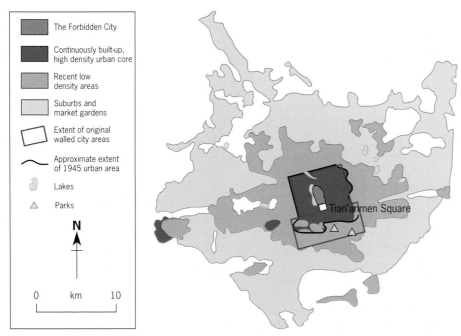

Figure 7.40 Urban structure of Beijing (*Source:* Burtenshaw, 1983)

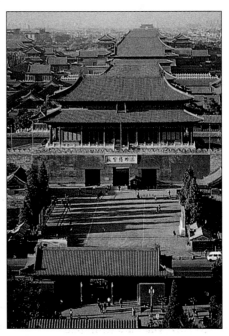

Figure 7.41 The Forbidden City, Beijing

The capital of one of the few remaining communist countries, Beijing has been developed since 1949 as a model socialist city. Its outer zones (Fig. 7.40) contain the more recently developed areas and include new lower-density residential areas, factories, offices and universities. The factory sector is largely confined to the east and south, in a planned attempt to avoid the spread of air pollution by the prevailing north-westerly winds. The outer zone includes satellite towns such as Shijingshan and Fengtai as well as suburbs, offices and intensively farmed market gardens.

Costs and benefits of tourism

Tourism in Beijing has brought both costs and benefits to the city, its inhabitants and the Chinese economy (Table 7.3).

Figure 7.42 Part of Tian'anmen Square, Beijing

Table 7.3 Costs and benefits of tourism in Beijing

Costs	Benefits
to Beijing's inhabitants increase in prices in city-centre shops	increase in employment opportunities (in construction, hotels, etc.)
loss of tranquillity in parks, gardens, museums and Imperial Palace	increase in demand for fresh produce (fruit, vegetables, animals) from market gardens and urban periphery
'alien' cultures, customs and values are introduced by foreign tourists	increasing opportunities to meet people from other cultures
inhabitants of some older housing forced to move; sites are redeveloped as hotels	
to Beijing's infrastructure water supply, electricity supply and sewage disposal placed under severe strain	income is available for improvements to the road network, the airport and the main railway station
historic buildings suffer from erosion (e.g. the steps of the Imperial Palace)	income is available for conserving buildings (e.g. the Imperial Palace, the Temple of Heaven)
hotels are built in the city centre instead of hospitals, schools, etc.	
tourist coaches, etc. add to traffic congestion and air pollution	
to China encourages excessive urban–rural migration (e.g. over 1000 people/week to Beijing)	more foreign companies invest in China
threat to Chinese culture as traditional forms of dance, etc. are overcommercialised	tourists bring much-needed foreign exchange to China

18a Which groups of people in Beijing (residents, shopkeepers, etc.) are most likely to benefit from the growth of tourism? Which groups are likely to be disadvantaged?
b How far do you agree with the view that the benefits of tourism to Beijing outweigh the costs and problems?

7.7 Transport

An efficient transport system, capable of moving people, materials and products quickly and cheaply, is the aim of all city planners, but is difficult to achieve in practice. Most cities experience large-scale transport problems, which can be seen in traffic jams, overcrowded trains and growing air pollution. Transport systems in cities are often inadequate to support people's ways of life both economically and socially. People's **mobility** (their ability to move from place to place) has been greatly reduced, and the **accessibility** of many places (the ease with which they can be reached) is decreasing. An extreme example of traffic problems can be seen in Mexico City (Chapter 2).

Transport in London

Figure 7.43 London

Resulting from the outward spread of homes and the persistence of city centre employment, journeys to work in London (Fig. 7.43) cause powerful morning and evening commuter flows. These surges of people move along roads (by car and bus) and rail networks. To these are added the many people seeking shopping facilities, entertainment and professional services in the city.

London's road transport problems include the slow speed of road traffic (less than 10 km/hr), large-scale traffic jams, air pollution and even gridlock (Fig. 7.44). Delays caused by traffic congestion are expensive. A 1995 CBI survey showed that businesses in the UK spend £37bn/year transporting goods, of which £15bn results from traffic congestion.

In the past, the London Underground system and the rail network proved quicker for travellers than road transport. However, a 1993 survey by University College London found that the journey times by car, bus, rail and Underground were about the same; massive overcrowding on the rail and Underground systems made them unpopular with many travellers. This makes it even harder to persuade people not to use their cars.

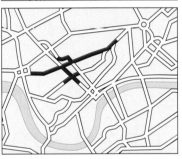

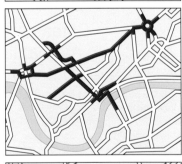

16.54

Rush hour. Major collision at junction of Cromwell Road and Earls Court Road

17.00

Junction completely blocked, the jam starts

17.10

Cars back-up at a rate of 6.6 km per hour. Warwick Road blocked

17.20

Hyde Park Corner jammed solid

17.30

Victoria at a standstill, cars entering area at 2200 per hour

Figure 7.44 Gridlock in central London: an example (*Source: The Guardian*, 14 May 1991)

Figure 7.45 Road traffic in the UK (*Adapted from: The Guardian*, 27 October 1994) (left)

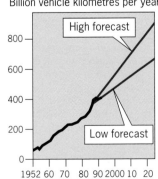

Carmageddon

Since 1965 the total UK road network has increased by 11% and traffic has grown by 153%.

Road traffic

Billion vehicle kilometres per year

Traffic facts

● 70% of households in Britain own at least one car. There are more than 20 million cars in use.

● There are 225 000 miles of British roads. Motorways make up less than 1% but carry 15% of all traffic.

● Car travel accounts for about 80% of personal travel. Eighty-nine out of every 100 business journeys and four in five of all shopping journeys over 2 miles are made by car.

● Since 1965, total road user taxation has risen from about £1 billion to an estimated £22 billion in 1993.

London's problems reflect the general UK trend towards car transport and the resultant massive increase in vehicle numbers (Fig. 7.45). However, large-scale road-building schemes – like the expansion of London's motorway ring road (the M25) – simply serve to release suppressed demand which rapidly fills the extra capacity. Until 1994, UK government policy favoured private road transport; more recently, however, attention has switched to improving public transport.

?

19a Draw a box diagram to show the main transport problems in cities like London.
b Draw a box diagram to show the main causes of these transport problems.

Solving urban transport problems

Many cities have introduced measures to try to solve their transport problems. These measures range from a complete ban on cars in city centres to the development of tighter controls on exhaust emissions and the development of new mass transit systems. It appears that there is no simple or single answer to the problems of urban transport. Rather, a combination of approaches is needed, and these may vary from city to city depending on the nature of specific local problems.

Figures 7.46–7.49 illustrate some of the approaches that have been either suggested or tried. Figure 7.50 points out that these approaches in turn generate further problems, especially in terms of access to transport by vulnerable groups such as the poor and the elderly.

Car bans pierce holes in urban smog blankets

Los Angeles, America's most polluted city, has begun a programme to reduce the infamous smog that blankets the city for four months a year. The primary target is the automobile, the pride and joy of most Angelinos. The city has a notoriously poor public transport infrastructure, but endless miles of highway

Since 1990, state and federal authorities have ordered progressively cleaner car exhausts. Every new car must be equipped with a catalytic converter and older cars must pass strict emission tests. Smog enforcement officers now use the latest technology, beaming infrared light across highways to detect carbon monoxide and hydrocarbon emissions from faulty exhausts.

By 1998, in an agreement with the motor industry, at least 2 per cent of new cars sold in the Los Angeles basin will be 'ZEVs' (Zero Emission Vehicles) – electric cars. Car manufacturers have fought the proposal, saying such vehicles are expensive and unworkable, but environmentalists have still

Cities across the globe are battling pollution, but some are more successful than others.

got 'ZEV Day' firmly marked on their calendars.

Measures to reduce the polluting power of the car are in place in parts of Europe and environmentalists say air quality has improved. In the Seventies, Freiburg, a city of 250 000 inhabitants on the edge of the Black Forest, was amongst the first German cities to restrict car use after acid rain began destroying the trees and threatened to undermine the forest's tourist trade.

A huge area of the city centre was turned into a pedestrian zone and almost all the rest has been 'traffic calmed'. Only 13 parking places were allowed for each 1000 of the population in the city centre. Trams, buses, walking and cycling are all heavily promoted.

Only one in 10 shoppers in the city centre uses a car, but trade has not been affected. Freiburg's 'environmental traffic management' programme is now being widely copied throughout Germany.

Large industrial cities are taking action too. In Athens, where up to 1000 deaths a year have been attributed to the *nefos*, a filthy smog that collects in the valleys, cars have been banned from a large part of the city centre this summer. This follows a scheme where cars with odd and even number plates were allowed in the city on alternate days. When a trial ban was enforced last year, pollution levels fell dramatically.

But many of the world's biggest cities have yet to take any action to reduce air pollution. And almost every large urban sprawl in the developing world – such as Bangkok, Jakarta, Manila, Bombay or Lagos – appears hopelessly mired in a pollution haze generated by permanent traffic jams, with no prospect of relief.

Figure 7.46 'Car bans pierce holes in urban smog blankets' (*Adapted from: The Observer*, 6 August 1995)

Manchester's supertrams: an alternative approach

The profitable Bury to Altrincham Metrolink recalls a leading Lancashire light of 19th century Utopianism

Manchester's new sleek grey Metrolink supertrams, which can travel at up to 100kph, have become the envy of many cities seeking to combat traffic congestion. Commuters and shoppers have now the option of travelling straight into the city centre by Metrolink from outlying centres such as Bury and Altrincham.

Research has shown 48 per cent of passengers had the chance of using a car, but preferred to leave it at home. Another major growth area came from young mothers with prams, and disabled people able to use the 'easy access' found at many stations. Metrolink stations are unmanned but controlled strictly. Every platform, ticket vending machine, lift, escalator and passenger emergency communications point is watched by video cameras, which also sweep strategic areas of track.

'We have been very, very pleasantly surprised by the number of letters and phone calls we've had, saying how safe people feel on the system,' said Mr Hibbert. 'Lone females feel safe travelling late at night, which I think is the touchstone of any system.'

The UK has yet to acquire the continental EC transport ethic, despite claims that supertram passengers from Altrincham take only 22 minutes in the rush-hour to reach Manchester city centre, compared with 52 minutes by car and 64 minutes by bus.

Figure 7.47 'Manchester's supertrams: an alternative approach' (*Adapted from: The Guardian*, 10 April 1993)

How to keep car drivers off the road

What can be done to encourage motorists to use more environmentally friendly modes of transport?

■ Transport consultant Bill Wyley argues that the cost of driving must be increased to control unsustainable traffic growth. He suggests that private car owners should pay a steep fee if they use motorways during the week, and commercial vehicles if they use them at weekends. He argues that most of the revenue raised should be ploughed into public transport to help fuel the resulting shift away from roads.

■ Transport 2000, the environmental pressure group, has devised an alternative transport package. The group wants Ministers to limit road spending to work on local bypasses and access roads and then to:

❑ Modernise London Transport services, which, it is claimed, would double the number of passengers within a decade.

❑ Introduce traffic-calming measures on 80 per cent of residential streets to encourage people to cycle or walk, rather than drive, distances of less than two miles – 80 per cent of all journeys.

❑ Introduce bus priority measures and frequent bus services to every town in Britain.

❑ Encourage a switch of freight from road to rail and water.

These measures, argues director Stephen Joseph, would result in less pollution, better access to facilities, less congestion and cleaner and greener cities.

■ Government scientists have warned that Britain's air quality has deteriorated dramatically as a direct result of traffic fumes. The introduction of punitive legislation, as in the United States, could help to reduce pollution levels. In the US, the world's leading 'car culture', new clean-air laws mean that state governments now face fines if they fail to meet national air quality targets.

Figure 7.48 'How to keep car drivers off the road' (*Adapted from: The Observer*, 17 October 1993)

Park and Ride schemes

Park and Ride schemes in the UK have been designed to persuade car drivers to leave their vehicles on the edges of cities and travel by public transport – usually bus – to the city centre. In this way, planners hope to reduce the numbers of cars in city centre streets.

The first successful daily Park and Ride scheme was introduced in Oxford in 1973, and is still functioning. By the mid-1980s, daily schemes were operating in Bath, Chester, Maidstone and Nottingham, as well as Oxford. In 1989, the Department of Transport calculated that road traffic would grow by between 83 per cent and 142 per cent between 1988 and 2025. This made it clear to planners in cities such as Bath and Bristol that it would be uneconomic to cater for traffic growth by building more roads. Local authorities therefore re-assessed their transport policies. Avon County Council published its Transport Plan in 1993, which put emphasis on discouraging car use in favour of encouraging walking, cycling and the use of public transport, with the development of Park and Ride being important in the latter.

Bath's first Park and Ride scheme was introduced over the Christmas period in 1981; it ran from the University of Bath to the city centre. In 1986 a daily service began from a purpose-built car park at Newbridge. This was followed by a Monday-to-Friday service from an upgraded site in Lansdown. Other Park and Ride schemes are planned (Fig. 7.49).

By 1999, 2800 people per week were travelling on the Lansdown service and 6700 on the Newbridge service. The Newbridge service is now so popular that demand exceeds the available car spaces, so much so that parked cars overspill on to surrounding roads. In total, some 250 car trips per day have been removed from the roads leading in to Bath, but there has been some increase in traffic on roads in the outer urban areas leading to the Park and Ride schemes.

Figure 7.49 Park and Ride schemes in Bath
Source: M. C. Cairns (1997) 'The Development of Park and Ride in Britain', Geography No. 354 Vol. 1.82 January p81–85. Fig. 2 p82.

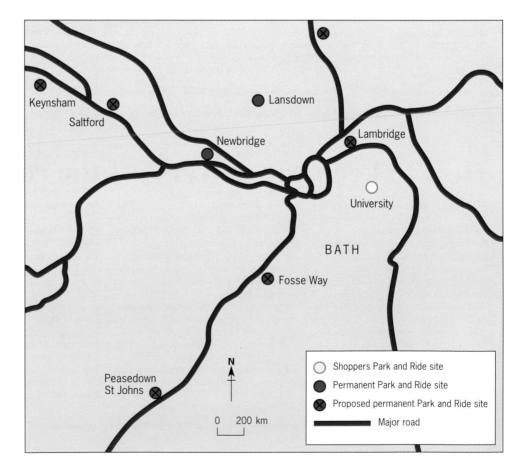

20 Study Figures 7.46–7.49.
a Make a list of the proposed solutions to urban transport problems, dividing them into the following categories: pollution control; vehicle control; public transport systems; pricing mechanisms.
b Identify the main advantages and disadvantages of each of these solutions. In each case, identify the groups of people that are likely to benefit/be disadvantaged.

'We need a car...'

If petrol rises to around £1 a litre and public transport becomes more convenient and reliable, the car will no longer be considered as king.

But Mr Snell, aged 45, said: 'I'm not sure if I could change my way of life. Over the past few years wages have been held in check. There's no way I would want road pricing schemes or anything that pushed up the costs. We need a car for shopping and, when I'm home, taking the kids to school.

'Without going into debt I don't think there could be much change for me. Yet I see the need for better public transport and less pollution. What do I do?'

Dorothy Whyte, aged 74, from Chiswick, west London, said: 'Putting petrol up might take people off the road but it will put other prices up.'

But she added: 'We'd have to keep ours even if things did go up. Our legs aren't as good as they were and a car gives us a sense of freedom.'

Figure 7.50 'We need a car...' (*Adapted from: The Guardian,* 27 October 1994)

Summary

- The economic bases of cities change over time and generate changes in the types and locations of employment within cities.
- The first wave of decentralisation was the movement of people away from the city centre into the suburbs.
- The second wave of decentralisation was the movement of manufacturing industry from the centre to the suburbs.
- Changes in the size and location of manufacturing industry in cities have major impacts on urban form.
- The informal sector is a very important part of many urban economies.
- The third wave of decentralisation occurred with the movement of some retailing from city centres to peripheral hypermarkets and out-of-town centres.
- Traditional city centre shopping areas have suffered from the growth of out-of-town centres, but are now fighting back through redevelopment projects.
- Office-based service industries are extremely important sectors of urban employment.
- City centre sites are attractive to offices because of the strength of their linkages.
- The fourth wave of decentralisation occurred with the movement of some offices away from city centres to the suburbs and edge-of-city sites.
- The growth of urban tourism produces both costs and benefits for local residents.
- Urban transport systems are often inadequate. This creates a range of social, economic and environmental problems.
- Proposed solutions to urban transport problems often create new and different problems.

8 Processes and planning

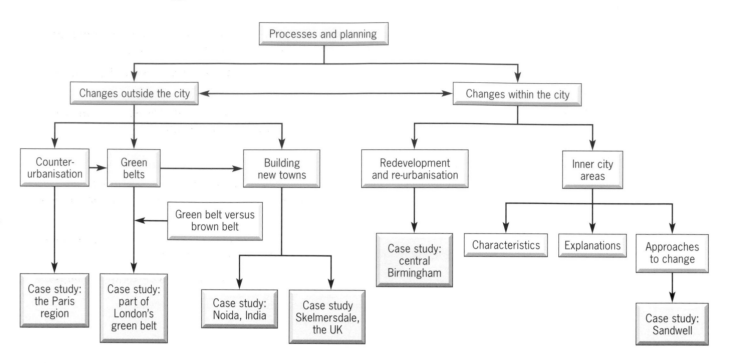

8.1 Introduction

This chapter focuses on recent changes in cities, in particular the processes of **counter-urbanisation**, redevelopment, re-urbanisation and planning. Counter-urbanisation is the process of population movement away from large cities to smaller towns, new towns and villages in the countryside. It has been a feature of large cities in EMDCs since the 1970s and is now being seen in newly industrialising countries (NICs) such as Brazil, Singapore and South Korea. Counter-urbanisation has had a big impact on both the large cities losing population and the small towns and villages in the countryside gaining population.

    Redevelopment, especially of city centres, has been one response by planners to try to halt, or reverse, the loss of population resulting from counter-urbanisation. Urban administrators and planners have tried to give their cities a facelift by redeveloping old-established central sites such as wholesale markets, railway stations and sometimes even industrial zones. Different approaches have been tried in different cities, but the general aim has been to revitalise the centre with new shops, services and homes to prevent more people moving away. In some cases, redevelopment work has been so successful that the city has started to grow again. This process is known as **re-urbanisation** (see Figs 1.14–1.15). A theme common to all these processes is the role of urban **planning**, and especially planning within the context of the urban region. Only in this way, it seems, can cities develop a momentum and structure to support them through periods of rapid change.

8.2 Counter-urbanisation

Counter-urbanisation was first recorded in the USA in the early 1970s when people began leaving large cities and moving out to smaller towns (sometimes new towns) and villages. This process is also sometimes called the **rural population turnaround**, because after years of population decline, rural

1 Study Figure 8.1.
a Make a copy of Figure 8.1 and shade in red the areas with a population increase of over 7 per cent between 1981 and 1991.
b Shade in blue the areas with a static or declining population between 1981 and 1991.
c Suggest reasons for these two patterns.

2 Compare your map with Figure 8.2. What relationships appear to exist between the changes you have mapped and the pattern of population density in 1991?

areas all over the world are now registering an increase in numbers. Census details for the last 25 years in countries like the UK, the USA and France show three main trends:

- a tendency for population to become more evenly spread across the national area as people move away from large urban concentrations;

- a decrease in the size of large settlements in the urban hierarchy as more people leave them;

- a **negative correlation** between population growth and settlement size – i.e. smaller settlements are growing faster than larger ones.

Causes of counter-urbanisation
There is no single, simple reason why people are leaving large cities and moving to smaller towns and villages. Rather, there is a combination of factors that include:

- improvements in transport, especially the construction of new motorways, and/or rail routes that enable longer-distance commuting;

- improvements in information technology such as faxes, e-mail and video-conferencing facilities;

- the growth of retirement migration;

Figure 8.1 Percentage population change in the UK, 1981–91   **Figure 8.2 Population density in the UK, 1991**

3a Explain how each of the causes listed on pp 128-30 contributes to the growth of counter-urbanisation in countries like the UK.
b Work in pairs to draw up a list of other possible reasons for the growth of counter-urbanisation.
c Which of the various explanations of counter-urbanisation do you think are the most important, and why?

4 Study Figure 8.3 and Table 8.1.
a Describe the pattern of the location of former residences of the people who moved to Liskeard between 1980 and 1995.
b Classify the main reasons for people leaving their original area into economic and non-economic reasons. Which seem to be the more important?
c Analyse the main reasons given for choosing the Liskeard area.

- government policies in some countries that are designed to encourage more people to live in rural areas;

- changing residential preferences amongst people of working age;

- the relocation of some offices, shops and factories to edge-of-city and greenfield sites;

- people's perceptions of the differences in quality of life between large cities and smaller towns and villages;

- improvements in health, education and social services in some rural areas.

Although the causes of counter-urbanisation will vary in individual cases, the process in general is an important one that will shape the form and function of many major cities. Counter-urbanisation affects both the large cities losing population and the towns and villages which receive an influx of population. As with all urban processes, both costs and benefits result – as can clearly be seen in the Paris region.

Table 8.1 People's reasons for leaving and for moving to Liskeard, Cornwall, 1980–95 (*Source*: 1995 sample survey)

	Reasons for leaving original area[a]	Reasons for choosing Liskeard area[a]
Required by employer	5	1
Voluntary move related to job or career	14	10
Unemployment	10	0
Housing	8	15
Change of lifestyle	21	22
Retirement	15	4
Family/health	8	10
Environment – social, physical	10	31
Other reasons	9	7

[a]Percentage of total sample

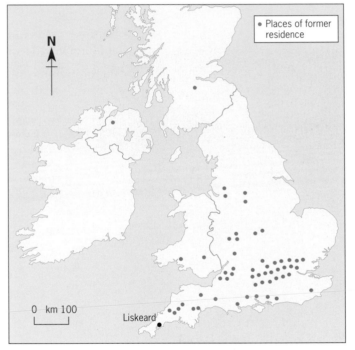

Figure 8.3 Places of former residence of people moving to Liskeard, Cornwall, between 1980 and 1995 (*Source*: 1995 survey data)

Counter-urbanisation in the Paris region

For much of recent history, Paris has attracted migrants from all over France – but particularly from its rural areas – and from other countries. However, a new trend became apparent in the 1970s when, for the first time, population began to decrease in the inner Paris area. By contrast, some of the fastest-growing areas were in the outer départements (administrative areas) of the Paris region.

The Paris region
The Paris region is made up of three main zones, Ville de Paris, Petite and Grande Couronne (Fig. 8.4).

Ville de Paris
The Ville de Paris (City of Paris) is the heart of the historic city containing most of the best known architectural monuments (Figs 8.5–8.6), cultural and

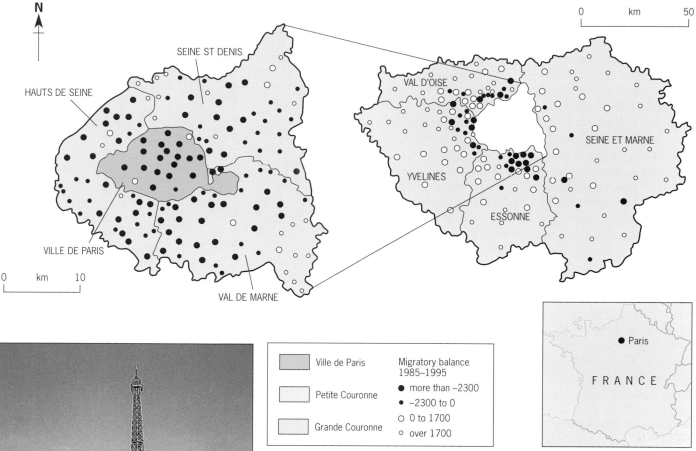

Figure 8.4 **The Paris region (*Based on:* Hull et al., 1988)**

Figure 8.5 **The Eiffel Tower, central Paris**

Figure 8.6 **L'Opéra Garnier, central Paris**

leisure facilities. It is also the business centre of the French economy and the location of the national educational and government institutions. Land values are extremely high and few people can afford to live in this area. Surrounding the historic core is a ring of 10 arrondissements (districts) whose housing and industry developed mostly between 1840 and 1914. These inner city areas have become run down and are in need of improvement and/or redevelopment.

Petite Couronne

Surrounding central Paris are the three inner suburban départements of Hauts de Seine, Seine St Denis and Val de Marne. Together, these comprise the Petite Couronne and consist of twentieth-century suburban development of flats, housing and industry. The Petite Couronne and the Ville de Paris together form the main built-up area of Paris.

Grande Couronne

The four départements of Val d'Oise, Seine et Marne, Essonne and Yvelines surround the two inner zones of Paris and, together with them, make up the Paris region. The outer zone, known as the Grande Couronne, is mostly farmland and forest, plus new towns such as Marne-la-Vallée and Cergy-Pontoise.

Population change, 1975–94

The population change between 1975 and 1994 in these three main parts of the Paris region can be seen in Figure 8.7. The population of the City of Paris fell from 2.3 million in 1975 to 2.0 million in 1994. Similarly, the population of the Petite Couronne fell from 3.9 million to 3.7 million over the same period. The decline in both areas was largely the result of inner city redevelopment. Slum areas were demolished in the 1970s to be replaced by office parks consisting of large high-rise blocks (e.g. La Défense) and cultural centres (e.g. the Pompidou centre). With high property values and rents, fewer people were able to afford to live in central Paris and many moved out to new towns, first planned as part of the Master Plan for Paris in 1976 (Fig. 8.8).

La Défense illustrates the nature of the redevelopment within the central and inner parts of Paris. Twenty-five tower blocks of offices, shops and apartments have been built. Over 20 000 people live here, linked by an express suburban railway and by the Metro to the city centre. However, in the construction of La Défense, 25 000 people were forced to move to other, usually outer, parts of the city and over 9400 buildings were demolished. In their place stand 1.3 million sq m of office space and 1.4 million sq m of apartments. Development still continues at La Défense with the building of the highest tower block in Europe, the Tour Sans Fin, which will be 1400 metres high when it is completed in 2001.

As more and more people left the two inner zones of the city between 1975 and 1994, the population of the Grande Couronne increased from 3.6 million to 4.8 million. The Paris Master Plan envisaged this growth as being concentrated in two 'development corridors', one to the north and one to the south of the River Seine (Fig. 8.8). Each of the growth corridors was planned to contain four new towns, each with a target population of 200 000. The new towns were to be separated by green open spaces such as the Plaine de Versailles. The two development corridors attracted most in-migration during the period 1975–94, and the new town of Marne-la-Vallée is developing rapidly into a Parisian garden city (Fig. 8.9). Marne-la-Vallée is situated 13 km east of central Paris. It has grown from 26 former villages, and now has six rapid express stations (RER), with four more

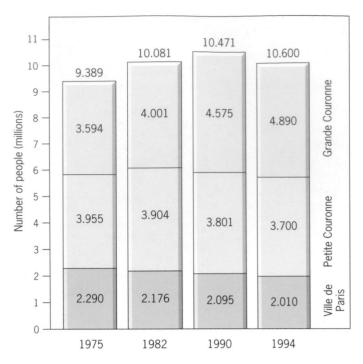

Figure 8.7 Population change in the Paris region, 1975–94 (*Source:* INSEE, 1995)

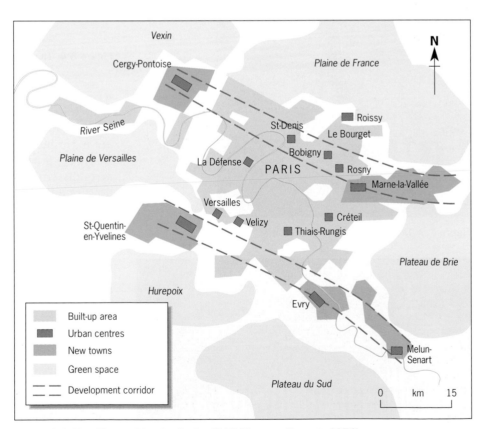

Figure 8.8 The Master Plan for Paris, 1976 (*Source:* Donert, 1974)

planned. It is also linked to the centre of Paris by the A4 motorway and a train de grand vitesse (TGV) station that opened in 1994.

Marne-la-Vallée is being developed in four main sectors (Fig. 8.9):

- Porte de Paris: the business centre, with a huge office development;

- Val Maubuée: an area with large parks, lakes, business parks and residential areas with pedestrianised streets, hypermarkets, schools and cultural centres;

- La Cité Descartes: the high-tech scientific centre based on electronics and computer technology; and

- Val d'Europe and Val de Bussy: with the EuroDisney theme park.

Marne-la-Vallée is typical of the newer towns that have grown up as people and industry have left the inner areas. By 1998, Marne-la-Vallée had over 1200 new firms employing 69 000 people. However, the newcomers have inflated property prices and their relatively affluent, car-based lifestyles have caused resentment in smaller villages whose shops and services have declined (Fig. 8.10).

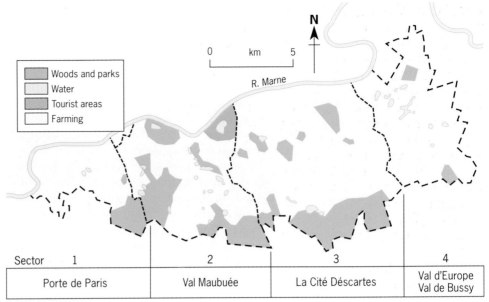

Figure 8.9 The four sectors of Marne la Vallée

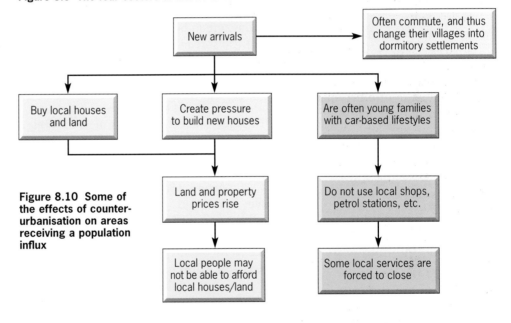

Figure 8.10 Some of the effects of counter-urbanisation on areas receiving a population influx

5a Using evidence from Figure 8.10 and the case study, draw up a table of the positive and negative effects of counter-urbanisation on towns like Marne-la-Vallée.

b Draw a diagram (similar to Figure 8.10) to illustrate some of the effects of counter-urbanisation on areas that have lost population, like central and inner Paris.

6 Study Table 8.2.

a Devise a graphical way to illustrate the population changes shown.

b Comment briefly on the patterns shown in your diagram, mentioning especially features such as cities with overall decline or growth and cities with the greatest/least inner city decline.

c How far do the cities in Table 8.2 seem to follow a pattern of population change similar to that of Paris?

Table 8.2 Percentage change in population in some major French cities, 1968–95 (*Sources:* Hull et al., 1988; INSEE, 1996)

	Urban region: overall percentage change			Inner area: percentage change		
	1968–75	1975–85	1985–95	1968–75	1975–85	1985–95
Lyons	3.6	−0.5	0.4	−11.1	−5.8	−1.2
Marseilles	5.9	0.9	−0.6	2.3	−3.9	−2.8
Lille	5.1	−0.1	−0.7	−8.8	−10.7	−5.2
Bordeaux	7.5	2.6	0.9	17.5	−6.7	−8.2
Toulouse	14.1	2.5	1.9	0.7	−8.1	−9.2
Nantes	11.8	2.5	2.1	−0.9	−6.2	−7.5
Nice	11.4	2.7	2.4	6.5	−2.3	−6.9

8.3 Green belts

As more and more people seek to leave large cities, there is enormous pressure for additional development in the **urban fringe** – that is, the area on the edge of, or just beyond, the built-up zone. Planners in cities all over the world realised that there was a risk of new urban developments eventually spreading and linking up with existing urban areas to create massive **urban sprawl**. Not only would this lead to the loss of valuable agricultural and recreational land, but it would create monster conurbations. To counter this tendency, **green belts** were established.

Green belts are areas around the perimeters of cities. They are made up of mostly open space – agricultural land and woodland – that is protected by planning controls from being built up. Green belts were designed to prevent further outward urban growth, but urban development sometimes leapfrogs over the restricted area and continues beyond it. The concept of green belts dates back to Greek and Roman times, but it was first applied in modern times in the UK, in the Greater London Plan of 1944. Within the plan, London's green belt was established together with a ring of new towns which were built beyond it. The aim of the new towns was to take people and industry from the bomb-devastated areas of inner London and re-establish them in completely new, planned settlements.

Today, green belts are generally recognised as having five main functions: to check the spread of further urban development; to keep neighbouring towns physically separate; to preserve the special character of towns; to assist in urban renewal; to provide an improved environment for recreation and leisure. In the UK, green belts cover 1.82 million hectares, or 12 per cent of the total land area (Fig. 8.11).

The green belt that surrounds a city (Fig. 8.12a) is only one variation on the theme of containing urban sprawl and providing access to open space. **Green wedges** (Fig. 8.12b) penetrate to the heart of a city, as in Copenhagen. **Green corridors** (Fig. 8.12c) have been created in Geneva to run straight through the city. The **green zone** (Fig. 8.12d) is similar to the plan proposed for open spaces in the Paris region. The **green buffer** (Fig. 8.12e) has been favoured in the Ruhr area of Germany to separate cities such as Essen, Bochum, Dortmund and Duisburg. In the Netherlands, a **green heart** (Fig. 8.12f) preserves open space in the centre of the urban region of the Randstad, and within the ring of cities from Amsterdam and Rotterdam to the Hague.

Figure 8.11 Major urban areas, green belts and new towns in the UK and Northern Ireland, 1988 (*Source*: Flint and Flint, 1989)

?

7 Study Figure 8.12. Outline the main advantages and disadvantages of each of the different approaches to 'green' planning described there.

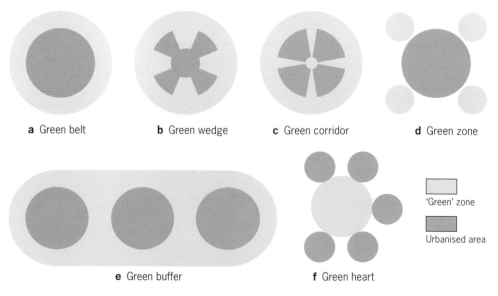

a Green belt   **b** Green wedge   **c** Green corridor   **d** Green zone

e Green buffer   **f** Green heart

'Green' zone

Urbanised area

Figure 8.12 Different types of green belt (*Source:* Burtenshaw, 1983)

Green belt problems in the UK

There is no doubt that green belts have had some success in containing urban sprawl in the UK. However, a recent report suggests that they may have outlived their usefulness and highlights the problems associated with them. Some of the most common problems are listed below.

- Much of the land in green belts is now actually **brown-belt** or **brownfield land** – that is, damaged or degraded land. As much as 20 per cent of London's green belt may consist of this type of land where sewage works, power stations, landfill sites and sand and gravel excavations are intermingled with abandoned, weed-ridden fields.

- Because green belts involve strict regulations on new or expanding industrial development, it has been speculated that jobs may have been lost as a result of prohibited developments. In the London area alone, it has been suggested that up to 100 000 jobs in manufacturing industry may have been lost since 1945.

- There is great pressure to release land within the green belt for housing, especially in attractive villages or sites close to transport links such as motorways, dual carriageways and railway stations.

- In some cases, developments such as the National Exhibition Centre near Birmingham (Fig. 8.13) have been allowed within green belts. Once this has happened, it increases the pressure for additional development close to that site.

- The existence of a green belt with its controls on development puts extra pressure on rural areas just beyond the edge of the green belt. Developers assess these areas with the intention of building housing estates, shopping centres and sometimes even whole new towns.

Figure 8.13 The National Exhibition Centre (left foreground) and Birmingham International Airport (right), in 1989

Part of London's green belt near Rickmansworth

Figure 8.14 shows a section of London's green belt located some 25 km to the west of the city centre. It is at the crossing-point of two key motorways, the M25 which circles the capital and the M40 leading to Oxford and Birmingham. There is intense pressure for the development of this area because of its proximity to the existing built-up area, to Heathrow airport (only 10km away) and Stockley Business Park. It is also an area in which the demand for leisure and recreational facilities is intense – as suggested on the map by the presence of a golf course, the museum and the aerodrome. Water-based recreational facilities are provided by the Grand Union Canal and some of the lakes along the Colne valley.

Local residents are already concerned about the number and extent of sewage works and industrial sites, especially in the valley-floor area. They are worried that there may be an increase in these brownfield land uses, with associated falls in house values.

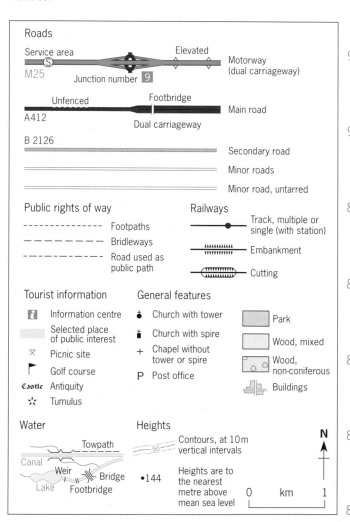

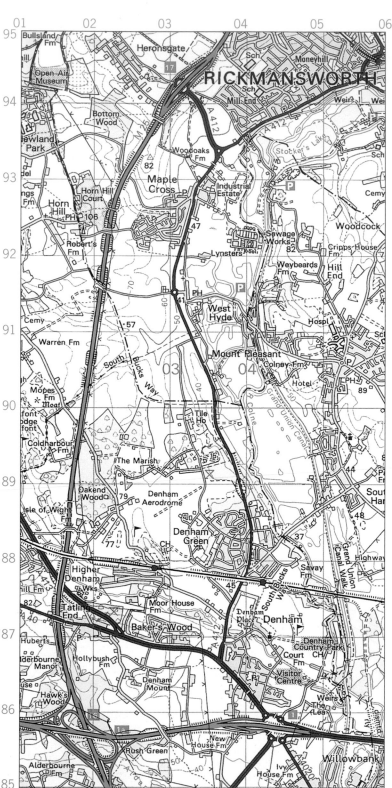

Figure 8.14 Extract from OS 1:50000, sheet 176

Being so close to two major motorways makes the villages in the area desirable sites for commuter housing, and there are regular applications for new housing schemes. The attraction of people and companies to the south-east continues to grow with developments such as the Channel Tunnel and Stansted and City airports. Many hi-tech companies in the London area already say that they have problems in recruiting staff as a result of housing shortages and high house prices. In a 1995 survey, 83 per cent of people in the London area said they wanted to retain green belts. However, in the same poll 55 per cent were also in favour of allowing more house building.

Some pressures on London's green belt are easing. For example, less land will be needed for farming and some sand and gravel quarries are nearing the end of their useful lives. One possible way of easing pressures on the green belt would be to use sites of former mineral workings for new housing, and to allow recreation and house building on low-grade farmland. The OS map extract (Fig. 8.14) and the questions will enable you to investigate some of these issues further.

?

8a Make a land use map of the area shown in Figure 8.14.
b Describe and explain the pattern shown on your map.
c Identify the main areas on your map with land uses that could create noise and pollution. Which of these do you feel are inappropriate to a green belt? Why?
d Outline the ways in which some of the problems of noise and pollution might be reduced in this area.
9a Locate a site on Figure 8.14 that you think would make a suitable location for a new hypermarket, to be used largely by shoppers with cars. Outline the reasons for your choice of this site in relation to factors such as: its accessibility to main roads and motorways; nearby land uses; slope and drainage.
b For the same site, outline the objections which would be raised by such a proposed development in London's green belt. Include factors such as recent trends in UK government policy towards green belts and hypermarkets, as well as the need to prevent the spread of brown-belt uses in the area.
10a Identify at least two grid squares on Figure 8.14 in which you think local planners might be willing to allow an expansion of housing. Your squares should be located on the edge of existing settlements where you think that new housing would not replace high quality farm land or re-creational open space. Now outline the case that a developer would put to justify development in one of the grid squares.
b Write a letter to the local press giving the objections that local people might have to this scheme.

8.4 Green belt versus brown belt

Figure 8.15 How brownfield land in the U.K. could be developed

The rapid development of land on the edge of large urban areas has created pressures on green belts in countries such as the UK, France and Germany. For example, in 1998, the UK government predicted that an extra 5.5 million new

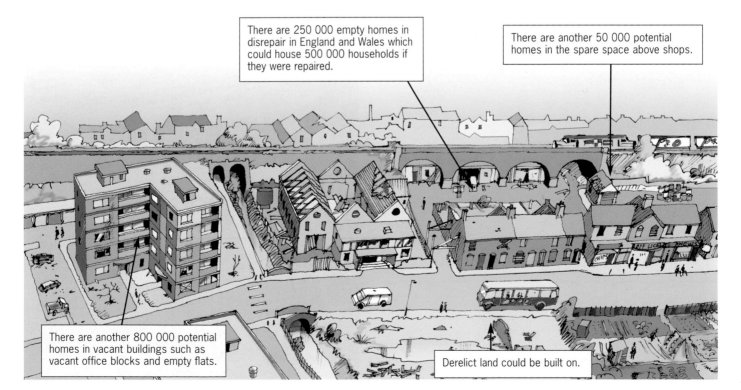

There are 250 000 empty homes in disrepair in England and Wales which could house 500 000 households if they were repaired.

There are another 50 000 potential homes in the spare space above shops.

There are another 800 000 potential homes in vacant buildings such as vacant office blocks and empty flats.

Derelict land could be built on.

homes would be needed by 2023. The homes would be needed because the number of single person households is growing, people are living longer and more people are migrating into south-east England. However, the government was keen to try and ensure that at least 60 per cent of the new homes were built on urban brownfield sites. Figure 8.15 illustrates some of the ways in which brownfield land in cities could be utilised.

House builders were far less keen for the majority of this new development to take place on brownfield sites. Brownfield sites are much more expensive to develop because the land is often polluted and so has to be reclaimed before it can be used. Also brownfield sites are often surrounded by derelict buildings and run-down estates, which again do not attract developers. However, these sites do have the advantage of existing infrastructure such as water, gas and electricity supplies, together with a road network. Developing brownfield sites would also help to reduce commuting and help to revive run-down parts of the urban environment. Greenfield sites, by contrast, are relatively cheap to develop, construction can take place quickly and the whole area can be planned from scratch. This has to be set against the loss of farmland, wildlife habitat and the tendency to encourage further urban sprawl.

8.5 Building new towns

One approach to the problems of pressures on the urban fringe and to the decay and dereliction in large cities has been to build new towns. New towns were an early solution to the problems of urban growth and have now been adopted in 71 countries (Figs 8.16–8.18). New towns are designed to be freestanding, self-contained and socially balanced urban centres. There are three main types of new town:

• New towns built to relieve overcrowding in cities and conurbations – for example, Telford in the UK, Jurong in Singapore and Noida in India.

• New towns built to develop new resources, especially minerals or timber. Noyabrsk and Tynda in Russia are in this group.

• New towns built to encourage people to settle in 'new' more remote parts of a country. Brasilia is in this group.

?

11a What are the main advantages and disadvantages of building new houses in the UK on
• brownfield sites and
• greenfield sites?
b What arguments would you advance to oppose developers who want to build on a greenfield site when they argue that there are not enough brownfield sites available?

Figure 8.16 Saltaire, England

?

12 Study Figures 8.16–8.18.
a What evidence is there on each photograph to show that the town was planned?
b What evidence is there on each photograph to indicate how long ago the town was planned?

Most new towns were designed on the basis of the **neighbourhood unit**. This is a small-scale residential unit in which it is hoped that people will feel 'at home'. The neighbourhood unit is large enough to form the catchment of a primary school, and to provide for the everyday shopping and welfare needs of the community. It is small enough for people not to feel isolated and lost. The design usually excludes through traffic, which is channelled out to ring roads.

Land uses in new towns are carefully planned to segregate housing from industry, and to provide easy access to green space for all the neighbourhood units. The town centre is usually a modern, covered shopping and office complex with bus and rail stations and associated car parks.

The case studies of Noida in India and Skelmersdale in the UK highlight some of the features and issues associated with the development of new towns.

Figure 8.17 Jurong, Singapore

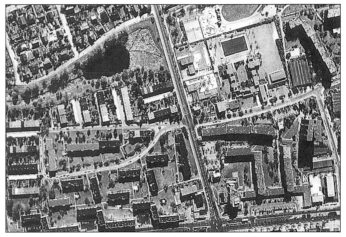

Figure 8.18 Skaaken, near Berlin

Noida: the New Okhla Industrial Development Area, India

Noida, the New Okhla Industrial Development Area, is a new town 12km south-east of New Delhi in India (Fig. 8.19). It covers 14 915 ha and was created in 1976 in an attempt to decentralise people and industry from New Delhi with its population of 5.9 million. It will provide homes at reasonable prices within a convenient distance of New Delhi and will house 5000 small industries that were operating illegally in the informal sector in New Delhi.

In the area covered by Noida, there are 50 pre-existing villages with a combined population of 42 000. Twenty-one of these villages will eventually be incorporated within the city – now about 70 per cent constructed. When finished, it will cover 20 per cent of the total project area. The remaining 80 per cent will be either green belt or agricultural land.

Figure 8.19 The location of Noida in India

13 Study Figure 8.20.
a Describe and explain the distribution of green belt land in Noida.
b Suggest possible reasons for the locations of small-scale and medium-scale industries in Noida.
c If Noida continues to grow and to attract people and industry away from New Delhi, which area of existing agricultural land do you think could be developed as a new sub-district? Make a tracing of Figure 8.20 and show the new sub-district centre and residential area.
d Explain carefully the reasons for your choice of sub-district location.

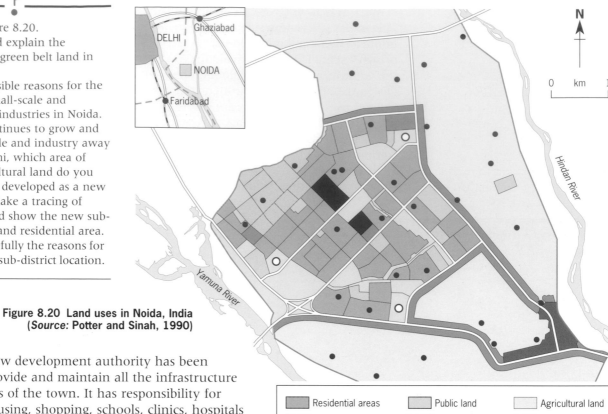

Figure 8.20 Land uses in Noida, India
(*Source:* Potter and Sinah, 1990)

A single new development authority has been formed to provide and maintain all the infrastructure and amenities of the town. It has responsibility for providing housing, shopping, schools, clinics, hospitals and services. In 1983 a Master Plan for Noida 2001 (Fig. 8.20) was drawn up that aimed to create a self-contained, socially balanced and well-designed community of 200 000 people by 1994 and of 500 000 by 2001. In order to achieve a socially balanced community, the development authority has built houses and flats for all income groups. Those for low-income groups are heavily subsidised by the Noida development authority (Fig. 8.21).

Noida is an example of a rapidly growing new town, founded on small-scale, informal sector industrial enterprises. The main phases of its development are summarised in Table 8.3. Its continued growth owes much to the government's desire to decentralise people and industries from New Delhi.

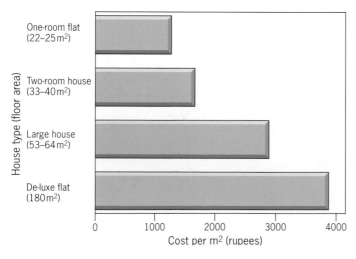

Figure 8.21 Housing in Noida, India
(*Source:* Potter and Sinah, 1990

Table 8.3 Phases in the development of Noida, India
(*Source:* Potter and Sinah, 1990)

Phase 1	1112 industrial sheds built. 4546 small industrial units built. By 1994 there were 3000 small firms in Noida, mainly in electronics, engineering and textiles. Aim to develop pollution-free enterprises.
Phase 2	125 medium- and large-scale factories built. Main banks and government departments opened offices.
Phase 3	449 units of the hosiery industry built covering 117 ha. Plans for establishment of film production centre. In order to remain within its 500 000 target, the Noida Authority restricts residential plots to members of the workforce and villagers forced to move when their land was acquired. This phase continues.

Skelmersdale new town, the UK

Skelmersdale new town is in Lancashire (Fig. 8.22), and houses some 42 000 people. It was planned in the 1960s as an **overspill town**, to take people and industry from the Merseyside conurbation.

Skelmersdale was designed as a series of 'villages' each separated from the others and from the town centre by an elaborate road and footpath network (Fig. 8.23). The footpaths take the longer, more decorative, planners' route, with the result that now residents walk on the roads to cut corners. The planners tried to re-create the street layouts of the industrial north, in the hope of building a sense of community spirit. Unfortunately, the results are that the view from one house is often the back of another; that people walk directly past each others' windows; and that houses open on to a complex warren of alleyways. Such a layout is ideal for vandals and almost impossible to police.

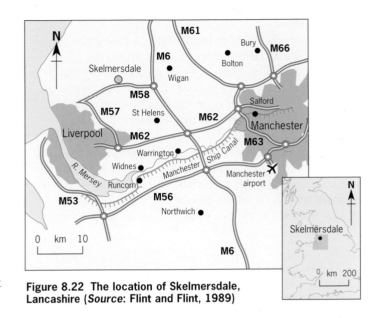

Figure 8.22 The location of Skelmersdale, Lancashire (*Source*: Flint and Flint, 1989)

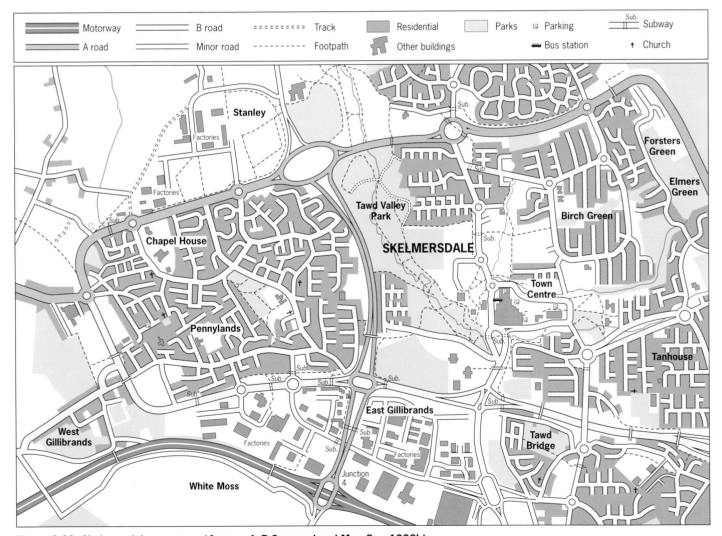

Figure 8.23 Skelmersdale new town (*Source*: A–Z Geographers' Map Co., 1996b)

Most of the houses and flats (Fig. 8.24) were poorly built and flat roofs leaked from the early days. Damp is a major problem in many houses and flats, causing carpets to rot and patches of black and green mould to form on walls.

The large estates were built with shopping parades, parks, pubs and community centres. However, the planned hospital was never built and key stores such as Marks & Spencer never moved into the town centre. Worse still, the factories, which had opened in the 1970s with government grants, were hit hard by economic recession in the 1980s. Most factories and many shops closed (Fig. 8.25) and unemployment rose. Skelmersdale never was self-sufficient in employment, and some people had always been forced to commute to work in Liverpool, Wigan or St Helens. However, factory and office closures in these areas in the 1980s

Figure 8.24 Housing in Skelmersdale

added to Skelmersdale's unemployment problem. The result was that by 1995 over 40 per cent of adults aged16–60 in Skelmersdale were unemployed.

Many people now feel trapped in Skelmersdale because they cannot afford a car to visit neighbouring towns. The existence of a 'captive' local population often results in high prices in the town's shops. The overall picture is one of high unemployment, few job opportunities and poor local medical, transport and educational services.

?

14 Compare approaches to new town development and problems in Noida and Skelmersdale under the headings: location; reasons for establishment; design and layout; provision of accommodation; employment changes; provision of services; and other issues or problems.

Figure 8.25 Boarded-up shops in Skelmersdale

8.6 Globalisation, redevelopment and re-urbanisation

The era of new town building is mainly over. In most EMDCs, attention in the 1980s and 1990s has swung to the need to revive and redevelop large cities. The aim has been to stop the loss of population, industry and employment by redeveloping the city, tackling housing problems and upgrading the city's image (see Figs 1.14–1.15). However, this redevelopment has had to take place within the context of the increasing **globalisation** of urban economies.

Globalisation is the process by which all cities have become part of the global capitalist economy. An important feature of globalisation is the mobility of investment, which can be switched from Europe to Asia to Latin America in a very short time. All cities, including cities in EMDCs, seeking to redevelop their economies and their built environments have to be able to attract this mobile investment.

Another feature of globalisation is the shift from manufacturing industry to service-based employment. For this reason, cities like Birmingham, which in the 1980s experienced serious economic difficulties as old industries declined,

Figure 8.26 New office buildings adjacent to Snow Hill Station, central Birmingham

Figure 8.27 Frankfurt book fair

have struggled to attract new service industries (Fig. 8.26) to compensate for the loss in manufacturing employment.

Re-imaging cities

Cities had to market themselves during the 1990s in order to attract investment. The idea of marketing cities is not new – many UK cities promoted themselves in Victorian times. Rather than simply advertise a city's virtues, modern place marketing tries to re-image the city – that is, to develop a new image for it. We can see this in the range of special events taking place in major cities worldwide, including festivals, trade fairs (Fig. 8.27) and conventions.

City advertising often goes hand-in-hand with the creation of a new urban landscape by the demolition of derelict factory sites and the construction of shopping malls, science parks and cultural and conference centres. Accompanying these developments there is often a growth of leisure and entertainment facilities as well as tourist attractions and business services. The aim is to provide cities with a new economic infrastructure geared to the needs of a **de-industrialised economy** (following the loss of manufacturing industry).

The re-imaging of cities in the UK involves an alliance of local city councils with private investors and developers. The role of some city councils has now expanded beyond the provision of education and welfare services to a more outward-oriented stance designed to attract investment from abroad. Consequently, the public sector has now taken on some of the features that were once seen as characteristic of the private sector – for example, risk-taking, inventiveness, promotion and leadership. City councils of this type are called **entrepreneurial**. They work to co-ordinate development between private investors and councils in order to attract external investment into the city that will benefit both local businesses and local councils. The degree to which this strategy is successful in attracting new jobs and additional investment, and in rebuilding the city, can be seen in the case of Birmingham.

?

15 Study a large city in your area which has undergone significant recent change.

a Draw a map to locate each of the changes you have identified (e.g. new shopping centres, business parks, office parks, new hotels, redevelopment in the CBD).

b For each change, find out: the previous land use; the reason(s) for the change; and its effect(s) on local people and the city as a whole. (You may need to refer to local newspaper cuttings – these are usually available in the reference library.)

c How far do you think the changes will help to make the city more attractive to foreign investment?

Redevelopment in central Birmingham

The loss of 191 000 jobs, mostly in manufacturing industry, between 1971 and 1986, encouraged Birmingham to seek new ways to create jobs. In its Economic strategy for Birmingham document for 1986, the council focused on two main strategies to generate jobs:

• fostering business tourism; and
• the creation of a new international city image.

In 1983, Birmingham had already taken the first step along this route by establishing the Aston Science Park (Fig. 8.28) next to Aston University. This alliance of the public (council) and private (university) sectors is an early example of what in the USA is called a **growth coalition** – that is, the interaction of the public and private sectors, together with the external promotion of the city and a commitment to **flagship schemes** (high-profile developments). As a result of its commitment to such entrepreneurial activities, Birmingham's financial investment in schemes of this type grew six-fold between 1981 and 1991.

Creating a new urban landscape

After 1986, image-building investment was concentrated in the central core which was seen as the key to stimulating and attracting investment (Fig. 8.29). Flagship projects included the International Convention Centre (see Fig. 7.35), opened in 1991. The aim of the city council was to create an urban space that was safe, visually exciting, pleasurable and profitable in order to attract potential investors. The designs of all Birmingham's flagship schemes are post-modern and re-employ past images and styles that are combined in new ways to integrate within each individual **townscape** (Figs 8.26 and 8.30).

Figure 8.28 Aston Science Park, Birmingham

The Heartlands initiative

The Heartlands scheme is an Urban Development Corporation initiative (see section 8.9) in the form of a partnership between the city council and five national development companies. The aim is to redevelop an 890 ha site of derelict and contaminated industrial land in the north-eastern part of the inner city, close to the city centre (Fig. 8.31). Heartlands has co-ordinated the redevelopment which includes improvements to the infrastructure, the development of campus-style

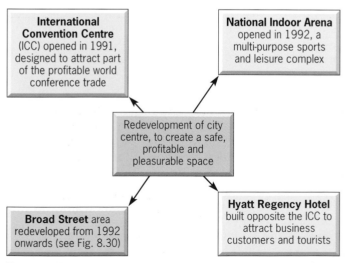

International Convention Centre (ICC) opened in 1991, designed to attract part of the profitable world conference trade

National Indoor Arena opened in 1992, a multi-purpose sports and leisure complex

Redevelopment of city centre, to create a safe, profitable and pleasurable space

Broad Street area redeveloped from 1992 onwards (see Fig. 8.30)

Hyatt Regency Hotel built opposite the ICC to attract business customers and tourists

Figure 8.29 Redevelopment projects in Birmingham's central core

Figure 8.30 Gas Street Basin, Birmingham

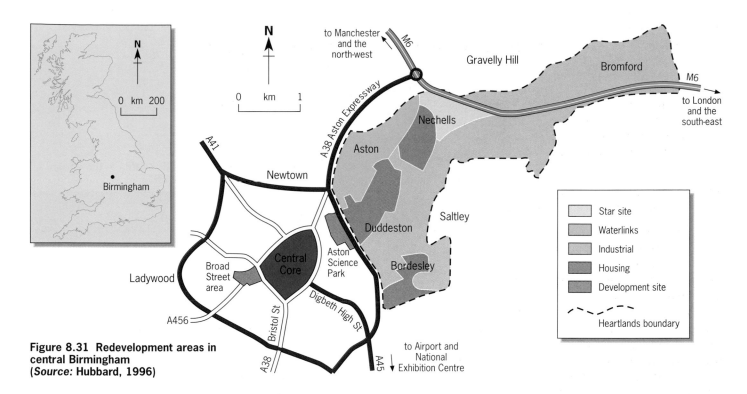

Figure 8.31 Redevelopment areas in central Birmingham (*Source:* Hubbard, 1996)

offices and the construction of a small amount of housing. Within Heartlands, there is a series of smaller initiatives each with its own character. The Waterlinks area, for example, is centred on the Birmingham–Fazeley canal and is a series of business parks and office developments with a lot of on-site parking and a variety of amenities.

Present problems

Large parts of the **urban fabric** of central Birmingham have been rebuilt, but other problems have been created. A survey in 1993 showed that conditions in some of the worst-off parts of the city had deteriorated because investment had been directed into the flagship projects.

New jobs were created within the Broad Street Redevelopment Area, but many are poorly paid and/or are part-time posts in hotels and nightclubs. The number of new jobs created in the Heartlands area by 1993 was small. Many of the firms that moved into Heartlands were simply relocating there from another part of the city. Birmingham has had some success in stimulating office employment in the central core, but faces strong international competition from other business centres in Europe, including Frankfurt, Lille, Marbella and Milan.

16a Why and how has Birmingham tried to redevelop its central areas?
b How successful do you think that Birmingham's redevelopment has been?
c How successful do you think it will be in the longer term?

8.7 Inner city areas

Inner city areas, in the UK, are areas of older – often nineteenth-century – residential and industrial development, lying between the central business district (CBD) and the suburbs of major cities. In the UK, about 4 million people live in inner city areas which are often described as having the following characteristics:

- Population decline: people of working age and with job skills tend to move out of inner city areas in search of work and better living standards.

- Economic decline: there are limited and decreasing job opportunities as factories and offices close (Fig. 8.32). Inner city areas generally fail to attract new industries because of their problems of dereliction and decline.

17 Study Table 8.4.

a From the table, select six indicators to represent the range of social and economic deprivation in Coventry.

b Explain the reasons for your choice of indicators.

c Rank each indicator from high to low in relation to deprivation, such that a rank of 1 is very deprived and 18 is not very deprived. Think carefully about each indicator as you assess it.

d For each ward in the city, add the six ranks together to produce a total rank score.

e Divide the total rank scores into six classes.

18a On a copy of Figure 8.34, draw a **choropleth map** to show the range of rank scores for deprivation.

b Describe the pattern of deprivation shown on your map. In particular, can you identify an inner city area with multiple social and economic deprivation? Are there other areas of the city with similar severe patterns of deprivation?

c What do you think are the causes of these patterns?

Figure 8.32 Derelict industry in Birmingham

Figure 8.33 Graffiti at the entrance to 1960s flats

- Physical and environmental change: conditions include much derelict land, vandalised and empty buildings, poor quality housing dating from either the nineteenth century or the 1960s (Fig. 8.33), and a marked lack of open space.

- An increase in poverty and deprivation: social conditions include a higher than average percentage of the poor, the elderly, the unskilled, ethnic minorities, single-parent families and the homeless. Inner city areas are often areas of multiple social and economic deprivation.

Table 8.4 Population change and selected socio-economic indicators for Coventry wards, 1991 (*Source:* HMSO, 1993)

	Percentage population change 1981–91	Percentage of persons in households with NC-born head[a]	Percentage unskilled workers	Percentage unemployed	Percentage households with no car	Percentage households without indoor WC	Percentage households owner-occupied	Percentage households renting from private landlord
Bablake	−6.1	1.7	6.5	10.2	33	0.2	80	7
Binley & Willenhall	+7.2	3.1	5.8	16.2	41	1.1	47	6
Cheylesmore	−7.3	5.9	6.1	12.5	34	1.1	81	11
Earlsdon	−11.5	3.6	2.1	8.1	27	1.4	83	12
Foleshill	−18.2	50.9	16.1	24.2	61	6.9	58	29
Henley	−8.1	3.7	8.6	18.2	45	0.4	47	6
Holbrook	−4.2	12.1	7.8	14.1	41	3.9	72	13
Longford	−7.1	10.9	8.9	15.9	46	6.2	63	11
Lower Stoke	−12.2	7.4	9.1	15.1	47	2.0	70	8
Radford	−12.6	12.1	12.2	18.3	51	3.8	52	14
St Michaels	−17.2	30.0	12.9	24.1	67	6.4	46	26
Sherbourne	−10.1	3.1	5.2	12.0	39	1.1	82	11
Upper Stoke	−11.1	12.2	8.4	16.2	51	3.2	70	10
Wainbody	+5.9	2.6	1.7	5.9	14	0.3	93	4
Westwood	−11.6	1.4	7.9	17.1	42	1.1	53	6
Whoberley	−11.2	3.6	4.2	13.4	39	2.4	85	10
Woodlands	+0.4	1.1	4.0	12.2	31	0.3	69	8
Wyken	+7.8	6.1	4.9	10.1	32	0.6	75	5

[a] New Commonwealth

Figure 8.34 The city of Coventry, showing ward boundaries (*Source:* Matthews, 1991)

Table 8.5 Percentage change in population in inner city areas of UK conurbations, 1961–91 (*Sources:* Matthews, 1991; HMSO, 1993)

	1961–71	1971–81	1981–91
London	–13.5	–17.6	–18.2
Birmingham	–8.3	–17.6	–19.1
Liverpool	–18.3	–26.6	–14.5
Manchester	–16.8	–24.5	–20.1
Newcastle	–17.8	–18.0	–19.7

Population decline

Inner city areas began losing population in the period 1951–61, but the effects of such losses were masked by high birth rates. However, after 1961 birth rates began to decline and the population losses became much more apparent (Table 8.5). Inner London, for example, lost over 1 million people between 1961 and 1991.

The main causes of population decline in inner cities were:

Improvements in transport

These allowed more workers to live further from their place of work and commute. In 1961, 30 per cent of UK households owned a car; by 1991, this figure had risen to 65 per cent.

Slum clearance and redevelopment

The aim of slum clearance and redevelopment schemes was to improve housing conditions in inner city areas. **Comprehensive Development Areas** (CDAs) were designated (Fig. 8.35), within which wholesale demolition took place prior to redevelopment. Residents had to move out of their homes before work began and not all were able to return because, after rebuilding, housing densities were usually much lower (Table 8.6).

The attraction of suburban lifestyles

The suburbs offered the promise of greater space and less pollution. There was a boom in new house building on cheap edge-of-city land, and this encouraged movement away from the inner cities.

Very serious job losses

Glasgow, for example, lost 60 000 jobs between 1961 and 1971, and London lost 243 000 jobs during the same period. Some writers have debated whether factory closures and job losses were a cause of people leaving inner city areas, or a result of a process that had already started. Probably it was a combination

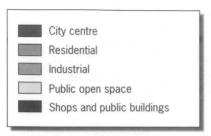

■	City centre
■	Residential
■	Industrial
□	Public open space
■	Shops and public buildings

Figure 8.35 Comprehensive Development Areas in Birmingham, 1975 (*Source*: Parke, 1975)

19a Use the data in Table 8.6 to draw **pie graphs** of the changing land use in Birmingham's Comprehensive Development Areas.

b Analyse the changes in land use within each CDA, outlining the main effects of the changes on people and on the environment.

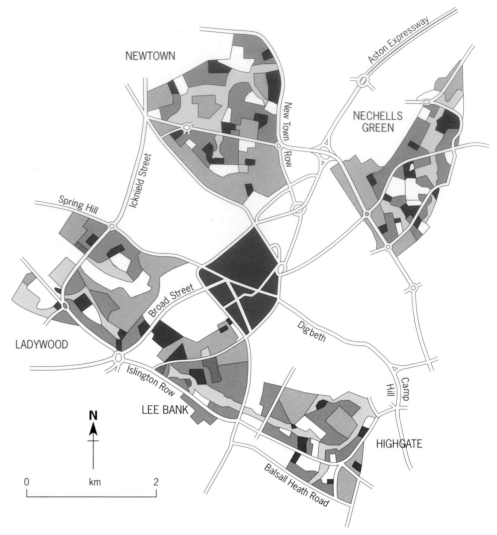

Table 8.6 Population change and percentage land use change in Birmingham's Comprehensive Development Areas (CDAs), 1949 and 1970 (*Source*: Birmingham Planning Department)

	Newtown		Nechells		Ladywood		Lee Bank		Highgate	
	1949	1970	1949	1970	1949	1970	1949	1970	1949	1970
Percentage of total land use										
Residential	41	26	44	30	48	30	45	24	43	29
Industrial	30	30	24	24	21	21	24	21	22	21
Open space	2	16	1	16	1	17	0	13	4	17
Others (public buildings, roads)	24	18	28	20	28	23	29	35	28	19

Population of CDAs	1949	1970
Newtown	28 125	15 400
Nechells	19 072	12 537
Ladywood	24 418	12 448
Lee Bank	14 797	6 531
Highgate	16 484	10 081

of the two. However, the results were dramatic because the loss of population was selective. Usually the younger, more skilled and more enterprising people left first, leaving behind an ageing population – often with low skills – to face serious problems in achieving a decent standard of living.

Not all migration in the period 1951–91 was away from UK inner city areas. From 1951 until the 1970s, there was an influx of new arrivals from the Caribbean, India, Pakistan and parts of Africa. Although members of these ethnic groups formed only 4 per cent of the total UK population in 1991, they do form significant concentrations in some inner city areas. For example, in Birmingham in 1998 ethnic minorities made up 42 per cent of the total population of inner city areas.

Economic decline

Inner city areas in the UK have experienced massive factory closures and job losses (Table 8.7 and Fig. 8.36). In some inner city areas, manufacturing industry has ceased to exist. The UK overall has experienced a serious decline in manufacturing jobs since 1951, but inner cities have borne the brunt of the losses, with a decline of more than 50 per cent (over 1.5 million jobs) between 1951 and 1995. The few gains in service industries have not made up for these losses. Inner cities have also seen the growth of part-time, low-paid female jobs (e.g. in restaurants and shops) at the expense of full-time male employment. Many of the men made redundant in inner cities were often unable to find other jobs.

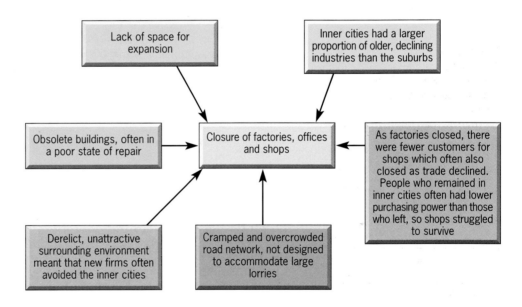

Figure 8.36 Reasons for economic decline in UK inner city areas

Table 8.7 Percentage change in employment in UK inner city areas, 1951–91 (figures in percentages) (*Source*: HMSO, 1993)

		Inner city areas	Overall
Total employment	1951–61	+1.0	+70.0
	61–71	–14.8	–1.3
	71–81	–14.6	–2.7
	81–91	–15.2	–3.1
Manufacturing	1951–61	–8.0	+5.0
	61–71	–26.1	–3.9
	71–81	–36.8	–24.5
	81–91	–39.2	–29.2
Private services	1951–61	+11.0	+14.0
	61–71	–15.3	+4.2
	71–81	–6.4	+14.4
	81–91	–5.7	+15.6

Figure 8.37 A tower block (now demolished) in the Kinghold estate, Hackney, London

Physical and environmental change

UK inner city areas typically consist of a mixture of some remnants of nineteenth-century industrial buildings and housing, together with some 1950s and 1960s redevelopment. Each of these two types of area has its own particular challenges.

The areas of nineteenth-century development often consist of boarded-up shops, houses and factories, intermixed with derelict land and old terraced houses. The housing that remains is often privately rented and is frequently overcrowded.

The 1950s and 1960s housing estates often include tower blocks of flats (Fig. 8.37), some of which have proved to have serious problems. Often the construction was of poor quality and the buildings have deteriorated with the passage of time. Some flats suffer from problems of condensation and dampness. They lack soundproofing and are poorly insulated and therefore expensive to heat. Residents on upper floors have to rely on lifts for access – particularly parents with prams and pushchairs, and the elderly. Frequently, the lifts break down or are vandalised, and vandalism in the corridors and stairwells is also common. Many residents are afraid of being mugged and the elderly and the infirm often feel trapped in their flats. There are few if any play areas for younger children, and no community facilities for young people or for the elderly.

The growth of poverty and deprivation

Inner city areas in 1991 housed about 7 per cent of the UK population, but they contained:

- 15 per cent of all unskilled workers;

- 33 per cent of all **New Commonwealth** residents;

- twice the national average of single-parent families; and

- three times the national average of long-term unemployed people.

However, it would be wrong to assume that all people in UK inner city areas are poor, or that all deprived people live only in inner city areas (see Chapter 5). Nevertheless, inner cities do contain serious problems of poverty and deprivation – as is shown by Figure 8.38, for example, in which the wards of Birmingham have been ranked from best to worst around five indicators of social deprivation.

?

20a Many of the 1950s and 1960s tower blocks are daubed with graffiti and neglected by the same people who before had taken care of their small, nineteenth-century terraced houses. Suggest possible reasons for this change in people's attitudes and behaviour.
b In the 1970s, it would have been cheaper to refurbish some of the old nineteenth-century terraced houses than to rebuild the area with tower blocks of flats. Suggest possible reasons why this did not happen.

21 Study Figure 8.38.
a Describe the pattern of social deprivation shown, paying particular attention to the location of the two types of most seriously deprived area.
b How far does the map suggest that Birmingham needs to widen its attempts to reduce deprivation beyond the inner city areas?

Deprivation index based on:
Male unemployment
Persons in household with New Commonwealth or Pakistani head
Overcrowded households
Social classes IV and V
Young, single-person households.

High ↑ Low

Figure 8.38 Social deprivation in Birmingham, 1991 (*Sources:* Matthews, 1991; HMSO, 1993)

Sutton Four Oaks
Oscott
Kingstanding
Sutton Vesey
Sutton New Hall
Perry Barr
Sandwell
Erdington
Stockland Green
Kingsbury
Handsworth
Soho
Aston
Washwood Heath
Hodge Hill
Shard End
Ladywood
Nechells
City centre
Yardley
Smallheath
Sparkbrook
Acocks Green
Sheldon
Quinton
Harborne
Edgbaston
Sparkhill
Fox Hollies
Bartley Green
Selly Oak
Moseley
Weoley
Bournville
Brandwood
Hall Green
Northfield
Kings Norton
Billesley
Longbridge

N

0 km 5

8.8 Explanations of the UK inner city problem

In the years after 1945, several different attempts were made to explain the nature and problems of inner city areas in the UK and the challenges they presented (Fig. 8.39). These explanations are important because they made a major contribution to the different development policies that have since been applied within inner city areas (section 8.9).

Explanations based on the quality of the built environment
Explanations based on the quality of the built environment were among the earliest to be suggested. First put forward in the 1940s and 1950s, these explanations regarded poor housing and the general run-down nature of the built environment as the principal challenges. The aim was to rebuild whole communities by means of large-scale slum clearance and planned comprehensive redevelopment schemes.

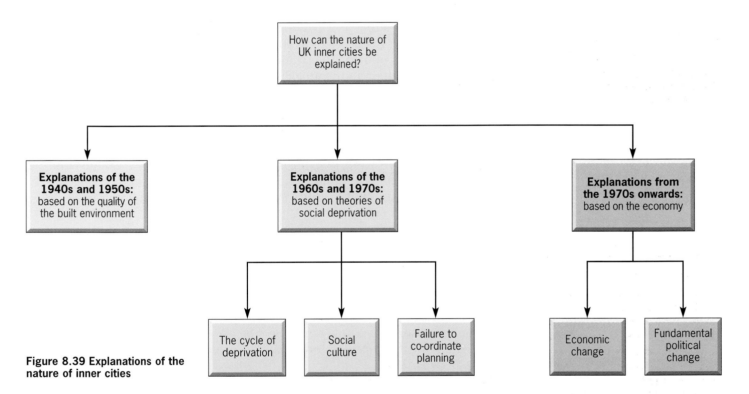

Figure 8.39 Explanations of the nature of inner cities

Explanations based on social deprivation
In the 1960s and 1970s, three further explanations were advanced, focusing on different aspects of the social deprivation apparent in UK inner city areas. These explanations concentrated on the challenges presented by particularly deprived groups or areas within the inner city and so are called area-based. The aim was to target special help to specific groups and parts of the inner city. The three main theories are discussed next.

The cycle of deprivation
This explanation argues that many inner city families experience severe poverty as a result of low wages or unemployment. This in turn leads to poor, often overcrowded, living conditions that frequently lead to ill health and so to poor school attendance. This in turn may lead to groups of people with poor skills whose chances of finding work become weaker. The whole process becomes a downward **cycle of deprivation**. The aim was to devise policies aimed at breaking this cycle by, for example, giving educational support.

Figure 8.40 Derelict pavilion in an inner city park, Walsall, West Midlands

?

22a For each of the explanations shown in Figure 8.39, outline: the perceived challenge; the aims of the policy; and the means by which these aims were to be achieved.
b Assemble evidence from this chapter in support of the view that inner city problems are inevitable in a capitalist society. How far do you agree or disagree with this view? Give your reasons.

Figure 8.41 Liverpool International Garden Festival, 1985

Social culture

This explanation argues that in inner city areas, anti-social attitudes may be passed on within families from one generation to the next. If one family member's lifestyle involves crime or vandalism, for example, other members of the same family may follow his/her example. The aim was to provide better social education for both children and adults.

Failure to co-ordinate planning

This explanation sees the challenges of inner city areas as stemming from a failure to bring together effectively the wide range of different agencies and departments working to improve conditions. Uncleared sites, derelict land and abandoned buildings, for example, are seen as evidence of planning failure (Fig. 8.40). The solution was seen to entail greater co-ordination between the various agencies working in inner city areas in the UK.

Explanations based on the economy

From the 1970s onwards, two further explanations were offered. Groups of researchers believed that area-based policies were unlikely to work because they simply moved the problem to another part of the city. These researchers saw the challenges of urban deprivation as a product of low income and a lack of wealth. The solution to the problem was thought to lie in the provision of employment. Two main views developed.

Economic change

One group of researchers saw inner city challenges as being the result of broader economic trends such as **restructuring** (investing in new goods and services), **re-organisation** (moving away from old inner city locations) and **rationalisation** (concentrating production in fewer, larger units). Hence the solution was seen as the provision of greater financial help to inner cities, in order to make them more attractive to industry.

Fundamental political change

Another, Marxist, group of researchers argued that inner city challenges were the result of the capitalist system of production. This in turn meant that large manufacturing industries in cities only profited by being able to create a pool of cheap, unskilled, expendable local labour together with cheap land. These resources of labour and land could be used or discarded in relation to economic cycles of boom or bust. These researchers believed that conditions in inner cities could only be improved by replacing a capitalist system with a socialist system of production.

8.9 Approaches to meeting the UK inner city challenge

There have been many attempts to improve the physical and social conditions within inner city areas in the UK. The first schemes, which began in the early twentieth century, concentrated on slum clearance. Later, in the 1960s and 1970s, Labour governments began the Urban Programme – a strategy designed to bring together central and local government in partnership to improve inner city areas. The Conservative governments of the 1980s began a series of initiatives such as City Action Teams (CATs) – which consisted of civil servants delegated to deal with inner city areas – and Task Forces – groups designed to develop bigger projects such as garden festivals (Fig. 8.41).

The two groups of projects with the highest profiles in the 1980s and 1990s were Enterprise Zones (EZs) and Urban Development Corporations (UDCs). EZs and UDCs were given extensive powers within their areas, largely

Figure 8.42 Waterside redevelopment, Cardiff Bay area

Figure 8.43 A new factory building, Cardiff Bay area

bypassing the usual local authority planning controls. After some initial success, many ran into difficulties during the recession of the early 1990s.

Enterprise Zones

Enterprise Zones were first established in 1981, when 11 EZs were set up, including Salford Docks adjacent to the Manchester Ship Canal. EZs were originally designed to encourage industrial growth, but many of them – like Telford – were not in inner cities, but were created to revive industry in peripheral areas. By 1990, there were 26 EZs throughout the UK, varying in size up to a maximum of 400 ha. Firms locating within the EZs were offered a range of financial and other benefits, including grants for buildings and machinery and a relaxation of planning regulations. The hope was to initiate regeneration by halting industrial decline and providing new employment opportunities.

Urban Development Corporations

Urban Development Corporations were property-led projects that sought to become catalysts for the development of inner city areas. Most UDCs were in areas that had suffered serious economic decline and had a high proportion of derelict land. Some had very little housing. UDCs had the power to acquire land and to create the conditions necessary to attract private investment by rebuilding infrastructure, designing attractive office and housing developments and in some cases – for example, in Cardiff Bay – making land available for industry (Figs 8.42–8.43). Between 1980 and 1998, 13 UDCs were established in England and Wales. Most of these have now been wound up and their responsibilities passed to local authorities. At designation, the largest in area (4858 ha) was Teesside and the UDC with the largest resident population (40 400) was London Docklands.

Action for Cities and the City Challenge Scheme

In 1988, the government launched its Action for Cities programme which was a series of proposals for action by different government departments in inner city areas. By 1991, the government had realised that local authorities had a role to play in inner city redevelopment and launched its City Challenge Scheme. In this scheme, a number of local authorities were invited to bid for a share of £82 million to be spent on projects in their area. The scheme was widely criticised for turning needed redevelopment into a kind of competition. In 1992 the scheme was wound up, and government attention moved away from inner cities to the urban fringe.

Figure 8.44 St Ann's Square, Manchester

?

---

23 Outline the main advantages and disadvantages of the Urban Renewal Area strategy adopted by Leeds City Council.

Other redevelopment strategies

Urban Development Corporations tend to be large-scale, high-profile projects, funded and controlled by central government. However, many local authorities throughout the UK have been striving for years to improve conditions in inner cities and other parts of the urban area. For example, in the 1960s, Leeds began a programme based on Improvement Grants, which made funds available for house improvement in certain parts of the city. The money was used for installing inside toilets in older houses, as well as improving roofs, walls, doors, windows and kitchens.

This initiative gave rise to two national programmes in the 1970s and 1980s: General Improvement Areas (GIAs); and Housing Action Areas (HAAs). The aim of both programmes was to improve existing houses and flats rather than try to demolish them as part of an expensive comprehensive redevelopment strategy. In addition to improvement grants, the GIAs and HAAs also included general environmental improvements such as landscaping, pedestrianisation (Fig. 8.44) and the provision of play spaces and off-street parking.

In 1985, Leeds City Council established ten Urban Renewal Areas (URAs), most of which were in inner city areas (Fig. 8.45). These URAs were larger than the GIAs and HAAs which ceased to exist nationally in 1991. Within the URAs in Leeds, housing improvement grants were available. Investments were also encouraged by housing associations and under the government Housing Programme.

Leeds has now formed the Leeds Partnership Homes programme which is a joint co-operative body involving the City Council and housing associations operating in the URAs. The Council provides the land and the housing associations use their funds to build new houses and flats (Fig. 8.46). This approach to redevelopment retains much greater local control, and is more democratic than UDCs, yet it reduces costs by attracting outside investment from housing associations. The partnership approach should mean that local needs get more attention – especially as regards housing and jobs. However, such initiatives are still small-scale and quite expensive. There is also still criticism that the needs of local people are not being fully met because some of the housing is expensive and few new jobs have so far been created.

Figure 8.45 Urban Renewal Areas in Leeds, 1985 (*Source:* Chaffey, 1995)

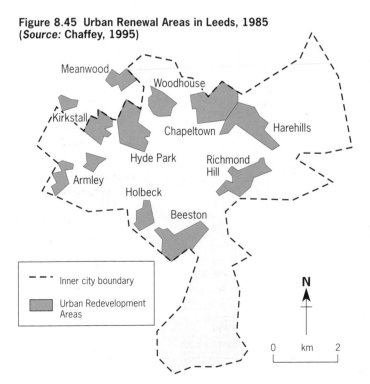

Meanwood
Woodhouse
Kirkstall
Chapeltown
Harehills
Hyde Park
Richmond Hill
Armley
Holbeck
Beeston

- - - Inner city boundary

Urban Redevelopment Areas

N

0 km 2

Figure 8.46 New housing adjacent to the River Aire, Leeds

The Single Regeneration Budget
From 1995 onwards, Single Regeneration Budget (SRB) schemes were introduced in selected urban areas of England and Wales. Local Authorities were invited to bid for central government funding which was intended to regenerate run-down areas, in similar ways to the City Challenge Scheme. The intention was that central government funding would attract additional private funding to aid in the regeneration process.

Sandwell

In 2000, Sandwell, in the West Midlands, (Fig. 8.47) had already had funding for the Black Country Development Corporation and the Tipton City Challenge. These schemes both ended in 1998. They were replaced by the SRB in which Sandwell was awarded £50 million over the four rounds of funding. This £50 million in turn attracted a further £200 million from the public and private sectors.

Round One of the SRB funding started in 1995, and Sandwell gained finance to focus on three areas: North Smethwick, Hateley Heath and Cradley Heath. The aims were:
• to promote economic regeneration;
• improve standards of education and training;
• improve the quality of life via health, housing and environmental projects.

In Round Two, in 1996, Sandwell gained £7.2 million to promote the voluntary and community sectors, in the period up to 2003.

A further £7.5 million was secured by Sandwell under Round Three. This money was targeted to help the young people of the area, particularly through improvements in education, health and training. Sandwell had the largest single award of £10.75 million under S.R.B. Round Four. This means that during the period 1998 to 2005 Sandwell will receive £75.45 million. The whole programme of redevelopment aims to enable local people to participate more effectively in the social and economic development of Sandwell, and to live more sustainable and healthy lifestyles.

Dereliction and environmental issues in Sandwell – success or failure?
SRB funding is just one way in which Sandwell has been trying to improve its environment (see Fig. 8.47). In order to have some measure of the degree of success achieved by the various initiatives it is important to identify the area's problems.

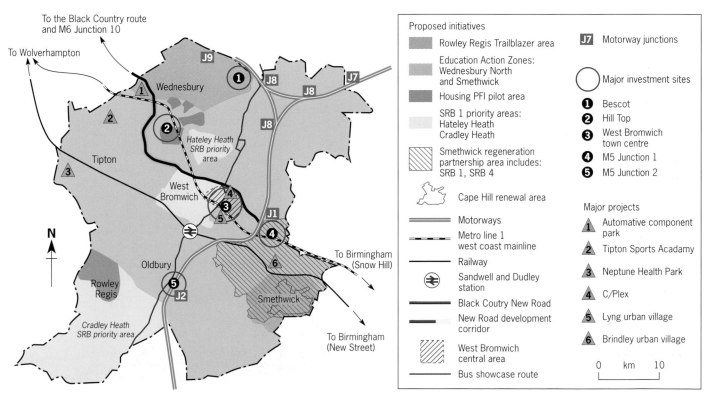

Figure 8.47 Sandwell in the West Midlands *Source*: **Sandwell MBC, 1999**

The need to transform Sandwell

Sandwell suffered high levels of social deprivation which were getting worse. In 1986, Sandwell was the 20th most deprived district in England; by 1998, it was the 7th. Alongside this, social deprivation the Borough's population fell by 6 per cent between 1981 and 1998, and a survey in 1997 found that a third of all households had incomes below £5500 per year. Nearly 25 per cent of the Borough's population in 1997 depended on Income Support; in 1998, 6.9 per cent of the population were unemployed (compared to a national average of 4.4 per cent). In 1997, 23 per cent of council housing was unfit and 20 per cent had no central heating. Many houses suffered from mould or rising damp, and Sandwell had the third highest rate of heart disease – 60 per cent above the national average. Educational achievement in the area is low compared to national averages.

An over-reliance on manufacturing industry added to Sandwell's problems. In 1998, 39 per cent of all jobs were in this sector compared to 18 per cent in Great Britain as a whole. Large areas of derelict and contaminated land were the result of former mining and industrial activity.

Sandwell's achievements

Much derelict and contaminated land has been reclaimed; for example, in the period between 1987 and 1997, 527 ha of land were reclaimed. Some of this land is now used for new industrial and business parks, and some has been used for new homes. Between 1986 and 1998, a total of 9714 new houses were built, including housing for rent units in Hateley Heath. Over 6500 new jobs were created between 1990 and 1999 as a result of the development of 22 125 m retail space and 397 new industrial units.

Council flats and houses were refurbished and some were transferred to housing associations or residents' shared ownership schemes. New primary schools were built and secondary schools refurbished whilst additional green spaces were created in congested areas such as Hateley Heath.

24a Work in pairs and rank Sandwell's problems in order of importance.
b To what extent has Sandwell succeeded in improving the quality of life for its poorest people?

Summary

- Counter-urbanisation was a major feature in most EMDCs and some NICs in the 1980s and early 1990s.

- Counter-urbanisation affects both cities which lose population and small towns and villages which gain population.

- Green belts were created to restrict urban sprawl, but they themselves have also created problems.

- New towns were seen as one solution to the problem of city growth, but they in turn have generated other problems.

- The globalisation of economic activity has often resulted in large-scale city centre redevelopment and the re-imaging of cities.

- UK inner city areas in the 1980s exhibited features of population decline, economic decline, environmental degradation, poverty and deprivation.

- Different explanations of the nature of the inner city challenge stress the built environment, social deprivation and economic failures. These evoke a range of responses.

- UDCs redevelop areas by using central government funds to attract private investment.

- UDC redevelopment of inner city areas brings both costs and benefits to local people and local environments.

- Alternative redevelopment strategies usually combine private investment with a degree of local control.

- It is very important that redevelopment schemes should meet the needs of local people.

9 The urban future

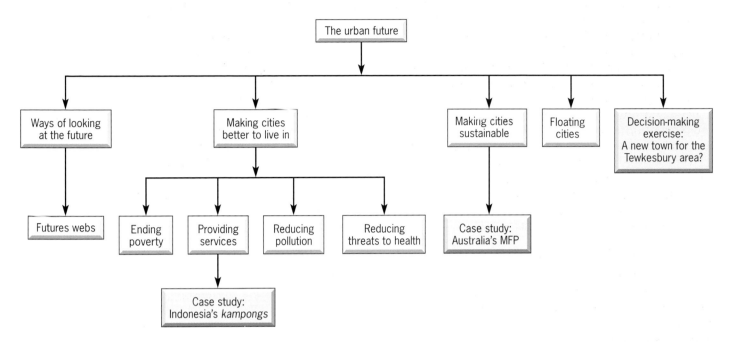

9.1 Introduction

This book has concentrated on an examination of the processes, policies and issues resulting from urbanisation. However, it is also important to consider the future of urban areas especially in our rapidly changing world. Looking at the future is not as simple as it sounds – if only because people have different ideas about what 'the future' actually means.

What do geographers mean by the future?
Geographers need to be aware of the different ways of looking at the future. This is particularly important in the context of planning situations. A decision which has short-term benefits, for example, may turn out to have long-term disadvantages. Four popular views of the future are shown in Figures 9.1–9.4.

Figure 9.1 The future is like a roller coaster
(*Source:* Flint and Flint, 1989)
This view of the future suggests that cities are on a fixed track which they have to follow. It implies that our path through the future has already been determined, but that we do not know where it will lead because it is dark. We may get occasional glimpses of the future in flashes of lightning, but we cannot do anything about it because we are locked into our seats.

Figure 9.2 The future is like a river
(*Source:* Flint and Flint, 1989)
This view suggests that managing the future of cities is like steering a boat down a river. The flow of the river broadly determines the direction we must take, but we can steer within the channel and look ahead to avoid hazards. If the river divides into more than one channel, we can choose between the various alternatives.

Figure 9.3 The future unfolds like a dice game
(*Source:* Flint and Flint, 1989)
This view suggests that the future for cities is entirely a matter of chance – just like a throw of the dice. We cannot influence the outcome, so we have to learn to accept whatever comes our way, whether it is good or bad.

Figure 9.4 The future is like an ocean
(*Source:* Flint and Flint, 1989)
This view suggests that the future of cities is like that of a ship on the ocean. There are many possible destinations and many different routes by which each destination can be reached. We can choose whichever future we want, if we work for it.

Futures webs

One way of trying to decide about the nature of the urban future is to use a **futures web** similar to the one in Figure 9.5. This particular web begins with growing urban pollution (in the centre) and shows some of its main effects. The boxes nearest the centre indicate the immediate (first-order) effects of the trend, and they are arranged in a roughly circular pattern. Each of these consequences in turn generates further effects and so there may be second-, third-, fourth- and even fifth-order consequences resulting from the initial trend.

?

1a Which of the four views about the future of cities do you most agree with?
b List the reasons why you reject the others.

2a Study Figure 9.5, then add more fourth- and fifth-order consequences of growing urban air pollution.
b Now select another aspect of urbanisation (e.g. re-urbanisation, traffic congestion, the growth of service industries, the challenges of urban inequality) and produce a futures web similar to Figure 9.5. Compare your web with that of others in the group and discuss how far you agree or disagree about the conclusions you have reached.

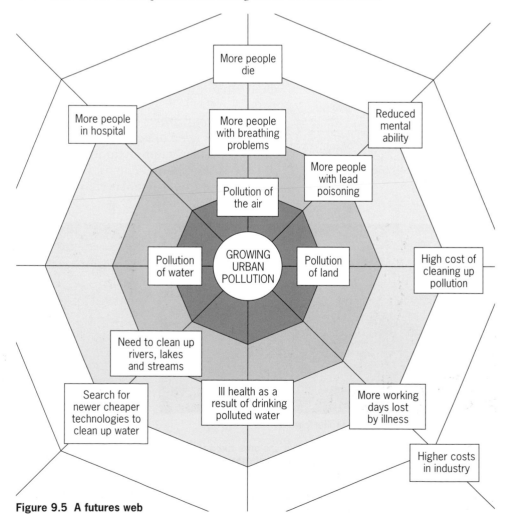

Figure 9.5 A futures web

9.2 Making cities better to live in

Despite many changes, cities all over the world are still makers of wealth, motors of invention and magnets for workers. In ELDCs, over 50 per cent of all gross domestic product (GDP) originates in cities, whilst in EMDCs the figure is 85 per cent (World Bank, 1996).

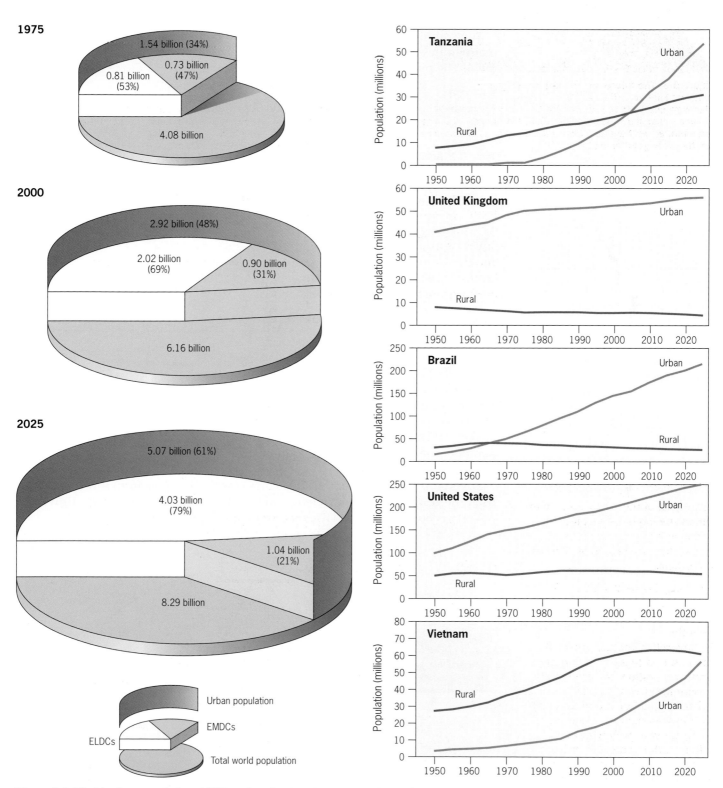

Figure 9.6 World urban population, 1975, and projections for 2000 and 2025 (*Source:* Annez, 1996)

Figure 9.7 Rural and urban population trends and projections for selected countries, 1950–2020 (*Source:* Hirsch, 1995)

Figure 9.6 shows the predicted trend in urbanisation in EMDCs and ELDCs. Figure 9.7 shows recent urban and rural population trends and projections in a range of countries. The continued growth and importance of urbanisation, especially in ELDCs is a striking feature of these predictions. The 276 million cities (cities with a population of 1 million or over) in the world in 1990 were home to 15 per cent of the world's population. However, the percentage of population living in these large cities varies both from country to country and from time to time.

The continued growth of the world's urban population has resulted in three main groups of problems which were identified in a World Bank report of 1996. The main groups of problems are:

• poverty;
• the need for service provision, especially of clean water; and
• the need to reduce pollution.

Table 9.1 Actual and projected rural and urban populations of selected countries, 1950–2020 (in millions) (*Source: Philip's Geographical Digest 1996–97*)

Year	Australia Urban	Australia Rural	Thailand Urban	Thailand Rural	Ireland Urban	Ireland Rural	Sweden Urban	Sweden Rural
1950	6.0	2.0	0.4	9.0	1.1	1.8	5.0	2.5
1960	9.0	2.0	0.5	10.0	1.4	1.6	5.5	2.0
1970	11.0	1.9	1.0	12.0	1.5	1.4	6.2	1.8
1980	13.0	2.0	3.0	15.0	2.0	1.5	6.8	1.6
1990	15.0	2.2	10.0	16.0	2.2	1.6	7.0	1.6
2000	16.0	2.5	15.0	20.0	2.5	1.6	7.1	1.4
2010	17.0	2.6	30.0	22.0	2.8	1.5	7.3	1.2
2020	20.0	2.4	45.0	25.0	3.5	1.4	7.5	1.0

Reducing poverty

In 1996, over 500 million people in countries all over the world were classed as poor and their numbers are rising. Over 300 million poor people live in towns and cities, mostly in ELDCs, but still over 15 per cent live in EMDCs. The poverty of these city-dwellers is one of the most difficult challenges facing planners concerned with trying to improve present and future life in urban environments.

Poverty in both ELDC and EMDC cities essentially stems from low income, itself the result of unemployment, underemployment and low wages. However, poverty is both a cause and a symptom of wider problems (Fig. 9.8).

?

3a Use the data in Table 9.1 to draw graphs of urbanisation trends for each country.
b Discuss the implications of the trends shown in your graphs and those shown in Figure 9.7 for urban planners focusing on developments up to 2020.

4a Outline the ways in which governments in both ELDCs and EMDCs could help people to break the cycle of poverty (Fig. 9.8).
b Why would it be difficult for governments to carry out such measures?

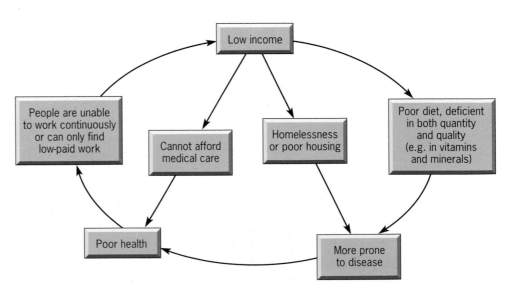

Figure 9.8 The cycle of poverty

People with low incomes may be homeless or forced to live in poor housing which may be damp, cold, overcrowded and not weatherproof. Conditions like these make people more vulnerable to diseases such as tuberculosis and pneumonia. People suffering from ill health often find it difficult to work continuously, or to find anything but low-paid employment. In this sense, poverty creates a downward spiral from which people find it hard to break free, wherever they live.

Poverty and a poor diet are often found together. People in extreme poverty are rarely able to afford to eat well, and their diet may be deficient in both quantity and quality. The lack of a balanced diet makes people more prone to ill-health, thus reducing their ability to earn money for food. Also, in these circumstances, people lack the money to pay for medicines and medical care which, in more and more countries, has to be paid for. Consequently, their health deteriorates further, as does their earning power.

Providing services

In ELDCs, poorer people live in slums and spontaneous settlements with unreliable water and electricity supplies, unpaved roads, uncovered drains and often few buses or other types of public transport. Each of these problems makes life more difficult for people who are already deeply burdened by poverty.

For example, the provision of safe, accessible drinking water is a basic commodity often denied to the urban poor. Where cities are unable to supply drinking water, street-sellers step in – but they sell the water at high prices. In Jakarta, water from street-sellers is 50 times the price of ordinary river water, whilst in Karachi the figure is 25 times higher. The result is a heavy cost to those people least able to pay. There is also a gender aspect to this burden, as water-carrying is traditionally regarded as women's work in many societies. In Chawana, a suburb of Lusaka in Zambia, women face a two-hour trip each day to fetch water.

Worse still, the only water available to the poor is often unsafe and this leads to diseases which impose yet another hardship on the poor. In the Middle East and North Africa, five of the six most common contagious diseases are water-borne (e.g. bilharzia). Children are the most frequent victims of such diseases and when they fall ill family members have to nurse them and so often forego potential outside income. One approach to solving the problem of how to provide cheap, safe water is the *kampong* improvement programme (KIP) of Indonesia.

Indonesia's *kampong* improvement programme (KIP)

This programme began in Jakarta in 1969 as an attempt to provide basic services such as clean water, sanitation and better roads to the *kampongs* (slum areas) of the city. Funding for the programme came from the World Bank (which provided 10 per cent), the Indonesian central government (30 per cent) and local authorities (60 per cent).

The aim of the programme was to use government investment to encourage people to improve their own environments. This has been achieved by employing local people to work on public projects such as installing sewers and clean water supplies, and building schools and clinics (Fig. 9.9). In this way, local people benefit by earning a wage for their work, by having access to basic services and facilities, and by enjoying better health and an improved environment.

The result is that people who originally could not afford to pay for improvements to their urban environment have been able to do so at relatively little cost to the central government. The World Bank estimates that countries only need to spend 0.2 per cent of their GDP over 15 years in order to be able to provide basic services to all the urban poor. By 1996, over 15 million people in and around Jakarta had gained access to improved basic services as a result of the programme.

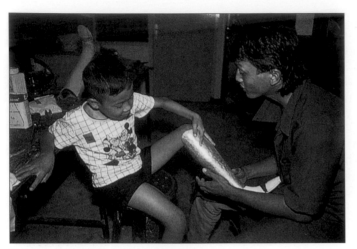

Figure 9.9 Inside a clinic in Jakarta

The World Bank also claims that with better services people in the improved *kampongs* spent the equivalent of US$20 on improving their homes and their surroundings. In some of the improved *kampongs*, new developments include parks and community schemes for the old and the very young.

?

5 What might be the main problems of trying to repeat the KIP project in countries such as the Philippines or Zambia? Make a list of all the problems you can think of, and compare your list with those of others in your group.

Figure 9.10 Air pollution by industry and road traffic causes breathing difficulties, particularly in children

?

6 Imagine that you are a planner in a city or town near where you live. What problems would you have in attempting to reduce air pollution? Draw up a table showing the main problems under the headings: economic, social and environmental.

Reducing pollution

Pollution is waste. The mounting costs of urban pollution represent a waste of human and physical resources. Dirty air shortens lives (Fig. 9.10); lead poisoning results in reduced mental capacities. Dirty water and uncollected garbage are breeding-grounds for disease. There is, therefore, an urgent need to reduce pollution of air, land and water.

Pollution claims a very high share of its victims from the urban poor. They are the city-dwellers most likely to rely on impure water or least likely to have access to proper sanitation facilities. The annual cost of air pollution from dust and lead in the three cities of Bangkok, Jakarta and Kuala Lumpur in 1996 was calculated to be US$5 billion – equivalent to 10 per cent of the total income of the three cities. Reducing pollution can save money.

Reducing threats to health

A World Health Organisation survey in 1996 found that the greatest threats to human health were soot, dust, lead and microbial diseases. However, the soot and dust can be removed from power plants and factories by relatively low-cost filtering systems. In future, such systems will become even cheaper and so even more attractive.

Lead poisoning does most damage to children. It affects 90 per cent of the children in African cities and 29 per cent of the children in Mexico City. Lead poisoning reduces children's powers of concentration and their motor skills. However, it is possible to reduce lead pollution dramatically by phasing out its use in petrol. Thailand made the switch to unleaded petrol between 1991 and 1996, and Malaysia is following this example. Lead pollution in many cities may also start to decrease if the number of cars in private ownership can be controlled, or if their access to city centres is restricted.

Microbial diseases are often transmitted by water. Improvements in basic services such as clean water are therefore important and should lead to a reduction in such threats to human health.

Urban planners all over the world are well aware that firms competing in a global market are not likely to be attracted to cities that do not offer clean water, reliable electricity, and good road and telecommunications systems. The problem is how to pay for these improvements. In some countries, such as Indonesia and Malaysia, the central government aims to raise the money to pay for the improvements. In other countries, such as Mexico and Argentina, private companies have been formed in order to improve the water supply to the nation's cities.

7a Study Figure 9.12. For each of the changes outlined in the diagram suggest the main challenges to their implementation. **b** How might these challenges be overcome?

9.3 Making cities sustainable

In addition to trying to improve living conditions in cities, the future will inevitably involve attempts to make cities **sustainable**. In this context, sustainable means city development that meets the needs of the present without compromising the ability of future generations to meet their needs (Brundtland Commission 1987). Ever since the creation of large cities with the development of industrialisation there have been worries over the environmental impacts of urbanisation. However the recent rapid growth of cities in ELDCs, with their huge challenges of ever increasing demands for housing, water, sanitation etc. have given an added dimension to concerns over the environmental impacts of urbanisation. The real problem lies with cities in EMDCs which consume ten times more resources per person than cities in ELDCs. Some writers talk about the **risk society**, which has emerged in cities in EMDCs. In such societies, technologies such as nuclear power and genetic engineering pose much greater ecological threats than the challenges of the past.

Agenda 21

In 1992, the Rio Earth Summit set up Agenda 21, in order to try to improve the sustainability of cities. Under this agreement, cities around the world agreed to develop plans to increase sustainable development within them.

Such plans typically include measures such as:

• increasing the area of green space within the city;

• promoting the recycling of waste;

• monitoring air and water quality;

• introducing more efficient public transport systems such as trams.

The car-dependent, decentralised, suburban city forms with their emphasis on consumption, typical of EMDC's are clearly wasteful of resources. Research in the USA and Australia has shown, for example, that large, sprawling cities are much more wasteful in their energy consumption than smaller, denser cities (Fig. 9.11). Academics and planners are concerned that the cities of the

Figure 9.11 The relationship between petrol consumption and urban density (*Source:* **Winchester and Chalkley, 1995**)

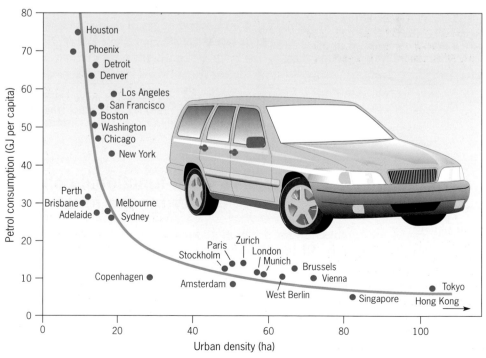

8 Study Figure 9.11.
a Divide the graph into three main sectors: sprawling cities with low densities and high rates of petrol consumption; relatively compact cities with medium rates of petrol consumption; and very compact cities with very low petrol consumption.
b What common features might explain why these cities are in these categories?

future should be environmentally sustainable, as well as economically efficient and socially equitable. Given the huge investment in suburbanisation it is unlikely that there will be an immediate turn-around in city design. Also, despite the growth in gentrification, it is unlikely that there will be a large-scale return of people to live in central and inner city areas. So, more likely is the **Multipli City** (Fig. 9.12). This is an area of small, relatively dense urban settlements, linked by improved public transport. Creating this system will not be easy in countries like the UK and USA, where car ownership is entrenched. The important fact about sustainability is that it is not simply about resources in isolation, but it is also linked to social and economic issues. All aspects of life in urban areas will have to change if sustainability is to be increased.

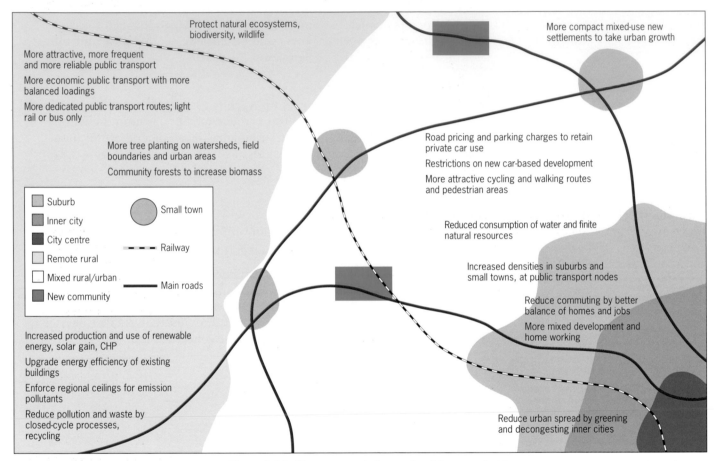

Protect natural ecosystems, biodiversity, wildlife

More compact mixed-use new settlements to take urban growth

More attractive, more frequent and more reliable public transport

More economic public transport with more balanced loadings

More dedicated public transport routes; light rail or bus only

More tree planting on watersheds, field boundaries and urban areas

Community forests to increase biomass

Road pricing and parking charges to retain private car use

Restrictions on new car-based development

More attractive cycling and walking routes and pedestrian areas

Reduced consumption of water and finite natural resources

Increased densities in suburbs and small towns, at public transport nodes

Reduce commuting by better balance of homes and jobs

More mixed development and home working

Suburb	Small town
Inner city	
City centre	Railway
Remote rural	
Mixed rural/urban	Main roads
New community	

Increased production and use of renewable energy, solar gain, CHP

Upgrade energy efficiency of existing buildings

Enforce regional ceilings for emission pollutants

Reduce pollution and waste by closed-cycle processes, recycling

Reduce urban spread by greening and decongesting inner cities

Figure 9.12 Changes needed to make cities sustainable.
(*Source:* Blavers (1999) Fig. 6.12 p282 'The unsustainable city' in S. Pile, C. Brook and C. Morney (eds.) Unruly Cities? : Order, Disorder. Open University Press, Routledge, London.)

Australia's multi-functional polis (MFP) – a city for the future

The new city is located at Gillman, a region 15 km north-east of the centre of Adelaide in South Australia (Fig. 9.13). The three main aims in the development of this city are for it:

• to be a centre for new science and technology;

• to be a model for twenty-first century planning, design and lifestyles; and

• to pioneer new types of development that are sustainable and sensitive to the needs of the environment.

The original idea for the MFP came from Japan, which sees Australia as having advantages of environment, space, amenities and lifestyle – as well as the opportunity for the growth of hi-tech industry.

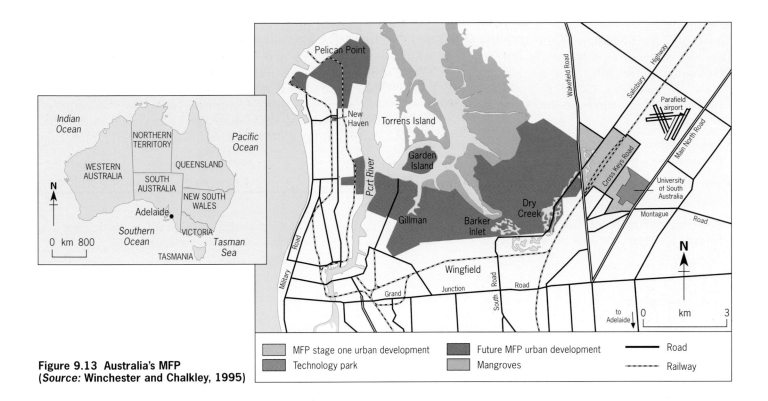

Figure 9.13 Australia's MFP
(*Source*: **Winchester and Chalkley, 1995)**

Australia was keen on the concept because it wanted to move away from a reliance on mining and farming which, in 1995, still accounted for two-thirds of the country's total exports. It is planned that the MFP will attract international investment to become a centre for new growth industries such as pollution monitoring, waste control and recycling.

The site and layout

The site chosen for this new town of the future is 2000 ha in size. Part of the area is an environmentally sensitive mangrove estuary (Figs 9.14–9.15). Part of the rest of the site is polluted land that for years had been used to dump waste. However, the first stage of the new town is being built on unpolluted land between Technology Park and Dry Creek (Fig. 9.13).

The city will be a series of linked villages separated by fields and lakes. A typical village will cover 36 ha, 50 per cent of which will be for housing, with 30 per cent for open space and 20 per cent for industry, commercial and community uses. There will be 35 dwellings per hectare which is significantly higher than in most Australian suburbs.

Figure 9.14 Mangrove estuary, MFP

The vision

The planning of MFP is dominated by the themes of technology and environment. It will be a wired city, with fibre-optic cables linking all households and businesses. This means that people will be able to do things such as pay bills, order goods and obtain train timetables without having to leave their homes. They will also be able to take part in education and training courses through these wired systems.

The plan is to produce an eco-sensitive city whose buildings and layout are energy-efficient. Solar heating, new building materials and high-efficiency appliances will all play a part in achieving this. The overall plan is to reduce energy consumption to one-half that of a typical Australian suburb and to ensure that 70 per cent of the energy used comes from renewable sources.

Figure 9.15 Garden Island, MFP

The future

So far, only the first phase of the MFP has been built. There are significant problems associated with its future development, especially:

- how to prevent damage to the environmentally sensitive estuary;

- how to attract increasingly mobile global investment in the face of stiff competition;

- how to achieve a social balance (younger, better-paid people are over-represented);

- how to prevent the new town from becoming a foreign enclave (one-half of its residents are from Japan and Asia).

To date, progress on the MFP has been solid but not spectacular. It may take until 2016 to reach its target population of 50 000. Currently, government and state funds are being used to clean up the polluted part of the site and to build infrastructure in the hope of encouraging private-sector investment. MFP does have the potential to show how a badly degraded site can be turned into an attractive, futuristic city.

9 Which of the various future problems facing the development of the MFP do you think will be the hardest to overcome? Explain your reasons for thinking this.

Providing new housing for the future

The recent development of new town ideas has not been confined to Australia. In the UK too there is renewed interest in the idea of new towns as a means of resolving some of the current urban problems (Fig. 9.16).

10a How far do you agree with the reasons given by the UK government in 1991 for the need to build 4.4 million new homes in England in the next 25 years?
b Tabulate the advantages and disadvantages of building new houses on: greenfield sites; land in existing urban areas.

11a What are the main arguments against the development of more new towns in the UK?
b How far do you agree or disagree with these arguments?

Key to the future?

… debate is growing about one of the most contentious environmental issues. The Government predicted in 1991 that 4.4 million new homes would be required in England alone over the next 25 years because of changing migration patterns, people living longer and a growth in single households. The big question is where they will be built. Builders want greenfield sites, while environmentalists prefer land in existing towns and cities.

There are doubts about whether there is enough suitable 'brownfield' land, and non-urban developments are being stonewalled by local authorities. So some people are beginning to ask whether more new towns, politically unfashionable for two decades, might provide part of the answer.

There is just a handful of new settlements under consideration now, and none is large enough to be described as a new town. Most are subject to particular circumstances that bypass the need for large-scale land assembly.

Concrete maker Blue Circle plans to build New Ebbsfleet beside a station on the high-speed Channel Tunnel rail link in North Kent. The new 'Euro-city' would provide 3200 homes and 20 000 jobs.

Property group Hanson Land is planning a £500m development outside Peterborough, Cambridgeshire. And insurer Eagle Star is behind a stalled development of 13 000 new homes in Micheldever, Hampshire. Opposition is fierce. It is led by the Council for the Protection of Rural England, which is against any large-scale development outside cities.

Tony Burton, its head of planning, says: 'Free-standing new settlements are least likely to be the way forward because of their urbanising effect and because they are counter to the Government's sustainability policy.

'If we're putting a huge new town in virgin countryside, that is less likely to get people out of their cars and more likely to generate traffic.'

This is a moot point. Supporters of new towns argue that if they are properly planned close to employment and other amenities, they can reduce commuting.

The green lobby argues that countryside the size of Bristol is disappearing under development each year, while the housebuilders counter that trying to force people into homes in areas where they don't want to live is undemocratic.

Figure 9.16 'Key to the future?' (*Source: The Observer*, 3 November 1996)

12a What are the main advantages for Japanese cities in the use of floating structures?
b What are likely to be the main drawbacks to this type of development?

9.4 Floating cities

For most of this century, land has been reclaimed from the sea and used for urban expansion. With improvements in technology, some schemes have become very large – over 900 ha of the site of Hong Kong's new airport, for example, are reclaimed land. In a dramatic new extension of this approach to solving development problems, some planners are now proposing that new cities be built on floating platforms on the sea itself (Fig. 9.17). These ideas are popular in crowded countries like Japan and the Netherlands where there is a shortage of suitable land for new urban development.

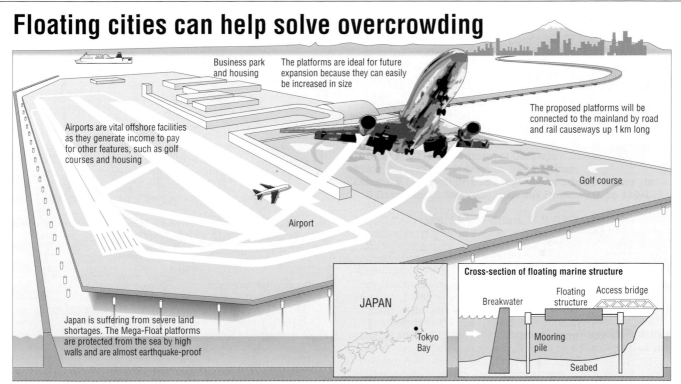

Floating cities can help solve overcrowding

Business park and housing

The platforms are ideal for future expansion because they can easily be increased in size

The proposed platforms will be connected to the mainland by road and rail causeways up 1 km long

Airports are vital offshore facilities as they generate income to pay for other features, such as golf courses and housing

Golf course

Airport

Japan is suffering from severe land shortages. The Mega-Float platforms are protected from the sea by high walls and are almost earthquake-proof

JAPAN

Tokyo Bay

Cross-section of floating marine structure

Breakwater

Floating structure

Access bridge

Mooring pile

Seabed

JAPANESE engineers are designing giant floating platforms several kilometres long so they can build tomorrow's cities on the high seas. The price of land is so high in the main urban areas of Japan that this now makes sound financial sense.

The massive platforms will be moored more than a kilometre offshore and connected to the coast by road and rail bridges. They will be protected from the ravages of the ocean by a shield of breakwaters.

The platforms will first be used as airports, harbours and factories. Some will also be used as holiday islands for watersports enthusiasts and for those who just want to get away from the crowded daily life in modern Japan. Floating golf courses are also a possibility. As an island nation with limited land

resources, Japan has had to depend greatly on its shallow coast waters. About half of the shallow sea area has already been reclaimed and it is thought that by the end of the millennium the rest will be turned into dry land.

With demand for land outstripping supply and with ultra-high-rise construction techniques yet to be proven, the only solution seems to be to build on top of the sea.

The Japanese minister of transport is promoting the research and development of ultra-large floating structures and a syndicate of 13 shipbuilders and 4 steelmakers has come together to realise the plan. The first full-scale demonstration is on schedule to be completed next year.

The emphasis on providing new facilities for airports and

harbours is not surprising considering that the transport ministry is promoting Mega-Float. However, these two uses also make sense for other reasons. Airports require huge amounts of land as do the shore facilities. They also generate a high income to pay for the hire of the platform.

The concept of Mega-Float has advantages compared to plans to accommodate Japan's growing population and expanding industry on solid ground. Almost all sea areas can be utilised regardless of their depth or geology.

The earthquakes that threaten parts of Japan cause virtually no damage to floating structures. They have almost no impact on the natural environment and may not change the ecosystem. The construction methods are cheap

and well understood. If the platform becomes overcrowded, it can be extended easily. Finally, if it turns out to be in the wrong place, it can be towed to a new site.

The first platform will be built in Tokyo Bay by joining together a series of smaller units. The engineers will use it to prove their system really works. In the meantime they are researching the internal structure of the platforms and how to moor such large objects securely.

Environmental assessments are also to be made, and then a large model, approximately 300 metres long, 60 metres wide and 2 metres thick, will be made by joining 9 floating units, each measuring 100 metres by 20 metres by 2 metres, on the sea to demonstrate the sea-joining technology, safety and endurance.

Figure 9.17 Proposal for a floating city in Tokyo Bay, Japan (*Source: The Sunday Times*, 19 May 1996)

9.5 Decision-making exercise:
A new town for the Tewkesbury area?

One way of evaluating the different types of housing and new towns needed for the future is by means of a decision-making exercise. In this exercise, you should imagine that you have been employed as a researcher by a Member of Parliament who is soon to visit the Tewkesbury area. She has given you the following brief.

Dear Researcher,

By now you will have accumulated quite a large amount of background material on the Tewkesbury area of Gloucestershire (Figs 9.18–9.22). I now need your help to prepare for my visit to the area. I will need to be prepared to answer questions on issues of local concern, and to express opinions that are based on the facts in so far as they are known. As you are aware, I have a reputation for expressing clear, logical views in a straightforward fashion.

I need you to prepare for my visit by investigating in particular the County Council's proposal to create a new town in the Tewkesbury area. I will be meeting two groups of people.

a Officials from the Gloucestershire County Council Planning Department who have advised on the need for the new town and recommended that it be sited near Tewkesbury.

b Officers from Tewkesbury Borough Council and other local people who oppose the idea of the new town.

1 Briefly outline the arguments that each of these two groups is likely to put to me either for or against the new town at Tewkesbury. As an MP, I have to balance local views with the national interest. Some key points seem to me:

• Are the reasons for assuming continued growth in demand for housing valid?
• Is the plan really based on the concept of sustainable development?
• Are the objections sensible and based on facts?

It seems to me that there are four possible positions I could take on the issue. These are:

a to support the proposed new town on greenbelt land near Tewkesbury;
b to support the idea of a new town, but oppose its location near Tewkesbury;
c to oppose both the need for a new town and its location near Tewkesbury; or
d to support the idea of a new town, but suggest that it be located on a brownfield site within the county (e.g. near Cheltenham or Gloucester).

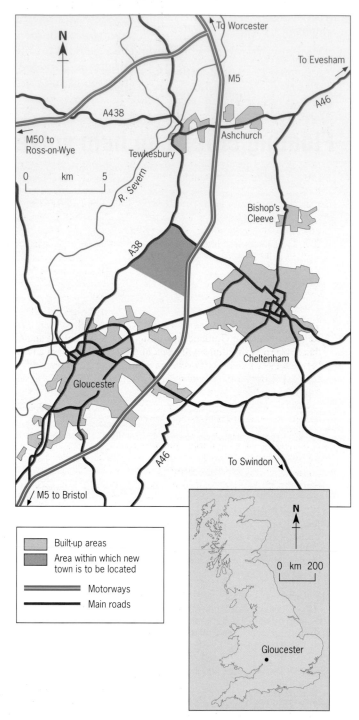

Figure 9.18 The location of the proposed new town in Gloucestershire

2 Suggest which one of the options **a–d** I should support. Present geographical arguments for the chosen option in the light of national needs and local circumstances. Explain why you think I should reject the other options.

Gloucester County Council is reviewing its Structure Plan. This provides a long term view of how housing, employment and shopping should develop in Gloucestershire between now and 2001. In doing this, careful consideration is given to environmental, economic and social factors.

Sustainable development is the guiding principle of the plan. This does not mean 'no development' but planning for new development in ways that protect and enhance the special local environmental qualities of the County as well as protecting the wider global environment. It is also about attracting new investment and jobs, and improving the quality of life for existing and future generations. We have called this approach 'Gloucestershire Living Sustainably'.

Why do we need all these new houses?

Regional Planning Guidance suggested that 53 000 new dwellings will be required between 1991 and 2011. (Dwellings refers to all types of houses including flats.) We have checked the figure carefully and believe that it is a correct reflection on the future demand for housing. Demand for these new houses comes from the existing population of Gloucestershire as it grows, as more people choose to live on their own, (partly as a result of the increased divorce rate), and as people live longer. We also need to take into account people who will move into the County from elsewhere for work and retirement.

Of the 53 000 dwellings, about 33 000 have either been built, have planning permission or have been identified in the local plans of the Borough and District Councils. This leaves land for about 20 000 dwellings still to be found. The key challenge is to accommodate the new development in a sustainable way.

Our suggestion for future development.

We are suggesting that there could be two new settlements in the County – one to the north of Gloucester between the A38 and the M5, wholly or partially in the Green Belt, the other to the west of the Stroud urban area.

It is intended that each new settlement would have approximately 3000 dwellings by 2011 (but with the potential to expand beyond then). This leaves about 14 000 dwellings to be built on other sites outside the Green Belt. The Borough and District Councils, guided by the policies of the Structure Plan, will identify sites in their local plans.

We believe that the majority of new development should take place close to the main urban areas of the County, to make it easier for people to reach their work, shops and leisure facilities either on foot, by bicycle or on public transport. If new development is scattered around the countryside, this is likely to increase commuting by car, worsening congestion and pollution.

We recognise that the proposals are contentious but none of them have been made without very careful consideration.

Will these proposals mean the loss of the Green Belt?

No, the Green Belt will remain between Cheltenham and Gloucester, and Cheltenham and Bishop's Cleeve. The primary reason for having a Green Belt between Gloucester and Cheltenham is to prevent the two towns merging. The importance of maintaining the separation between these two settlements is recognised. However, one of the identified 'areas of search' for a new settlement does include land within the Green Belt but because of its location, it would not cause Cheltenham to merge with Gloucester or Bishop's Cleeve. Furthermore Central Government has suggested that we may need to review some existing green belt boundaries.

What can the Structure Plan do for Gloucestershire's economy?

The Structure Plan can ensure that a sufficient amount of land is made available for future employment development. It is important to provide this land in the right places. We believe, and past experience has shown, that most employers want to locate in or close to Gloucester and Cheltenham, and generally near the M5 corridor.

However, some small scale employment will be permitted in some larger villages to help improve the rural economy.

Figure 9.19 Planning for the future: an extract from Gloucestershire County Council's Structure Plan, 1996

Figure 9.20 The proposed new town: extract from Gloucestershire County Council's Structure Plan, 1996

The proposal for a new settlement within Tewkesbury Borough (to the north of Gloucester, in the area between the A38 and the M5) not only helps to meet the housing and employment needs of Tewkesbury Borough but also a proportion of those of Cheltenham Borough and Cotswold District (where environmental factors limit the acceptability of development) during the Second Review Plan Period. It will also accommodate a proportion of Gloucester City's development needs after 2011, in the context of severe constraints to the city's continued expansion after that date.

We believe the settlement should be roughly equidistant from Gloucester, Cheltenham and Tewkesbury/Ashchurch and we should expect the developer(s) of the settlement to contribute to the provision of high quality public transport (in the first instance, bus) services to these and other important employment centres.

Nevertheless, the settlement's good access to the M5 and close proximity to both Gloucester and Cheltenham mean that there are excellent prospects for attracting employment to locate within the settlement, so that the community will become progressively more self-contained as it grows larger, while continuing to rely on established urban centres for a proportion of its employment and service needs.

We believe that this new settlement should be located either wholly or partially within an area of land currently designated as Green Belt, where very strict controls on new development operate at present.

It will be necessary for Tewkesbury Borough Council to re-draw the north-western boundary of the Green Belt in the context of its Local Plan, so that the new settlement can be established either wholly or partially on land removed from the Green Belt.

GLOUCESTERSHIRE GRIDLOCK

- Thousands of houses
- More cars
- New settlements
- Less green fields
- More congestion

Is more development really necessary? Where should new houses go? Who decides?

Gloucestershire County Council has drafted its new **Structure Plan** to guide development in the County to 2011. Known as the **Second Review**, it is out for consultation now. This sets out new housing targets for the Districts, including Tewkesbury Borough. The County proposes to add 12100 houses between 1991–2011 to the Borough's present 31000 houses (**approximately 40% increase**).

Tewkesbury Borough Council is critically questioning the whole basis of the Structure Plan – the figures, the assumptions, the implications – **but we need your help and support**.

The County Council Proposals affecting your Borough include:

- Concentration of **new development** into the **Severn Vale**.
- **5800 extra new houses** in the Borough to 2011, made up of –
- A **new settlement in the Green Belt** of at least **3000 houses** to the north of Gloucester between the M5 and A38 – (with potential to expand to **10000 – plus 45ha of industry**)
- Plus another 2800 new dwellings to find.

Tewkesbury Borough Council urges the County Council to:

- Reconsider the overall housing numbers (**53000 in Gloucestershire up to the year 2011**) – are they really needed?
- Protect the Green Belt – the critical gap between Cheltenham and Gloucester, and Cheltenham and Bishop's Cleeve.
- Distribute the necessary development more fairly around the County.
- Recognise the environment of the Vale and the quality of life of its residents needs as much protection as other areas.
- Make use of redevelopment sites for housing.
- Analyse the impact of more cars – is public transport a realistic alternative?
- Give further thought to jobs – where are people going to work?

Figure 9.21 'Gloucestershire gridlock' (*Source:* Tewkesbury Borough Council, 1996)

Figure 9.22 Executive summary of Tewkesbury Borough Council's objections to the new town proposal, 1996

Executive summary of objections by Tewkesbury Borough Council to proposed new town in their area

The Council commissioned Professor David King of Anglia Polytechnic University to examine the County Council's projection work in detail. On the basis of his advice, the Borough requests the County to re-examine these issues in particular.

* The Borough Council sees no justification for new settlements. The County should plan for zero in-migration after 2001 rather than the substantial in-migration of the present plan.

* No consideration appears to have been given to the environmental impact of new settlements.

* It is very unlikely that any new settlement could be self-contained in employment, so it would generate large volumes of commuters adding to existing road traffic problems. It would also become a dormitory town which would not be in keeping with the existing settlement pattern.

* The area of the proposed new town is green belt and as such it should be conserved and protected — not developed.

* The Borough Council accepts the need for some new housing in the area. It has however identified a number of brownfield sites in Cheltenham (close to the railway station, and also the former bus station now a car park) which could provide many additional dwellings rather than building a new town.

* Building new settlements, especially close to a motorway, only encourages even more in-migration to an area like Tewkesbury. The Council's plan would accommodate incomers without providing necessary new housing for local people.

9.6 Conclusions

We hope that, as you have worked your way through the various sections of this book, you will have realised that – in the realm of urban geography – facts, concepts and definitions may be concrete but interpretations of that evidence will vary. Interpretations change over time, and, as a result, so also do approaches to dealing with urban change.

Approaches to solving the challenges of urbanisation vary greatly from time to time and from place to place. For example, tower blocks of flats were seen as an appropriate response to the UK housing shortage of the 1950s. However, by the 1960s and 1970s, the social problems engendered by tower blocks had become apparent and they were condemned, often by the same politicians who had encouraged their initial construction. Yet attempts to predict how cities will change in the future and to provide for the needs of future societies must continue because buildings last much longer than their builders. Moreover, the pace of change is quickening. Only by trying to understand and to explain the changes accompanying urbanisation will future generations be able to plan for change in the city.

The urban future is one which concerns everyone who is a responsible human being. Most of us will live our lives in cities and we should be particularly concerned for those people who live in areas with very high population densities, whether they be in Bogotá, Bombay or Birmingham.

The final decision-making exercise (Chapter 10) shows how extremely difficult it is to determine priorities and to improve conditions with limited financial resources in cities with extremely high population densities. If we can make cities habitable places for all people, then we will have helped in a small way to improve the world. In developing our ideas about the urban future, the understanding provided by geographers, as outlined in this book, will make a valuable contribution to human development.

Summary

- People have different ideas about what the future means, especially in terms of its geography.

- Urbanisation remains one of the dominant trends in world geography.

- Urbanisation continues to generate problems related to poverty, health and the provision of housing, education and other services.

- There are several experimental schemes which try to provide services for people in urban areas at low cost.

- Pollution of air, land and water remains a major problem in many urban areas, despite attempts to reduce it.

- Future cities will need to be much more sustainable than existing ones.

- The ability of governments, like that of the UK, to build most new developments on brownfield sites is under very close scrutiny.

10 Decision-making exercise: Calcutta, India

In this exercise, you should imagine that you have been employed as a consultant by the Calcutta Municipal Authority, to advise them on the relative merits of a range of projects designed to improve the city's environment. The Municipal Authority has given you the following brief.

Dear Consultant,

You will have accumulated a large amount of background material relating to Calcutta, including the following:

- A Data File containing some basic facts about Calcutta (Table 10.1) and a listing of the nature, causes and extent of some of the city's main environmental problems (Table 10.2).

- A Map File showing the main features of the city's urban structure, land uses and employment; together with maps of mains water and sewerage provision and areas with particular environmental problems (Figs 10.1–10.4).

- A Photo File showing some of the different types of housing and problems in Calcutta (Figs 10.5–10.15).

- A Project File, listing the projects for environmental improvement which we, as the Municipal Authority, have to consider.

We now need your expert help in reaching decisions about the projects. As you will see, each project is costed, but the Municipal Authority has a strict budget limit which is the equivalent of £30 million. This is a particularly large amount for a city like Calcutta, and it is seen as a one-off expenditure designed to bring big improvements to the city's environment. We must ensure that the money is allocated carefully between projects that will bring the maximum benefit to the largest number of people in the city. We must also be very clear why we have selected certain projects and not others.

As you will know, there are two main groups of environmental problems (called the Brown Agenda) facing cities in ELDCs such as Calcutta:

1 traditional environmental health problems resulting from the lack of sewage or water services to large numbers of people; and

2 more recent environmental problems arising from industrialisation and transport, including the pollution of air, land and water.

The Municipal Authority is keen to address both groups of problems; however, our main priority is to improve conditions for some of the poorest groups in the city, many of whom are homeless or live in bustees (spontaneous settlements).

You will also note that Projects 3 and 7 involve the possibility of additional funding in the form of aid from the UK and the US. However, there are strings attached to this aid. Therefore, we need you to consider carefully the issues involved in these projects. In general, the Indian government and the Calcutta Municipal Authority are happy to receive aid from other countries, but we would prefer to decide ourselves the ways in which the aid is to be spent. With these factors in mind, therefore, we need you to assess the situation carefully and advise us (as detailed overleaf).

- Write a brief summary of the city's environmental problems, highlighting those you feel require the most urgent action in order to improve living standards for the poorest city-dwellers.

- Compile a matrix assessing the advantages and disadvantages of all the proposed projects. In each case, point out which groups in society, such as the poorest or the homeless, will benefit most from the project.

- Suggest an allocation of the £30 million between a selection of the projects, explaining the reasons for your allocation. You will also need to include a specific case for adopting or rejecting Projects 3 and 7 which involve aid from the UK and the US.

Data File

Table 10.1 Some basic facts about Calcutta

Situation	At the mouth of the Ganges (the largest river system in India), with the city's highest point only 10 m above sea-level.
Population	10.96 million (1991), India's largest city. Contains 20 per cent of West Bengal's population, and 40 per cent live in slums (*bustees*).
Population density	Varies from 7228 per sq km to 162 866 per sq km in some places.
Infant mortality rate	102 per 1000 live births (1998).
Main causes of death	Diarrhoea, diphtheria, tetanus and measles, largely resulting from poor sanitary conditions and overcrowding.

Table 10.2 Some of Calcutta's main environmental problems

Sanitation	Thirty per cent of the population have no latrine. 500 000 people live and sleep on the city's roads. Calcutta is trying to build public lavatories as part of the Bustee Development Programme.
Water supply	Seventy per cent of the population have access to piped water, although as many as 35–45 households may use the same tap. The pipe network is 150 years old and so there are many leaks and breaks which allow pollutants to enter the water supply. During the monsoon, flooding causes the surface water to become contaminated by sewage and garbage. The contaminated water transmits gastro-enteritis and related diseases.
Air pollution	Sixty per cent of the population suffer from a respiratory infection (1992 data), mainly due to pollution by sulphur dioxide (SO_2) produced by the chemical and engineering industries, the power stations, and the emissions from buses and trucks (whose numbers grew by 78 per cent between 1980 and 1989). Suspended particulate matter (SPM) is a big problem arising from coal burning and 200 000 tonnes are emitted each year. Poor people use coal and charcoal for cooking and this adds to air pollution, especially in winter when there is often a temperature inversion. In 1990, 177 000 tonnes of carbon monoxide (CO) were emitted, half of it coming from motor vehicles. (Vehicle registrations doubled during 1980–89.) The other major sources of CO are industry and homes.
Noise pollution	Ten per cent of the population suffer hearing loss as a result of noise pollution. The most important noise source is transport, deriving from poorly maintained vehicles and roads.
Industrial development	In 1990, Calcutta had 11 516 large and small industrial units. A number of these produce toxic chemicals and are located in densely populated residential areas.
Key problem	**Lack of financial resources to improve the urban environment.**

Map File

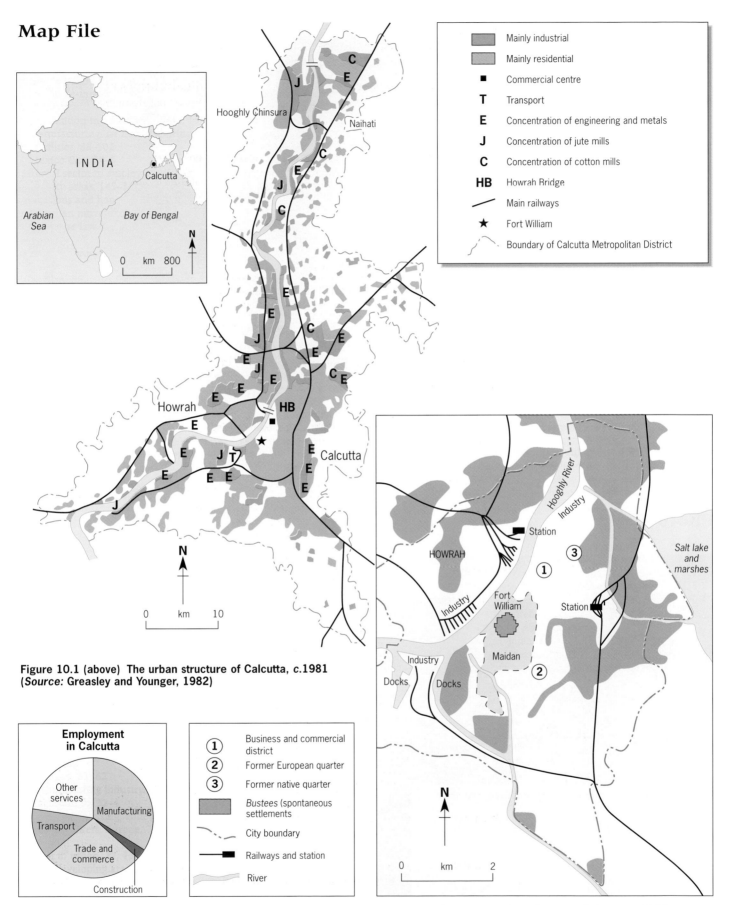

Figure 10.1 (above) The urban structure of Calcutta, *c.*1981
(*Source:* Greasley and Younger, 1982)

Figure 10.2 Land use and employment, Calcutta, *c.*1986
(*Source:* Nixon, 1987)

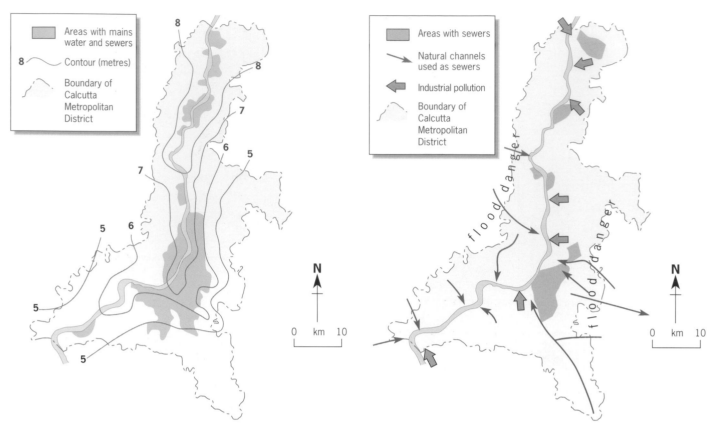

Figure 10.3 Calcutta: contours and areas with mains water and sewage, c.1990 (*Source:* Knapp et al., 1991)

Figure 10.4 Calcutta: location of main environmental problems, c.1986 (*Source:* Nixon, 1987)

Photo File

Figure 10.5 Rush hour in Chowringhee Road, Calcutta

Figure 10.6 Traffic congestion, Calcutta

Figure 10.7 Modern apartment blocks in a residential suburb, Calcutta

Figure 10.8 Older apartments with shops beneath, Calcutta

Figure 10.9 Small apartments in an old apartment block, Calcutta

Figure 10.10 High-density housing in a bustee, Calcutta

Photo File

Figure 10.11a Living in a *bustee*, Calcutta

Figure 10.11b Living in a *bustee*, Calcutta

Figure 10.12 Pavement-dwellers in Calcutta

Figure 10.13 Homeless people sorting rubbish in Calcutta

Figure 10.14 Street food, Calcutta

Figure 10.15 Beggars in Calcutta

Project File

Project 1

This project would repair leaks and breaks in the network of water pipes throughout the city. This would cost £5 million and would improve the safety and quality of the water supply to one-quarter of the 70 per cent of the city's population who have access to piped water. This would lead to significant reductions in infant mortality and a general improvement in community health. It would also provide much-needed employment for some of the city's jobless. The project would be organised and run by the Calcutta Municipal Authority who would identify the areas for priority action. Top priority would be given to stopping industrial pollutants such as cyanide and benzene entering the water supply.

Project 2

This project aims to provide low-cost, methane-burning, cooking stoves to over 500000 poor households in the city. The purpose is to persuade people to stop using coal and charcoal as the main fuels for cooking and heating. In this way, the air pollution in the city – especially that caused by sulphur dioxide (SO_2) and suspended particulate matter (SPM) would be reduced by over 20 per cent. The new stoves are relatively cheap, but they would still need to be subsidised to a cost of £1 million, in order to make them affordable to the poorest groups in the city. In many cases, the stoves would have to be given to families, who would also have to be instructed in how to use them and persuaded that they were a good alternative to the traditional coal and charcoal. A further £0.5 million would need to be allocated to the project in order to subsidise the sale of the canisters of gas to people over the first five years of the project.

Project 3

The aim of this project is to reduce some of the worst air pollution in Calcutta. The project would cost £10 million, half of which is available in the form of aid from the UK and the US for the installation of filters on all the coal-burning power stations in the city. These filters would remove all the sulphur dioxide (SO_2) and most of the suspended particulate matter produced by the power stations. However, a condition of the aid is that the money can only be spent on air filters, which must be purchased from companies in the UK and in the US. The project would give a big boost to reducing (SO_2) pollution in Calcutta, and thus would help the 60 per cent of the population suffering from respiratory infections. However, it would do nothing to reduce any of the other sources of (SO_2) pollution – nor would it help to reduce any other kinds of air pollution. However, the benefits of the project would accrue to all the city's population.

Project 4

The aim of this project is to construct a network of storm drains at a cost of £18 million to remove the worst of the flooding in the monsoon season. The system of storm drains would be built across the whole city in order to prevent contamination of surface water by sewage and garbage. Such contamination contributes to ill health and especially to the high rate of infant mortality. Over 15 000 poorer people would be employed during the construction phase of the project, thereby adding greatly to their household incomes. Whilst the project would undoubtedly cause widespread disruption to the city during the construction phase – especially in the centre – it can be argued that the long-term benefits in improved public health would be well worth the cost of disruption. The £18 million also has to cover the cost of additional pumps required to remove some flood water from the low-lying city centre.

Project 5

This project aims to provide basic latrines for 80 per cent of the people who currently have no latrine. The project would cost £2 million, and would be an extension of the Bustee Development Programme which has already built some public lavatories. The project would build banks of latrines in locations central to those parts of the city lacking basic amenities. Over £1.5 million of the total will be needed to install the sewage systems or septic tanks necessary to service the latrines. Whilst not a particularly glamorous project, it has the potential to improve the quality of life and general health of over 2 million of the city's poorest people. In addition, some of Calcutta's unemployed and underemployed people would be able to obtain work building the sewers and latrines. However, because the system of sewers in the rest of the city is old and run-down, there is a fear amongst planners that the additional strain on the system resulting from the improvements might lead to the collapse of large parts of the main network.

Project 6

This project would cost £6 million and aims to provide low-cost accommodation in simple flats for about 80 000 of the 500 000 people who have no homes. The main costs – about 70 per cent of the total – will be in purchasing land within the city on which to build the flats. However, the construction costs will be kept to a minimum by employing some of the homeless people, who will thus gain additional income. The flats will be of a very basic construction, consisting of two rooms with their own cold water supply and a shared toilet. Income from renting the flats will not be high because of the extreme poverty of many of the occupants, so an additional £1 million will have to be set aside for maintenance of the flats. Once construction of the flats ceases, some of the occupants will again have little or no income, so rents must reflect their inability to pay large sums. Improvements in general health, particularly infant and maternal mortality, should be among the benefits of the project.

Project 7

This project aims to construct a new mass transit light railway system in part of central Calcutta at a cost of £20 million, half of which would come from the UK and the US. Again, a condition of the aid is that the money is only spent on this project and that the rails, locomotives and carriages for the network are purchased from UK or US companies. The construction of the light railway would create over 1000 jobs, mostly for local people who would benefit from this additional income. The project would also help to reduce air pollution, especially by sulphur dioxide (SO_2) and carbon monoxide (CO), by providing people with an alternative to cars and buses. Fares on the new light rail system would have to be subsidised to the extent of £2 million over three years (not subsidised by the UK or the US) in order to encourage large numbers of people to abandon cars, buses and motor cycles. However, the project clearly would not reduce air pollution from other sources, and may cause some unemployment amongst rickshaw-pullers and others employed in the transport industry.

Appendix

Questionnaires on office activity

Introduction

Whilst many students carry out questionnaires to investigate shopping habits, relatively few investigate the rapidly expanding area of office activity. The growth of service industries in the UK has led to a massive increase in the number, type and location of the offices housing these activities. As Chapter 7 explains, there are many different kinds of offices, from banks and building societies to estate agents, architects and city housing and social service departments. When investigating offices, it is usually best to select only one or two types of office activity to study, otherwise the sample size becomes unrealistic. Thus, for example, a study of the reasons behind the location of financial offices in a city centre could involve:

- the definition of 'financial' offices – e.g. banks, insurance companies, insurance brokers and building societies;

- the selection of a sample group to whom the questionnaire would be sent; and

- the drawing up a questionnaire to ask the reasons behind the location of the particular office.

Similarly, a study comparing a sample of a particular group of offices in a suburb with a sample in the city centre might involve the first two elements outlined above, together with a questionnaire designed to highlight the similarities and differences between suburban and city centre offices.

These are just two ideas from a range of possibilities for investigations of office activity.

An example of a questionnaire

The following questionnaire covers a very wide range of topics, and would need to be amended in the light of the specific aspect of office activity under investigation. However, this questionnaire may prove to be a useful starting point for fieldwork studies on offices.

Name of fieldwork investigator:

_____

Date of interview: _____

Name and address of company:

_____

_____

Nature of business of the company:

_____

_____

1 What is the size of the office (sq m)? _____

2 How many people are employed in different grades within the office (e.g. clerical, administrative, management, cleaning, etc.)? _____

3 Is this the only office of the company? Yes ☐ No ☐

4 If not, where are the others? _____

5 Is this a branch of another company? Yes ☐ No ☐

6 If so, where is the head office? _____

7 How satisfied are you (very satisfied, satisfied, unhappy, very unhappy) with the present accommodation in terms of:

size; ☐ ☐ ☐ ☐

layout; ☐ ☐ ☐ ☐

space; ☐ ☐ ☐ ☐

services (e.g. parking, security); ☐ ☐ ☐ ☐

rent; ☐ ☐ ☐ ☐

heating/air conditioning. ☐ ☐ ☐ ☐

8 Do you own the office or rent it? Own ☐ rent ☐

9 If rent, how frequent is the review? _____

10 What do you think are the main advantages and disadvantages of locating in this site in terms of:

contacts with clients/suppliers; _____

rent; _____

ability to recruit a range of staff; _____

services; _____

other factors (please specify). _____

11 What do you think is the most important single reason for your present location?

_____

_____

12 Have you considered relocating? If so, when and to where?

_____

_____

13 Where are decisions about location made (e.g. locally; at the head office)?

_____

14 What percentage of the staff travel to the office by:

car; _____

bus; _____

train; _____

bicycle; _____

on foot; _____

other (please specify). _____

15 Do most staff live locally (within 10km) or travel from further afield? Locally ☐ Further ☐

16 How many parking spaces are reserved for the company? _____

17 Are these for staff or clients? Staff ☐ Clients ☐

18 What are the three main external organisations with which you are in most regular contact?

_____

_____

_____

19 Do you have face-to-face meetings? Yes ☐ No ☐

20 What are the advantages of face-to-face meetings over other forms of communication such as video-conferencing or fax?

_____

_____

21 What services (e.g. security or typing) are available in the current office building?

_____

_____

References

Alexander, I (1979) *Office Location and Public Policy*, Longman.

Annez, P (1996) 'Livable cities for the twenty-first century', *Siemens Review*, Vol. 62, June/July, pp 5–9.

Berry, B J (1977) *Contemporary Urban Ecology*, Macmillan.

Beck, U (1992) *Risk Society: Towards a New Modernity*, Sage, London

Blakemore, H and Smith, C T (eds) (1992) *Latin America*, 3rd edn, Methuen.

Blowers, A (1999) 'The unsustainable city?' in S Pile, C Brook and C Money (eds) *Unruly Cities? Order, Disorder*. Open University Press, Routledge, London

British Association (1950) *Birmingham in its Regional Setting*, British Association.

Brown, L A and Moore, E G (1985) 'The intra-urban migration process: a second perspective', *Geografiska Annaler*, Vol. 67B, pp 1–13.

Burdette, M C (1988) *Zambia: between two worlds*, Avebury.

Burtenshaw, D (1983) *Cities and Towns*, Bell and Hyman.

Carter, H (1983) *An Introduction to Urban Historical Geography*, Arnold.

Carter, H (1990) *Urban and Rural Settlements*, Longman.

Chaffey, J (1995) *A New View of Britain*, Hodder & Stoughton.

Chauncey, G (1995) *Gay New York; The Making of a Gay Male World, 1840–1940*, Flamingo, Glasgow

Chilton, R (1986) 'Age, sex and arrest trends for 12 of the nation's largest central cities' in J M Byrne and R J Sampson (eds) *The Social Ecology of Crime*, Springer, New York

City of Birmingham, Planning Department (1993) *The Birmingham Plan: Birmingham Unitary Development Plan 1993*.

City of Birmingham, Planning Department (1996) *Report on housing conditions*.

Clarke, W A V and Cadwallader, M T (1973) 'Residential preferences: an alternative view of intra-urban space', *Environment and Planning A*, Vol. 5, pp 693–703.

Daniel, P and Hopkinson, M (1991) *The Geography of Settlement*, 2nd edn, Oliver and Boyd.

Daniels, P (1987) *The Service Industries*, Cambridge University Press.

Dickenson, J (ed.) (1996) *A Geography of the Third World*, Routledge.

Donert, K (1974) 'Regional developments in France', *Geofile*, 107, Thornes.

Downs, R M and Stea, D (1973) *Image and Environment*, Arnold.

Drakakis-Smith, D (1987) *The Third World city*, Methuen.

Duncan, T L C (1971) *Measuring housing quality*, Occasional Paper No. 20, Centre for Urban and Regional Studies, University of Birmingham.

Ellis, B (1987) *The West Midlands*, Cambridge University Press.

Everson, J and Fitzgerald, B P (1969) *Settlement Patterns*, Longman.

Fielding, G H (1975) *Geography as Social Science*, Harper & Row.

Flint, D (1987) *Progress and Change in Developing Countries*, Blackwell.

Flint, D and Flint C (1989) *British Issues in Geography*, Collins.

Garreau, J (1991) *Edge City: Life on the New Frontier*, Doubleday, New York

Geographers' A–Z Map Co. (1996a) *Great Britain Road Atlas*.

Geographers' A–Z Map Co. (1996b) *Southport Street Atlas*.

Gloucestershire County Council (1996) *Structure plan*.

Greasley, B and Younger, M (1982) *Population and Urbanisation*, Harrap.

Guy, C (1994) 'Whatever happened to regional shopping centres', *Geography*, Vol. 79, Part 4, pp 293–312.

Harris, C O and Ullman, E L (1945) 'The nature of cities', *Annals of the Academy of Political and Social Science*, Vol. 242, pp 7–17.

Healey, M J and Ilberry, B W (1990) *Location and Change*, Oxford University Press.

Hirsch, P (1995) 'Urbanisation and development', *Geography Review*, Vol. 8, No. 4, pp 18–23.

HMSO (1993) *1991 Census of population in England and Wales*.

HMSO (1995) *Report of the census of distribution and other services*.

Hoyt, H (1939) *The structure and growth of residential neighborhoods in American cities*, Federal Housing Administration.

Hubbard, P (1996) 'Re-imaging the city', *Geography*, Vol. 81, Part 1, pp 26–36.

Hull, A, Jones, T and Kenny, S (1988) *Geographical Issues in Western Europe*, Longman.

Humphreys, K, Mason, P and Pinch, S (1983) 'The externality fields of football grounds: a case study of The Dell, Southampton', *Geoforum*, 14, pp 401–412.

Hutman, E Blauw, W and Saltman M (eds) *Urban Housing Segregation of Minorities in Western Europe and the United States*, Duke University Press, Durham

Imrie, R (1996) *Disability and the City: International Perspectives*, Paul Chapman, London

INSEE (Institut National de la Statistique et des Etudes Economiques) (1995) Première (84), Juin.

Kearsley, G (1983) 'Teaching urban geography: the Burgess model', *New Zealand Journal of Geography*, Vol. 75, pp 10–13.

Knapp, B, Ross, S and McRae, D (1991) *The Challenge of the Human Environment*, Longman.

Knox, P (1976) 'Environmental quality in Sheffield', *Scottish Geographical Magazine*, Vol. 92, pp 101–107.

Knox, P (1996) *Urban Social Geography*, 3rd edn, Longman.

Lenon, B and Cleves, P (1994) *Fieldwork Techniques and Projects in Geography*, Collins.

Matthews, H (1991) *British Inner Cities*, Oxford University Press.

McInnes, A (1980) *The English town 1660–1760*, Historical Association of London.

Murdie, R A (1969) *Factoral ecology of metropolitan Toronto*, Research Paper No. 116, Department of Geography, University of Chicago.

Nixon, B (1987) *World Contrasts*, Bell & Hyman.

Orleans, P (1973) 'Differential cognition of urban residents', in R Downs and D Stea (eds) *Image and Environment*, pp 120–123, Aldine.

Park, D C, Radford, J.P and Vickers, M H (1998) 'Disability studies in human geography' in *Progress in Human Geography*, 22, 208-33

Park, R E, Burgess, E W and Mckenzie, R D (eds) (1925) *The city*, University of Chicago Press.

Parke, J M H (1975) *The redevelopment of Birmingham's inner city*, unpublished MA thesis, University of Birmingham.

Peach, C (1998) 'South Asian and Caribbean ethnic minority housing choice in Britain' *Urban Studies*, 35, 1657–80

Philip's Geographical Digest 1996–97, Heinemann.

Potter, S and Sinah, J (1990) 'Noida: a planned industrial township south-east of Delhi', *Geography*, Vol. 75, pp 63–65.

Pritchard, R M (1976) *Housing and the Social Structure of the City*, Cambridge University Press.

Rae, J H (1983) *Social deprivation in Glasgow*, Glasgow City Council.

Robinson, R (1995) 'Unit F: Settlement', in M Witherick (ed.) *Environment and people*, pp 430–509, Thornes.

Rogers, A (1995) 'Christaller's central place theory: a fresh look', *Geography Review*, Vol. 9, No.1, pp 10–12.

Simmons, J (1964) *The changing pattern of retail locations*, Research Paper No. 92, Department of Geography, University of Chicago.

Smith, C J (1980) 'Neighbourhood effects on mental health', in D Herbert and R J Johnston (eds) *Geography and the Urban Environment*, vol. 3, pp. 363–415, Wiley.

Tyre, R (ed.) (1993) *Merry Hill impact study*, DoE, HMSO.

Ward, P M (1990) *Mexico City: the production and reproduction of an urban environment*, Belhaven.

Warf, B (1990) 'The reconstruction of social ecology and neighbourhood change in Brooklyn', *Environment and Planning D*, Vol. 8, pp 73–96.

Waugh, D (1987) *The World*, Nelson.

West, R C and Angelli, J P (1966) *Middle America*, Prentice Hall.

Winchester, H and Chalkley, B (1995) 'A city for the future', *Geography Review*, Vol. 9, No. 2, pp 2–6.

Winchester, H P M and White, P (1998) 'The location of marginalized groups in the inner city', *Environment and Planning D: Society and Space*, 6, 37–54

World Bank (1996) *World Development Report: workers in an integrating world*, Oxford University Press.

Yiftachel, O and Hedgcock, D (1993) 'Urban social sustainability: the planning of an Australian city', *Cities*, 139–157

Glossary

Ableist geography A type of geography which assumes that all people are able bodied and none suffer from disabilities.

Accessibility The ease with which people can get to a particular place. Places with good accessibility include city centres, because so many roads and railway lines converge there.

Aided self-help scheme A method of improving conditions in spontaneous settlements in ELDCs. The government begins the process of improvement by installing electricity, a clean water supply and sewage disposal facilities. This encourages local residents to improve their homes by their own efforts – for example, by using bricks and concrete to create better housing.

Amenity A facility provided to improve the quality of the environment – for example, a park, a playground or a golf course.

Ancillary linkage A connection that is formed between offices and other businesses, such as cleaning firms and restaurants, that provide services for the office and its workers.

Axial belt The zone that is the most important part of a country, or region, containing its largest cities and main industries and, often, the majority of its population.

Backward linkage A connection between a factory and the individuals and companies that supply it with materials, equipment and services.

Bid–rent curve A graph that shows the different amounts of rent that a range of urban land uses can afford to pay. Retail shops, for example, can afford to pay a higher bid rent than industrial or residential land uses.

Binary (bi-primate) pattern A pattern that is dominated by two major elements. For example, a country's urban structure is binary if it is dominated by two principal cities.

Birth (of a firm) The development of a new company within part of a city. Some new companies are 'born' when employees leave an existing firm to set up on their own. Others are created by individuals or groups who set up a new business for the first time.

Breaking point A point on the boundary between the trading areas of two adjacent towns, calculated using a formula incorporating the population sizes of the towns and the distance between them. People on one side of the breaking point will shop in town A, whilst those on the other side will shop in town B.

Brown Agenda The range of environmental problems facing cities in ELDCs, including traditional environmental health problems, such as sewage disposal, and more recent problems resulting from industrialisation, such as air pollution.

Brown belt Land lying within a **green belt** that has already been damaged or degraded by activities such as quarrying, landfill and the construction of power stations and sewage works.

Brownfield site An urban area that used to have old factories and houses, but where these buildings have been demolished prior to redevelopment.

Bustee Strictly speaking, a *bustee* is a village in India, but the term is more commonly applied to the slums and spontaneous settlements of Indian cities such as Calcutta.

Central business district (CBD) The central area of a city, dominated by department stores, specialist and variety goods shops, offices, cinemas, theatres and hotels.

Central place A settlement that provides goods and services. It can vary in size from a village to a large city.

Choropleth map A map in which each area is shaded according to the amount of a variable that it contains – for example, a map of population density showing the number of people per sq km in each census district within a city.

Comparison goods These are **high-order** (usually expensive) **goods** such as antiques, jewellery and some electrical equipment. They are called comparison goods because people like to compare prices, quality and other features before buying them. Comparison goods are usually sold in shops in city centres or large **out-of-town shopping centres**.

Competitive linkage A link, usually in the form of information, between offices that are competing for the same business. Because of the strength of competitive linkages, many offices locate near each other to keep an eye on their competitors.

Complementary linkage A link between different types of offices that helps them both to operate more efficiently or profitably – for example, when a bank employs an advertising agency.

Component A part that is produced to be assembled with other parts into a finished product – for example, tyres and windscreens are two components of car manufacture.

Comprehensive Development Area (CDA) An area, usually in the inner city, where the whole urban landscape was demolished before being rebuilt on a planned basis by the council or city government.

Conurbation A large urban area formed by the coalescing of several urban centres, or the outward expansion of one major centre.

Counter-urbanisation The movement of people away from towns and cities to live in villages and small towns in the countryside.

Cycle of deprivation A sequence of events experienced by disadvantaged people in which one problem leads to other problems and so makes things worse.

Death (of a firm) The closing down of a company when it goes out of business.

Decentralisation The movement of people, factories, offices and shops away from city centres towards suburban and edge-of-city locations.

De-industrialised economy An economy in which the importance of the manufacturing sector has declined, as factories have closed, and the importance of the service sector has increased.

Deprivation The degree to which an individual or an area is deprived of services and amenities. There are many different types and levels of deprivation including poor and overcrowded housing, inadequate diet, inadequate income and lack of opportunity for employment.

Disamenity An element that most people do not wish to live near – for example, a very busy main road, a factory that pollutes air and water, an abattoir.

Dominant group A group of people with the money and political power to influence the allocation of housing resources in their favour.

Dot map A map showing the distribution and quantity of a variable by means of dots. For example, to show the location of burglaries in a town over a given time-period (one dot for each burglary); or the distribution of population in a city (in this case, each dot will represent a selected number of people).

ELDC An economically less developed country – for example, India, Mali and Zambia. In ELDCs, many people still live in poverty; the economy may have only small industrial and service sectors.

EMDC An economically more developed country – for example, the UK, the US and Japan. EMDCs have developed both manufacturing and service industries and most people enjoy a relatively high standard of living.

Entrepreneur An individual who starts, manages and controls an enterprise and bears some of the financial risks involved.

Externality An outcome of an activity by an individual, group or institution that affects the welfare of other people. Externalities may be good (see **positive externality**) or bad (see **negative externality**).

Favela A Brazilian term for a **spontaneous settlement** or slum, where most of the homes are built from scrap materials.

Filtering A process by which social groups move from one residential area to another, leading to changes in the social nature of residential areas.

First wave of decentralisation The movement of people away from locations close to the city centre, out into the suburbs.

Flagship scheme A high-profile development, designed to encourage investment in an area and to be a model for further developments.

Forest belt An area of forest in a zone around a city, often forming part of the **green belt**, and intended to stop urban sprawl and to provide recreation zones for city-dwellers.

Formal sector The employment sector comprising jobs that are usually permanent, with set hours of work, agreed levels of pay and sometimes pensions and social security rights.

Forward linkage A link between a factory and the individuals or companies that purchase its products.

Fourth wave of decentralisation The movement of offices away from city centres to sites out in the suburbs or to office parks in edge-of-city locations.

Futures web A diagram showing the expected consequences of a major development. Boxes close to the centre of the web indicate immediate effects; and boxes further away indicate longer-term effects.

Gatekeeper An institution, or its representative, which acts in various ways to restrict people's access to different types of housing. Landowners, estate agents, mortgage lenders and housing managers are all gatekeepers.

Gentrification A process by which run-down houses in an inner city or other neglected area are improved by relatively affluent people who move there for easier access to the jobs and services of the city centre.

Ghetto An urban district containing a high proportion of one particular ethnic group. The term ghetto comes from the district of Geto in medieval Venice which was reserved for Jews.

Globalisation The process by which all cities become part of the single world economy. Thus, for example, money from Japan or the US may be invested in projects in cities in countries as far apart as the UK and China.

Gravity model A model, based on Newton's Law of Universal Gravitation, that is used to predict the degree of interaction between settlements.

Green belt An area around a city, composed mostly of parkland and farmland, in which development is strictly controlled. Its purpose is to prevent the outward growth of the city and, often, to prevent two or more cities from coalescing to form one huge urban area.

Green buffer An area of open space, composed mostly of parkland and farmland, in which development is strictly controlled. It runs between and around cities to provide most people with access to green space.

Green corridor An area of open space, composed mostly of parkland and farmland, where development is strictly controlled. Green corridors run in parallel lines, usually between different urban areas, keeping them separate.

Greenfield site An area, usually on the edge of a city, that has not been developed for housing, industry or transport. The area may still be farmland, which gives it its name.

Green heart An area of open space, composed mostly of parkland and farmland, where development is strictly controlled. The green heart lies at the centre of a series of surrounding towns.

Green wedge An area of open space, composed mostly of parkland and farmland, where development is strictly controlled. Green wedges spread outwards from the city centre.

Green zone An area of open space, composed mostly of farmland and parkland, where development is strictly controlled. Usually, there are several green zones arranged in circular fashion on the edge of a city.

Growth coalition A form of public–private partnership or **joint venture** in which public (often council) organisations and private companies work together in a common project.

High-order good/service A good or service, usually expensive, that people buy only occasionally – for example, furniture, computers and jewellery. High-order services are usually located in larger towns and cities accessible to large numbers of people.

Hinterland The name given to the area around a settlement which comes under its economic, political and social influence. The same area is also sometimes called the **sphere of influence** or **urban field**.

Industrial estate An area of factories and warehouses, usually purpose-built, in a particular part of a city. Industrial estates are usually planned and separated from residential areas; they often have a wide range of different types of industry.

Informal sector The employment sector comprising jobs that are usually not permanent, have no set hours

of work or levels of pay and do not provide pensions or social security rights – for example, selling water or matches, or shining shoes.

Information linkage A link between firms for the purpose of exchanging information. Most companies depend heavily on their information linkages to keep them up to date with market trends.

Intra-urban movement Movement that stays within the urban area – for example, people moving house within the same city.

Inverse-care law This law states that the availability of medical services is inversely proportional to the needs of the population – i.e. the greater the need, the fewer the medical services, especially general practitioner surgeries.

Joint venture A project that is developed by a partnership between one or more private companies and the local government of the city. The aim is to combine money and expertise from both private and public sources.

Leapfrogging The process by which members of an ethnic group move out from a ghetto into the suburbs. Leapfrogging is not sectoral and can involve a move to a suburb in any part of the city.

Linkage A link between different companies, or different parts of the same company. There are several types of linkage – see **ancillary**, **backward**, **competitive**, **complementary**, **forward**, **information** and **supply linkages**.

Low-order good/service A good or service, usually inexpensive, that people buy on a regular, often daily, basis – for example, newspapers, bread and milk. Low-order goods and services are usually purchased from shops located in suburban or neighbourhood centres close to where people live.

Megacities Cities with a population of over 10 million.

Mental map A mental map shows an individual's remembered perceptions of an area – the relationship between one part and another, and the details of each part. Distances and directions are often inaccurate, but the details are a useful source of information about how people see the world and the environments in which they live and work.

Micro-region A basic planning unit of cities in the former Soviet Union. Each micro-region consisted of blocks of flats, together with a primary school, shops, industries and recreation areas.

Migration The movement of people from one area to another, usually involving a permanent change of home. In ELDCs, many people are still migrating from the countryside into the cities.

Mobility The ability of people, or companies, to move from place to place. The ease with which people are able to move within cities has been reduced by the increasing volume of traffic and has been improved by better public transport.

Multipli city The idea for a city of the future which would consist of an area of small, relatively dense urban settlements, linked by improved public transport.

Muted group A group of people lacking the money and political power to influence the allocation of housing resources. As a result, they have the poorest housing or become homeless.

Natural increase/growth The increase in a population resulting from internal growth (i.e. the excess of births over deaths) rather than from migration.

Negative correlation An inverse relationship between two variables under examination. For example, in a comparison of population growth with settlement size, a negative correlation would exist if the smaller settlements were growing faster than the larger ones.

Negative externality An unpleasant outcome for other people of an activity by an individual, group or institution – for example, the fumes from a factory or noise from an airport.

Neighbourhood unit The basic building unit for planned new towns, designed to provide people with a safe, traffic-free environment and access to all frequently needed services such as primary schools, shops and clinics within walking distance.

New Commonwealth The more recent members of the Commonwealth, including countries such as India and Pakistan and the West Indian islands.

New town A planned urban centre, designed to be freestanding, self-contained and socially balanced.

Out-of-town shopping centre A large group of shops built either on a site at the edge of the urban area or on the site of a former large industrial complex. Such centres usually have large car parks, a pedestrianised, air-conditioned environment and over 100 shops.

Overbounded A city is overbounded when its administrative boundary is much larger than its built-up area. In these circumstances, the city may contain quite a lot of agricultural land.

Overspill town A town that expanded by taking people who were forced to move out of nearby cities as a result of slum clearance and redevelopment schemes.

Over-urbanisation Over-urbanisation, found in some cities in ELDCs, occurs when the rate of population growth, boosted by in-migration from surrounding rural areas, is more rapid than the growth of the city's economy. The result is that the city is unable to provide sufficient jobs and housing.

Petty commodity sector This is another name for the **informal sector**. Jobs in this sector are usually not permanent, have no set hours of work or levels of pay and do not provide pensions or social security rights – for example, selling water or matches, or shining shoes.

Pie graph A diagram in which a circle, representing the total of the values, is divided into sectors, each being proportional in size to the value it represents.

Place utility An assessment of the advantages and disadvantages of different parts of an urban area, made by individuals. The assessment of place utility is a very personal thing.

Planning Attempting to carry out a programme of work, such as building a new town or protecting historic buildings, by following an agreed set of guidelines, design or plan.

Positive externality A beneficial outcome for other people of an activity by an individual, group or institution – for example, an individual who endows a city art gallery contributes to the cultural development of local people.

Post-industrial cities Cities where manufacturing has ceased to be the main factor in economic, social and cultural change. Instead tertiary, quaternary and quinary activities take over as the bases of urban economic growth.

Primacy The degree to which one city dominates the urban system of a country. In many ELDCs, the primacy of the capital city is very marked.

Primate city An urban centre that dominates a country's urban system, with a population much greater than that of the next-largest city.

Primate pattern A pattern of urban settlements within a country or region in which one city dominates the whole urban structure.

Rancho The name given to a spontaneous settlement in cities such as Caracas in Venezuela.

Random sample A method of sampling based on the use of random numbers (Appendix A2). The use of random numbers avoids problems of bias in sample selection.

Range of a good/service The maximum distance that people will travel to obtain a particular good or service. In general, people are prepared to travel further for higher-order goods than for lower-order goods.

Rationalisation An economic process whereby production is concentrated in fewer, larger units in order to make production more efficient and more economic.

Recreation A short-term leisure activity involving trips from home – for example, to a leisure centre or cinema.

Redevelopment The rebuilding of parts of a city. Sometimes large areas are completely demolished before being rebuilt; sometimes all or some of the old buildings are retained and modernised to combine the best features of the old and the new.

Re-organisation A change in the way in which a company or area is structured and run. Most re-organisations are designed to improve efficiency. The term is also used to describe the movement of companies away from older inner city locations.

Restructuring An economic process of changing investment within a company or area towards new goods and services and away from old ones.

Re-urbanisation The process whereby towns and cities which have been experiencing a loss of population are able to reverse the decline and begin to grow again. Some form of city centre redevelopment is often the catalyst that starts re-urbanisation.

Risk society A society in which technologies, such as nuclear power and genetic engineering, become more and more important and so pose greater risks than in the past.

Rural population turnaround A halt in the decline of population in rural areas, followed by a growth in the rural population.

Scattergraph A type of graph used to plot the relationship between two variables as a series of points. For example, a scattergraph of settlement hierarchy would show the relationship between settlement size (population) and number of functions.

Second wave of decentralisation The movement of factories (and their associated jobs) from sites close to city centres, out into the suburbs.

Service sector That part of the urban economy comprising service industries – i.e. those which meet people's everyday needs. Services include the provision of food (shops, restaurants), education (schools), medical care (hospitals) and entertainment (cinemas).

Single Regeneration Budget (SRB) A scheme for urban redevelopment in the UK, whereby local authorities were invited to bid for central government funding.

Site-and-services scheme A method of encouraging housing improvement in poor areas of cities in ELDCs.

The government provides the land for a new development and installs services such as water and electricity. Local people can then obtain a plot in the scheme for a low rent and build their own houses.

Socio-economic status A collective term to describe a person's income, wealth, education and occupation.

Sphere of influence The name given to the area around a settlement which comes under its economic, political and social influence. The same area is also sometimes called the **urban field** or **hinterland**.

Spillover The process by which people move out from a **ghetto** into adjacent parts of the urban area, but in a distinctly sectoral pattern. As a result, minority groups tend remain in the same sector of a city.

Spontaneous settlement A squatter settlement or shanty town containing self-built houses made of scrap materials such as corrugated iron and plastic; the settlement usually lacks piped water, an electricity supply and sewage disposal facilities. Spontaneous settlements are numerous in cities in ELDCs and are illegal because the residents neither own the land on which the houses are built, nor have permission to build there.

Squatter settlement Another name for a **spontaneous settlement**.

Suburbanisation The process by which people, factories, offices and shops move out of the central areas of cities and into the suburbs.

Supply linkage A link that develops when a company grows big enough to attract into its area some or all of the companies which supply it with goods and services – for example, stationery, furniture and computers.

Sustainability Long-term management of the environment of an area in order to maintain its natural resources.

Systematic sample A method of sampling based on the use of a standard interval for the selection of the sample – for example, every tenth person, or the land use every 0.5 km.

Third wave of decentralisation The process by which some shops have left city centre locations for sites in the suburbs or on the edge of the city where they may be more accessible to customers.

Threshold population The minimum number of people required to support a particular good, shop or office. For example, large stores such as Boots or Marks & Spencer have a threshold population of over 100 000, whilst shoe shops have a threshold population of about 25 000.

Tourism A leisure activity involving a stay away from home – for example, to visit cities in a foreign country.

Townscape The physical appearance of the urban landscape, including the form and arrangement of its buildings and spaces.

Transfer (of a firm) The movement of a company from one part of a city to another.

Transition zone The area around the CBD. It is a zone of mixed land uses, ranging from car parks and derelict buildings to slums, cafes and older houses, often converted to offices or industrial uses.

Underbounded A city is underbounded when its administrative boundary is much smaller than its built-up area.

Underemployment The situation when people do not have fulltime, continuous work, and are usually only employed temporarily or seasonally.

Unemployment A lack of employment, or the ability to secure paid employment.

Urban agglomeration A very large built-up area, with extensive areas of housing, industry, retailing, manufacturing and recreational facilities.

Urban doughnut The internal structure of some cities in EMDCs in the twenty first century, whose CBD has emptied of people and economic activity. It has become the empty heart of an urban area.

Urban fabric The buildings and spaces that make up the physical structure of a city, including houses, shops, offices, factories and open spaces.

Urban field The area around a settlement which comes under its economic, political and social influence. The same area is also sometimes called the **hinterland** or **sphere of influence**.

Urban fringe The area at the edge of the built-up part of the city. The fringe is usually a zone of mixed land uses, from shopping malls and golf courses to farmland and motorways.

Urban hierarchy A system of urban centres in a region or country with a size distribution from the largest to the smallest, and a functional distribution from the most specialised to the least specialised.

Urbanisation The process by which more and more people live in towns and cities. By AD 2000, over half of the world's population will live in urban areas.

Urban morphology The form or shape of a town and the arrangement and layout of its buildings and spaces.

World cities Very large cities which are centres of global capitalism, where command and control of the global economy is exercised. They are important within the world economy, not just within the economy of one country. World cities include London, Tokyo, New York and São Paulo.

Zone in transition The area around the CBD. It is a zone of mixed land uses, ranging from car parks and derelict buildings to slums, cafes and older houses, often converted to offices or industrial uses.

Index

Published by Collins Educational
77–85 Fulham Palace Road
London W6 8JB

www.CollinsEducational.co.uk
On-line support for schools and colleges.
You might also like to visit
www.fireandwater.co.uk

An imprint of HarperCollins*Publishers*

© HarperCollinsPublishers Ltd 2001

First published 1998. Reprinted 1998.

ISBN 0 00 711427 3

Corrin Flint and David Flint hereby assert
their moral right to be identified as the
Authors of this Work.

Edited by Cover(2)Cover a.t.e.

Designed by Jerry Fowler; Sara Kidd

Picture research by Caroline Thompson

Computer artwork by Jerry Fowler,
Malcolm Porter

Index by Ann Kramer

Printed and bound by Printing Express,
Hong Kong

Author dedication
This book is dedicated to Lucy.

Acknowledgements

Every effort has been made to contact the
holders of copyright material, but if any
have been inadvertently overlooked the
publishers will be pleased to make the
necessary arrangements at the first
opportunity.

The publishers would like to thank the
following for permission to reproduce
photographs:

Aerofilms Ltd, Figs 3.2, 3.15, 4.7, 7.8, 8.13,
  8.28.
Ancient Art & Architecture Collection,
  Figs 1.1, 2.4.
Andes Press Agency/Carlos Reyes Manzo,
  Fig. 2.21.
Associated Press AP Photo, Fig. 6.18.
Bildflug 1989 Hansa Luftbild Munster.
  Reproduced by permission of
  Senatsverwaltung fur Bauen, Wohen
  under Verker-vom, Fig. 8.18,
Bridgeman Art Library, Figs 1.4a, 1.4c.
Robert Brook, Figs 7.22, 8.24, 8.25.
Cadbury's, Fig. 2.12, 2.13.
Cardiff Bay Development
  Corporation/Corfforaeth Datblygu bae
  Caerdydd, Figs 8.42, 8.43.
J Allan Cash Ltd, Figs 7.15, 7.37, 7.39, 8.26.
Collections/S Walsh, Fig. 3.1, D Bowie,
  Fig. 3.3, M St Maur, Fig. 3.5, B Shuel,
  Fig. 6.6.
Colorific!/R Bishop, Fig. 1.3, R Singh,
  Fig. 1.20, D Marvin, Fig. 1.22, D.
  Hunstein, Fig. 2.10, S Benbow, Fig. 2.25.
Corbis-Bettmann, Fig. 4.8.
James Davis Travel Photography, Figs 7.35,
  7.36, 8.5, 8.41.
Environmental Images, Fig. 6.17.
Mary Evans Picture Library, Figs 1.4b, 1.11,
  1.13, 2.9, 3.17, 4.13.
Eye Ubiquitous/G Wickham, Fig. 7.1, P
  Thompson, Fig. 7.2.
Focus Housing Association, Fig. 5.32.
Getty Images *Telegraph*, Fig. 2.7.
GettyOne Stone, Figs 5.38, 6.8, 6.30.
Sally & Richard Greenhill Photo Library,
  Fig. 8.33.

Sonia Halliday & Laura Lushington, Fig. 2.2.
Robert Harding Picture Library/G A Mather,
  Figs 3.16, 5.2, R Richardson, Fig. 5.14,
  Grieves, Fig. 7.3.
David Hoffman, Fig. 5.35.
Hulton Getty Picture Collection, Fig. 2.11.
Hutchison Library/I Lloyd, Figs 5.5, 5.25, 5.30.
Image Bank/G Rossi, Fig. 5.23, A Pistolesi,
  Fig. 6.27.
London Aerial Photo Library, Figs 1.5, 1.9,
  1.10.
Magnum Photos/F Scianna, Fig. 6.21.
Merry Hill Centre, Figs 7.17, 7.19.
MFP Corporation Australia, Figs 9.14, 9.15.
Ministry of Defence, Singapore, Fig. 8.17.
NRSC, Fig. 8.16.
Panos Pictures/M Schlossman, Figs 5.28, 9.9.
Refuge Assurance, Figs 7.32, 7.33.
Rex Features Ltd, Figs 6.4, 6.12, 9.10.
Spectrum Colour Library, Figs 3.4, 4.1, 4.2,
  4.6, 5.29, 6.3, 6.13, 7.13, 7.28, 7.41, 7.42,
  8.30.
Still Pictures/M Edwards, Figs 1.19, 1.24,
  2.23, 2.26, 3.20, 4.25, 4.26, 6.15, 10.6,
  10.7, 10.11a, 10.11b, 10.12, 10.13, 10.14,
  10.15, D Hoffman, Fig. 5.1, M Ostergaard,
  Fig. 5.3, M Wright, Fig. 5.26, H Notocny,
  Fig. 5.27, J Maier, Fig. 7.4, D Drain,
  Figs 8.32, 8.40, P Harrison, Fig. 10.10.
Stock Market Photo Agency Inc., Figs 4.18,
  10.5.
Travel Ink Photo & Feature Library/C
  Marshall, Fig. 1.2.
TRIP Photo Library/Dinodia, Fig. 4.21, B
  Turner, Figs 7.31, 10.9, Roberts, Figs 8.6,
  8.27, 8.37, G Horner, Fig. 8.46, H Rogers,
  Fig. 10.8.
Woodfall Wild Images/M Barlow, Fig. 3.13.

Cover photo: Aerial of tract housing, USA
(Getty Images *Telegraph*).

Maps
Figs 4.3 and 8.14 reproduced with the
permission of the Controller of Her Majesty's
Stationery Office. The products include
mapping data licensed from the Ordnance
Survey. © Crown Copyright 2000.
All rights reserved. Licence number
100018599.